THE ANTICLOCKWISE PROPOSAL

A Travel Adventure Around the World in Eighty Diamonds

For David 'Tommo' Thompson.

Copyright

The Anticlockwise Proposal:
A Travel Adventure Around the World in Eighty Diamonds

ISBN: 978-0-6451187-5-9
Imprint: Simon Michael Prior
10 9 8 7 6 5 4 3 2 1

CONTENTS

1. STRANGERS

LATITUDE: 43° 29' 15" S
LONGITUDE: 172° 32' 15" E

Strangers.

Strangers beside me, behind me, facing me.

Strangers, perching on the long, grey rows of identical chairs.

A bearded man wearing spectacles, carrying an overcoat.

A young couple clasping two tired, floppy children.

A brace of older ladies quietly flipping the pages of their paperbacks.

All strangers.

I scraped my fingers through my hair and stared at the carpet.

That January evening in 1998, everything changed.

For two years, Fiona had accompanied me everywhere.

Every adventure. Every disaster.

Every border. Every country.

We'd fled London and travelled the world.

We'd traversed Pacific islands and pursued the Queen of Tonga.

We'd slept at the foot of a glacier, hunted kiwis and helicoptered onto the tallest mountains in the Southern Hemisphere.

She'd always been beside me to prevent my stupid mistakes.

Beside me to shout, "Far out, Simon."

Beside me to encourage me to experience new countries, to learn dairy farming, even to become a stadium rock star.

And now...

Now, I'd abandoned her on the friendly side of passport control, and I sat in Christchurch Airport surrounded by strangers.

I stared at the Air New Zealand plane on the tarmac as if my forthcoming circumnavigation would provide the answer to our predicament.

Our lives here lay amongst majestic, snow-capped mountains, opaque, ice-blue lakes and endless, deep-green forests. My passport-stamping appointment at the New Zealand High Commission in London would allow me to stay here forever, but the scenery couldn't pay the bills.

We had scant savings, unsustainable income and no future.

Do we belong here anymore?

CRACKLE

"Ladies and gentlemen, flight NZ201 to Brisbane is ready to board all remaining passengers. Please have your boarding passes ready and your passports open at the photo page."

I glanced back towards Fiona's last known position, picked up my cabin baggage and joined the end of the queue.

The queue for the flight to my first destination.

Queensland, Australia.

Where the sun always shone, everyone always said, "G'day," and every animal was out to kill you.

2. KYLIE MINOGUE

LATITUDE: 37° 55' 28" S
LONGITUDE: 164° 23' 8" E

Row twelve contained a young lady in the window seat, and a middle-aged man in the aisle.

"Hi," I said to him, "excuse me; I'm in the centre."

The man nodded and stood. I stuffed my bag under the seat as unobtrusively as I could and juggled my book, wallet and passport while completely failing not to bump elbows multiple times with both my neighbours.

My possessions suitably filed, I sat back, commandeered both armrests and glanced out of the window.

The girl to my left gripped the laminated safety instruction card and clenched her teeth. Her shoulder-length, dark-brown hair partly concealed her pale-skinned face, and small wrinkles appeared in the corners of her eyes.

She sucked in a breath. "First time flying."

"Definitely not." My head shook rapidly, and I watched for her reaction. "I'm a world traveller. I flew from London originally, and I've lived in New Zealand for the last year. Now I'm circumnavigating the globe anticlockwise on a cheap ticket my travel agent found, through Australia, Hong Kong and England, then I return via Los Angeles."

She rubbed her hands along her trousers and exhaled. "I meant, it's my first time flying."

"Oh, sorry." I blushed.

JOLT

The plane retreated from the air bridge, and she glanced at the flashing lights on the tarmac.

"I've never left New Zealand before, so I'm excited and scared." She chewed the inside of her cheek and pointed to the aisle. "What are they doing? Is everything okay?"

"It's the safety demonstration. They're informing us what to do in the event of an emergency."

She leant forward and concentrated as the crew took up their safety-speech stance, legs slightly apart, one hand tucked behind their backs, gleaming, white teeth broadcasting confidence at their charges.

"Ladies and gentlemen, though you may have flown with us many times, every aeroplane is different. Please watch our crew carefully as they guide you through the safety features of this aircraft."

The tall, attractive cabin crew member clacked and unclacked her demonstration seatbelt clasp. I'd received instruction in this activity multiple times, so I studied her face and wondered how many pots of dark-brown foundation she exhausted each week. The girl next to me continued to grasp the safety card, and her gaze see-sawed between the flight attendant's props and the symbols of the brace position. As the demonstration progressed, she groped under the seat for her lifejacket.

I leant back and interlocked my fingers behind my head. "Don't worry. If we do have an emergency, I'll remind you where everything is."

Her eyes widened, and she tilted her head. "Have you experienced a plane disaster?"

I cast my mind back to watching the pig-scaring airport manager on the runway in Tonga, dive-bombing the bulls on a training flight above Fiona's father's farm and plummeting hundreds of feet in a tiny propeller plane crossing the strait between the New Zealand mainland and Stewart Island.

"Um, no. But I've flown enough times to be familiar with the procedure."

The plane bumped along the taxiway. My neighbour rubbed the seat arms.

I leant towards her. "Let's talk about something to distract you from flying. I'll start. My name's Simon."

She smiled. "Nice to meet you. I'm Kylie."

"Like Kylie Minogue?"

She rolled her eyes, flicked her hair back and laughed. "Yes, like Kylie bloody Minogue."

I winced. "Sorry, you must hear that all the time. Are you travelling to Brisbane for a holiday, or to visit relatives, or…?"

She grinned. "Emigrating. I'm an accident and emergency nurse. My friend works at Brisbane's Princess Alexandra Hospital, and she's secured me a job. I can't wait to start; they pay twice what I earn here. Plus, it's Queensland, right? Sun, sea, sand and surf. And the other 's'." She giggled and clutched her fists to her chest. "I've watched every travel programme about it on the telly."

The plane slowed, semicircled and paused. Kylie relaxed her grip on the safety card. "How about you? Why are you flying to Australia tonight?"

"Immigration forced me out of New Zealand. I've lived with my girlfriend, Fiona, on her family's dairy farm for the last year, and played guitar in pubs for pocket money. But my visa expired, so I had to say goodbye."

"Oh, no. Did you have to break up with her?"

I pressed my hand to my chest. "No, thank goodness. They've granted me a new permanent visa, but it must be validated offshore; they can't stamp it in New Zealand. That seems crazy, but it's"—I formed air quotes with my fingers—"the rules."

"You have to fly out of the country to be allowed to fly back in again? Wow."

"I know. I'll be overseas for a few weeks, and we couldn't afford for both of us to travel, so I've left her behind."

My eyes closed as I pictured Fiona hugging me at the airport, then I bit my lip as I realised that, while I'd been chatting with Kylie, I hadn't missed her as much as I should have.

The engine noise increased, and the seat pushed into my back. Kylie's knuckles whitened as the plane took off and circled, then the window offered passengers a view of Christchurch's twinkling streetlights. I watched the red-and-white glow of cars travelling along a main road, and my chest tingled as I wondered if Fiona was driving one of them.

Kylie inclined her head towards her lap. She looked up again, and moisture glistened in her eyes.

"Are you okay?" I asked. "What's wrong?"

"I've left my boyfriend behind too. Although, he's really my ex-boyfriend. Gosh, that's the first time I've said that." Her mouth straightened. "We've been going out since school. But he'll never achieve anything, never go anywhere. He lives with his parents, works in his dad's shop and drinks every weekend with the same mates. Our families expected us to marry, breed a family and grow old living in the same bloody suburb. But I want more from life; I want to experience other countries. Then, last week, the police arrested him for drunk driving, which was the last straw. I finally plucked up the courage to move to Australia, so I dumped him."

"Gosh. That's brave." I raised my eyebrows. "I reckon everyone expects Fiona and me to tie the knot as well. But she's only 24."

"Same age as me." Kylie smiled and nodded. "I'm starting a new job and a new life in a new country. Maybe I'll meet one of those hunky, tanned surf patrol guys like on *Baywatch*."

The plane levelled, and the seatbelt sign extinguished.

"Erm, how did your boyfriend take the news?" I asked.

"Badly. When I told him my emigration plans, he threatened to kill himself and screamed he couldn't go on without me. He said he'd book a flight and come too. But he never will; it's all drama. He's history. He's excess baggage."

She pressed her lips together and closed her eyes. I glanced to my right, as the crew member with perfect, brown makeup parked the aroma of hot food alongside us.

≈ ≈ ≈

"Ladies and gentlemen, this is First Officer Mark Fraser speaking from the flight deck."

The cabin lights illuminated, and I opened one eye.

"We trust you've enjoyed flying with us tonight. The weather in Brisbane this evening is fine—29 degrees with a light south-easterly breeze. We're about to begin our descent, and we'll have you disembarking at a quarter to midnight. On behalf of Captain David Watson, the flight crew and myself, may I thank you for flying with Air New Zealand, and we look forward to seeing you again next time you travel."

Kylie stretched and bumped my shoulder. "Oops, sorry."

She yawned, gazed out of the window and shielded her eyes. "It's black. Where's Brisbane?"

I checked my watch. "It's still half an hour until we land. Are you excited?"

Kylie jiggled in her seat. "I can't wait. My friend's meeting me at the airport, then tomorrow we're shopping for bikinis and catching some sun on the beach before I start work." She plucked a small mirror from her bag and checked her hair. "Is someone collecting you?"

"Yep, Tommo, an old friend from London. He's an Aussie, originally from Perth. We haven't seen each other for two years. I'm staying a couple of weeks, and he'll show me around."

"Would you like to meet up on my day off? You could bring your friend too."

I smiled and nodded. "That'd be lovely. How do I contact you?"

"I'll write down the phone number of the nurses' quarters. I'm not sure where I'm staying yet, so it's best if you ask for my friend, Leanne Cheng."

She tugged out a pen and a small address book, tore off a page and copied down a string of digits. "Here you go. I think that's how you dial the number locally."

"Thanks, Kylie. Wow. Now I know two people in Brisbane."

She smiled. "And so do I."

≈ ≈ ≈

I waited beside her as the baggage carousel creaked around the central metal platform, accompanied by the perfume of rubber friction. A black holdall, a battered, grey suitcase and a pushchair reappeared for the third time.

Kylie crossed her arms and tapped her foot. "How long do bags take to come? I've seen these before."

I laughed. "At every airport I've been to, anywhere in the world, there are always three, sad-looking cases rotating around and around with nobody claiming them."

Kylie stood on tiptoe and glanced left and right. "But who'd leave the airport without their child's pram?"

A fresh batch of luggage approached from behind the black plastic flaps that divided us mere passengers from the baggage handlers who briefly had complete control over our life's possessions. The moving conveyor belt paraded items in front of us as if we were contestants in *The Generation Game*.

"Here's mine," called Kylie. She yanked a dark-green backpack from the carousel and threw it over her shoulder. "My friend'll be outside. Can we offer you a ride anywhere?"

"I'll be fine. Tommo's picking me up."

"Thanks for the chat and for helping me feel safe on the flight. Make sure you call me."

"I will. Good luck with your new job."

She exited through the green channel.

I glanced up at a wall clock and thought about Fiona.

Fiona.

She'd be asleep in a cosy, warm bed. Not standing in an unfamiliar airport at midnight waiting for a bag.

My backpack joined the luggage assortment waltzing along the conveyor, and I plucked it from the carousel, marched towards the exit and hoped I'd be able to find Tommo.

≈ ≈ ≈

It wouldn't have mattered if I owned an empty bag or a suitcase stuffed with machine guns and cocaine; I always speed-walked through the green channel and avoided eye contact with the border security officers.

I scurried after the super-organised line of people who'd populated their arrival cards in advance. Fiona always completed these for me, so the orange slip in my hand was probably wrong.

A strong Australian accent. "Good morning, sir. Your incoming passenger card, please."

Morning? I suppose it must be after midnight.

I stared at the exit, blocked by his shaved head and blue uniform. "Nothing to declare."

He ran his finger down the side of my card where I'd ticked 'no' against every question. "No fruit, vegetables, animal or plant matter?"

"No, none."

12

"Have you visited a farm in the last seven days?"

I had a flashback to burying my face in Jazz the farm dog's fur.

Was it yesterday? When I said goodbye to Fiona's parents, played the concert at the agricultural and pastoral show, had the crowd up and dancing, then dashed to the airport, hugged Fiona until she turned blue and boarded the plane for Brisbane?

"Oh, yes. I have been on a farm. In New Zealand."

"I see, sir. In which case, please remove your shoes."

3. ARACHNAPHOBIA

LATITUDE: 27° 24' 11" S
LONGITUDE: 153° 6' 57" E

I frowned and glanced at my feet. "Pardon? Remove my shoes?"

Have we suddenly entered a mosque?

The border security agent pointed. "Your shoes. Take them off. Anyone who's been in an agricultural environment seven days prior to entering Australia must have their footwear fumigated."

"Oh. Right."

I sat and unlaced my Timberland hiking boots.

"Wait there, please, sir."

The officer clumped away while my fellow passengers filed past my plastic seat of shame. My cheeks reddened; I leant on my elbows and inspected the white linoleum floor between my knees.

I sighed and wished Fiona were here. She'd have anticipated this and would've brought clean footwear.

My eyes closed, and I imagined she was sitting in the next chair.

The agent stood over me.

"All done, sir. Sorry for the wait. Straight through the green channel when you're ready."

"Thanks." *Yay! Australia, here I come.*

I burst through to the arrivals hall and scanned the lingering relatives for Tommo's six-foot frame, wide grin and curly, blonde hair. Nobody fitting that description waited inside, so I marched through the sliding doors and exited into the warmth of a Queensland summer's night.

14

Taxis collected passengers. Bus doors opened as people disembarked or boarded. I stared along the concourse, but nobody fitted Tommo's description.

I almost returned inside to ensure I hadn't missed him when the blare of a *Dukes of Hazzard* dixie klaxon shattered the night air.

DAH-DAH DAAAH DAAAH DAAAH DAH-DAH-DAH DAAAH DAAAH DAAAH DAAAAAH

A lifted pickup truck with tyres as big as minor planets swerved across both lanes of airport traffic, deposited two wheels on the pavement and advertised an orange, red and yellow flame design along the side of the white bodywork. I grinned and shook my head as I recognised the driver.

"Tommo!"

"Simon, why the hell are you standing around in the street like a hobo? Chuck your stuff in the tray and climb in."

I threw my backpack over my head and reached up to open the door. The car had no side steps, and I awkwardly knelt on the sill, pulled myself over the threshold and fell into the footwell.

Tommo laughed. "Bloody shortarse. Shit, it's good to see you."

I origamied into the seat, slammed the door and tugged on the seat belt. We lurched off the pavement and joined the airport traffic.

≈ ≈ ≈

Tommo shouted above the engine revs. "Sorry I'm late. I had to drop a girl home. Then she invited me in and, you know how it is."

I grinned. *Same old Tommo. A different girl every week. Possibly every night.*

His Queensland surfer-hair waved in the breeze as his right arm hung out of the driver's window.

"What've you been up to? I haven't seen you for ages."

The approaching car headlights made me blink. I'd missed his friendly Aussie accent, which instantly transported me to a world of wet T-shirt competitions, loud live bands and nights of drunken dancing.

"Yeah, last time we spoke, you were leaving London for your home in Perth, and you gave me expert advice about how you nipped to France to obtain a six-month tourist visa so you could stay in England longer."

"That's right, you'd shacked up with that Kiwi girl whose visa ran out."

"Still am."

"Still shacked up with her? She must be good. About time you tied the bloody knot. How long's it been now?"

We centrifuged a roundabout, possibly on two wheels. I glanced over my shoulder to ensure my baggage remained in the tray and my belongings weren't bouncing along the verge.

"Erm, Fiona and I've been together for over two years. A year in London, then another in New Zealand."

"Two years?" He shook his head. "I think my longest relationship lasted two months. What've you been doing in New Zealand?"

"Milking cows and playing guitar. Living with Fiona's parents."

"Bloody hell, you're middle-aged. What happened to party Simon who danced and drank all evening, collapsed on my sofa for the night and then woke up and did it all over again?"

"He's still here. Hiding deep inside somewhere."

We paused at a traffic light, and the potent scent of unfamiliar tropical plants wafted through the open passenger window as if we were motoring through the Chelsea Flower Show.

"We'll have to drag him out. Find you a nice holiday girl and have some fun."

Oh, no. There's no word for fidelity in Tommo-speak.

"You've been in Brisbane a while, haven't you?" I asked. "How come you didn't stay in Western Australia?"

"Long story. I returned from London to Perth, then at my mate's birthday party I chatted up this English girl. Long, blonde hair, great body, looked like the chick from Abba. Anyway, she tells me she wants to cross Australia to the east coast and, if I give her a ride, she'll pay for petrol. We hooked up. I mean, who could resist? We cruised over, carried on through Melbourne and Sydney, then ended up in Brisbane with no money between us.

She found a job working at a bar with accommodation thrown in, and I crashed for a while."

Tommo threw his left arm in the air, thumped the dashboard and exhaled. "Shit, that was the nearest I've ever come to settling down. I almost bought a pipe and bloody slippers."

I laughed. "You're not still living with her, are you?"

"You're joking. I've had"—he released the steering wheel and counted on his fingers—"eight girlfriends since. Nine if you count last night's chick."

My head shook as I recalled more than one occasion in London when I'd distracted one girl at Tommo's front door while another departed via the rear exit. I wondered if these talents would need to be employed again over the next couple of weeks.

The multi-lane freeway which backed onto floodlit yards of commercial buildings reminded me of a British motorway, and I realised I hadn't seen a road with more than one stream of traffic for over a year. This was nothing like the winding lanes of rural New Zealand I'd driven with Fiona.

I pressed my lips together and glanced into my lap.

Fiona. About time you tied the knot.

≈ ≈ ≈

Tommo's aerial twanged as he swerved the truck into a space under his house. "Welcome home. Grab your stuff, and I'll show you your room."

17

My baggage had managed to remain in the tray during the exciting journey, although it seemed to have been slammed against the side several times. I glanced up at the lights shining from Tommo's home. I'd entered plenty of houses with no upstairs; many houses in New Zealand fell into that category, but no downstairs? Tommo led me up exterior stairs, and I grasped the wooden handrail until a splinter stabbed my palm. He held open an insect screen, and I crashed my backpack onto his kitchen floor.

"What's in there?" he asked. "A dead body?"

"It's my dive gear. I thought we might enjoy some scuba while I'm here."

"Great idea. The last time we dived together was in the bloody English Channel. It'll be warmer here, anyway."

I planted my hands on my hips and glanced around at peeling paint, broken kitchen cupboards and gaps where architraves should've been. "Um, nice house. D'you own it?"

"Yep. I buy up old wrecks, live in them while I'm renovating, sell them and move on. I rent out the spare room to a mate. He's not here as he's FIFO, so you can have his room."

"FIFO?"

"Fly in—fly out. He works in the mines. So, he's ten days on, ten days off. He earns bloody good money, but it's not a lifestyle I could subscribe to. No women in the mines; I wouldn't survive. Anyway, dump your stuff and help yourself to whatever you can find. I'm going to crash out. It's been a big day."

"Me too. I slept for about two hours on the plane. See you in the morning."

I turned, laughed to myself and shook my head.

Tommo. Goodness knows what the next few days'll bring.

An absent mining worker's possessions surrounded me as I lay on the bed and listened to the swoosh—swoosh—swoosh of the ceiling fan.

Night insects scratched high-pitched squeaks outside.

I turned to my right and stared at where Fiona's face should've indented the pillow, inhaled through my nostrils and dreamt of smelling her shampoo.

I'm two thousand kilometres away from you, in another country, in a strange house, staying with a drinking buddy I haven't seen for two years who wants to set me up with a holiday date. I miss you.

I sat bolt upright, as a spider the size of a scalp massager ambled across the ceiling.

4. BOW BABES

LATITUDE: 27° 32' 1" S
LONGITUDE: 153° 4' 24" E

The giant arachnid paused close to the ceiling light and wiggled some of its appendages.

Shit.

I crabbed off the bed and ran into the living room.

"Tommo, quick. Help."

A door swung open, and a boxer-shorted Tommo rubbed his eyes.

"What the hell's wrong? You look like you've heard a banshee."

I jabbed my finger behind me. "There's a humongous great big vast huge giant man-eating spider on my ceiling. Help me kill it. D'you have spray? Or a swat? Maybe a cricket bat?"

Tommo grinned and nodded. "I know there's a spider. She lives here."

I waved my arms. "She? What d'ya mean—she? It's a bloody enormous gigantic hairy monster and we need to kill it."

He patted the air with both hands. "Calm down, calm down. You can't kill her. That's Sweetykins."

I gaped. "Sweetykins? You've named it?"

"Yep. She's a huntsman. She won't harm you. She comes out at night and eats the other spiders which will hurt you, such as redbacks and white-tails. Ignore her and go to sleep."

"I thought every spider in Australia killed humans with one bite. How the hell do I sleep with a spider the size of a twelve-inch record staring at me?"

"Huntsmen aren't poisonous. Don't disturb her. She'll be gone by the morning."

"Don't disturb her? What about *her* disturbing *me*? And how the hell d'you know it's a she? Have you taken it out on a date or something?"

Tommo laughed. "Nah, she's not my type. Doesn't shave her legs."

"Very funny. So, she's not dangerous?"

"No more dangerous than any other woman I've lived with."

"I puffed upwards and shook my head. "You Aussies keep some odd pets."

Sweetykins watched me climb back into bed. I left the bedside lamp on in case she decided to consume me during the night.

≈ ≈ ≈

TZZZEEEEEEE.

TZZZEEEEEEEEEEEEEEEE.

TZ TZ TZ TZZZEEEEEEEEEEEE

The sound of an extremely enthusiastic dentist operating somewhere in the house woke me, followed by an expletive which didn't sound like words a professional dentist would normally use. The sun beamed through the open windows and projected striped, diagonal patterns on the wall. Sweetykins had vanished, and I lifted my bedcovers to ensure she hadn't secreted herself there. I decided the drill noise came from underneath me, so I walked through the kitchen doorway and down the outdoor stairs.

Warm, subtropical air filled my lungs. A tree which thrived despite obvious lack of care broadcast a strong fragrance from its red-and-cream patterned flowers. Tommo's wooden house, painted in assorted shades of green from peppermint toothpaste through to traffic light, stood in a row of similarly decorated residences. Most of them needed further applications of Dulux in the not-too-distant future.

None of them had a downstairs.

Tommo's bare, shoeless legs poked out from under his car.

I addressed his toes. "Hey, Tommo. How come none of these houses has a downstairs? All the living and sleeping areas are upstairs, and underneath there's car parking and storage."

"Morning, Simon," said Tommo's voice. "They're called Queenslanders. It's an iconic local design. Sea breezes blow under the house and keep it cool."

"I've never seen them anywhere else."

Tommo shuffled out, sat up and ruffled his hair. He grinned at me. "Look at you, with your T-shirt and ripped denim shorts. All you need's a suntan and you'll be a native. The chicks are gonna love you. You had a good sleep, anyway."

"What time is it?"

"Ten o'clock. I'm fixing the wiring on the ute. Neither of the brake lights work, and while I'm under here, I thought I'd mount some spotties on the roo bar."

"Jeez, I need to learn Australian. I know a ute's what we call a pickup truck, but what are spotties and roo bars?"

He stood and slapped his hand twice on a wide, black, metal tube across the front of the vehicle. "This is a roo bar."

"Where I come from, we call it a bull bar. Let me guess. 'Spotties' are those big headlights?"

"Yep. Spotlights. Could you stand at the back and tell me if the brake lights work?"

"Sure."

He climbed in the driver's seat and pumped a pedal while I walked to the rear of the car and confirmed two reds showed.

"Now," said Tommo, "let's test these new babies. Could you stand in front?"

I stumped around to the bonnet and held my hand to my eyes as two massive, white spotlights blinded me as if I'd been caught crossing no man's land between North and South Korea.

Yellow and orange blobs danced in my vision.

"Yep. They're working."

"Great. We'll need them tonight."

"Tonight? What's planned for tonight?"

I imagined he proposed to illuminate Sydney Opera House single-handedly.

"I thought we'd drive to Byron."

"Byron?"

"Byron Bay. It's a town across the border of New South Wales. You wanted to go diving, so I rang up and booked on tomorrow's boat. The chap told me we might see manta rays."

"Wow, are you serious? I haven't dived since Tonga, over a year ago. And I've never seen mantas. I can't wait."

"Cool. Oh, and on the way, we'll stop at the beach and check out the babes. See if we can pick up a couple for the evening."

I shook my head. "You can pick up however many girls you like, but I have a steady girlfriend."

"You've a girlfriend in New Zealand. You need another one here."

I sighed. "How long's the journey?"

"About three hours. Straight down the Pacific Highway. We'll grab food at Macca's."

I scratched my head. "If it's straight down the highway, why do we need the big spotlights?"

"We'll arrive after dark when the roos are feeding. They don't possess road sense, and I don't want to smack into one at a hundred kilometres per hour."

He stood with his hands on his hips, studied the recent additions, grinned and nodded.

"Plus, they look the dog's bollocks, don't they? Chicks love these big off-road trucks. You good to go? I'll grab my thongs."

I had a brief, unwelcome vision of Tommo in a tiny, G-string bikini bottom before remembering thongs was the Australian word for flip-flops.

Packing for the trip took one minute, as I hadn't unpacked from the flight. I threw my dive bag in the back of the ute and hopped in. The dixie horn echoed around the carport, and I ducked down, as I wasn't sure the neighbours appreciated Tommo's departure announcement.

≈ ≈ ≈

Tommo's vehicle had been invented before air-conditioning, so we opened the windows of the cab and dangled our arms as we drove. A sliding window between us and the tray of the pickup allowed some of the 38-degree breeze to hairdryer through.

The car wouldn't squeeze under the max headroom sign in the drive-through, so we circled and searched for a space. McDonald's suddenly seemed attractive as my tummy rumbled. I wondered if the company owned a system which pumped delicious smells into the car park.

Inside the restaurant, a group of orange-vested tradespeople munched breakfast and drank steaming coffee. Several families queued at the counter, and the staff shouted food orders at each other like Nasdaq traders on Black Monday.

Tommo pulled cash out. "What'll you have?"

"A bacon and egg McMuffin and a hash brown, please. And a coffee."

He leant on the counter. "Two bacon and egg McMuffins, two hash browns and two coffees, please, love."

The server blushed and smiled at Tommo. She swivelled and grabbed our meals, filled cups with coffee from a dispenser, and clipped on plastic lids. As she slid our trays across the counter, I could've sworn she fluttered her eyelashes. What was it with Tommo and the ladies? He hadn't brushed his hair or shaved, and they still loved him.

I broke flakes from my hash brown and tasted the salty vegetable oil. After a year of living in remotest New Zealand, three and a half hours from the nearest fast food outlet, I wasn't sure whether my stomach had braced itself sufficiently for the assault of Tommo's daily diet.

Tommo winked at a young lady on the next table, who turned to her friend and giggled. He grinned at me and nodded his head to the right twice. "What d'ya reckon? One each?"

The girls dumped their rubbish and departed.

He shrugged. "Ah, well. Plenty more fish in the sea."

I glanced over my shoulder. "Yes, where is the sea? I always thought Brisbane was on the beach. The ads on the telly for Australian tourism and Paul Hogan spouting, "Come and say G'day," all show bikini-clad, stunning girls jogging along wide, saffron-coloured sands. It's the same on the soap opera *Home and Away*. But all I've seen are suburbs and freeways."

"Brisbane's nickname's the River City. The beaches they show on TV are Goldie or the Sunny Coast."

"Goldie?"

Tommo laughed. "The Gold Coast. We'll stop on the way to Byron. That's where the babes hang out. And the Sunny Coast's north of Brisbane. The Sunshine Coast."

I took a bite of McMuffin.

The Sunshine Coast. What a fantastic name for a location.

"Will we have time to visit the Sunshine Coast while I'm here too?"

Tommo scrumpled his wrapper and stuffed it in his empty hash brown bag. "Of course. I'm happy to go anywhere for ladies."

≈ ≈ ≈

Subtropical sun fried my left arm Kellogg's logo-colour as we dodged around trucks. After a year living in remote, rural West Coast New Zealand, where the main highway travelled over single-lane, road-rail bridges, I leant forward and stared open-mouthed at the Australian traffic. A distant cluster of skyscrapers blurred through the heat haze.

"Is that where we're headed?"

"Yep. Surfers Paradise. Sun, sea and sand. It's a perfect afternoon to chill on the beach and watch the talent."

Two large parrots skrarked overhead as we crossed a river and paused in traffic. I glanced at the water and observed a small, white boat with a shirtless young man at the wheel and a pair of bikini-clad women riding in the front. They clinked wine glasses, and I smiled.

Tommo laughed. "Are you checking out the bow babes?"

I swivelled my head away from the window and cleared my throat. "Bow babes?"

"The chicks riding in the boat's bow. Plenty more once we reach the sand. I bet you can't wait to feast your eyes on the Aussie girls."

"Um, they do look attractive in their bikinis."

"That's the spirit."

The traffic inched forward. I glanced up at balcony-festooned apartments and watched daily life on the Gold Coast: a man sipping from a bottle and reading a newspaper, two older ladies leaning over a balustrade above him, a young boy patting a small dog.

Tommo swung the wheel as we passed a sign advertising an enticing-looking housing development called Paradise Waters, then the road skirted a wide beach fringed by tired, dusty palm trees. Teenagers in singlets and shorts pointed at Tommo's flame-adorned vehicle, and he grinned and waved.

"Your car certainly attracts attention," I said. I smiled and waved too, although I wasn't sure why.

Tommo nodded. "That's the idea."

He cruised the beachfront and rubbernecked. "Any spaces?"

"Yep. Oh, it's for disabled people. I'll keep looking."

Lifeguards in bright-yellow polo shirts watched the sea from small towers. I thought of Kylie and wondered whether she'd find her *Baywatch* dream man here. Groups of people scattered across the wide, flat beach, but they didn't crowd each other. Not like in England, where, on a hot, sunny day, families guarded their square metre of pebbles with a fortress of beach chairs, umbrellas, towels, picnic hampers, possibly even boiling oil, and valiantly fought off marauding intruders attempting to pillage their space.

I pointed. "She's moving her car."

A lady in a small Mazda indicated and pulled out in front of us.

I held one finger flat to my mouth. "Will this truck fit?"

"Only one way to find out." Tommo grinned, drove in forward and bumped up the kerb. His car rested at an angle with one wheel on the pavement.

"No worries." He high fived me, and I opened my door and plummeted the six feet to the ground.

Tommo rummaged through the pockets of his swim shorts, which exhibited an orange graphic of tanned ladies decorating a palm tree-fringed ocean. "D'you have any dollars? We'll need to feed the meter."

"Yep. Hold out your hands."

I tugged coins from my denim shorts and tipped them into Tommo's cupped palms. He emptied my pile onto the pavement and sorted through them, then threw a couple back at me. "New Zealand money. Won't work too well here. All right. That's $3.20. How much is the meter?"

"It's $1.80 per hour. We've enough for almost two hours."

"That'll do. The meter maids'll top it up."

I frowned and shrugged. "Meter maids?"

"Goldie meter maids. World famous since the 1960s."

I had a vision of ladies wearing outfits from *Grease*, singing *You're the One That I Want,* as they danced ensemble down the pavement.

"I've never heard of meter maids. What are they?"

"D'you have your camera? I'll take a photo of you with them." He grinned. "Just don't send it to Fiona."

We locked the dive gear in the front seats, grabbed our towels and headed for the beach.

I paused at the top of steps leading to the sand and breathed salt air into my nostrils. The cries of gulls and the screams of children blended into the background noise of the towering, constant, pounding surf. Black dots of surfers bobbed over the crests. With each wave, a few of them rode towards the beach with varying degrees of success, and I couldn't work out how they didn't all smash into each other.

The sun prickled the back of my neck. "Damn," I said. "I didn't bring sunscreen."

"They'll have some at the lifeguard tower," said Tommo. "But don't worry. At this time of day, it's easy to find shade."

He pointed. At every place where a skyscraper overlooked the beach, the wide, golden sand lay in shadow.

"Gosh, I didn't expect that. I guess it's handy. You can choose to lie in the shade of a tall building, or work on your tan between them."

"I think we should set up exactly there." Tommo pointed at a patch of sand precisely equidistant from two pairs of girls lying on their towels. He jumped down the steps, kicked off his thongs and led me towards his chosen location. I observed he strategically placed his towel close enough for conversation, far away enough not to be blatant. I wondered if he came here every weekend to find an evening date. He stripped off his singlet, and I pulled off my T-shirt and denim shorts.

Tommo pointed at my crotch and laughed.

5. BUDGIE SMUGGLERS

LATITUDE: 28° 0' 3" S
LONGITUDE: 153° 25' 38" E

I glanced down. "What's funny?"

"Look at your budgie smugglers. We'll have to score you a pair of boardies."

I squinted at my black swimming trunks.

"Budgie smugglers?"

"Budgie smugglers. Your swimmers." He grinned and glanced at the girls. "Just don't become too excited watching the ladies. Everyone'll know about it. D'you wanna jump in for a swim?"

I eyeballed the rollers. Spray flew up as each wave hit the beach, in a white noise of salt water.

"Is it safe?"

Tommo pointed. "See those red-and-yellow flags in front of the lifeguard tower?"

"Yep." Two sticks speared into the ground with a pennant at the top of each.

"That's where it's safe to swim."

I scratched my head, swivelled my gaze to the lifeguard tower and back to the flags. Two bare-chested, tanned, muscly men wearing blue shorts mounted a beach buggy and patrolled along the sand. This was all very *Baywatch*.

"How do the lifeguards know the crocodiles aren't in that section?"

Tommo frowned, then punched my arm and grinned. "Ya big galoot. The sea in Surfers Paradise isn't dangerous because of crocs. It's the rips."

"Rips?"

I wondered if rips were a formerly unknown Australian sea creature even more dangerous than the crocs.

Tommo nodded. "Yep, the rips. I'll show you."

We scuffed down the beach and stopped a short distance away from the lifeguard tower.

Tommo pointed at a wide line of blue water, which stretched away from the shore perpendicular to the sand. "See that? That's a rip. Drags you out. Those people are too close to it. They should keep between the flags where the lifeguards can watch them."

"If they swim into the rip, it'll sweep them away and no-one'll ever see them again?"

"They're foreigners; might've never seen the ocean before in their lives; they holiday here and don't have a clue. If you're ever caught in a rip, don't fight it 'cos you can't. The sea's stronger than you. Swim parallel to the beach until you're out of it and then swim back in. The lifeguards rescue hundreds of people every year who don't know that."

We walked back to the flags, and I scanned the waves. "There aren't any crocs?"

Tommo grinned. "Nah, mate. The sharks ate them all." He ran into the sea, and I followed him.

Tommo dived through the first wave and surfaced. The next breaker knocked me flat. I stood, choked, and fell over again. We crashed around in the surf until it exhausted us, then lay in the shallows. A small crab popped out of a hole and washed away with the incoming wave.

"Not a bad life, is it?" said Tommo. He tossed his blonde hair back and flicked water behind him. Two ladies in matching red swimsuits sprinted into the sea and jumped the waves.

"D'ya think you'd ever move to Australia?" he asked. "Sunshine, surf and the chicks, can't beat it."

"I hadn't considered Australia. Fiona misses England. After I return from my world trip, we'll need to make some decisions. I love helping her dad on the farm and playing guitar in pubs, but without a proper job I can't do those forever."

"How old are you now?"

"Twenty-nine."

"Getting on, Simon. You'll be in your thirties soon, and then it's all mortgages and nappies. My brother's thirty-four and he's so bloody married, he's put on about fifteen kilos."

30

I wrapped my arms around my knees and stared at the waves. Seagulls ark-ark-arked above me and soared sideways on thermals like discarded paper wrappers. I dug a small hole in the sand with my fingers. "D'you think I should ask her?"

The red-swimsuit girls exited the sea. Their long, wet hair snaked over their bodies, and I glanced away.

"Ask her what?"

"Ask her if she'll marry me?"

Tommo's eyebrows shot up. "Marry her? Is she the one?"

"I guess so. I mean, we're sitting here, and you're checking out these stunning girls, and I can see they're attractive to look at, but I'm thinking about Fiona, and how I wish she were enjoying the surf with me. I suppose she must be."

"Bloody hell, mate, you are serious about her. You could do the whole bended knee thing in the airport when you return. That's what my brother did with his girlfriend."

"Did she say yes?"

"She slapped him around the head, told him to stop embarrassing her and dragged him out of the arrivals hall. They're still married today."

We both laughed. Tommo stood. "Come on. You might be dreaming of walking up the aisle, but I'm not, and there are chicks waiting."

We strolled back to our towels and sat facing the sea.

"G'day, ladies," Tommo called to one pair of girls. "D'you have any sunscreen we could borrow? We seem to have forgotten ours."

I blushed and looked away. I wondered if he'd just invented this chat-up line or whether he had a selection.

The girl threw her arm around her friend and kissed her on the cheek. "Get lost, creep. We're together."

Tommo turned away. "Maybe not them. You have a try with the other two."

I opened my eyes wide. "Me? No way."

"Fiona'll never know. Surely she wouldn't object to you talking? Ask them if you could borrow some sunscreen."

"Really?"

"Yep. What's the worst that could happen?"

I stood, placed my hands on my hips and surveyed the beach. *Fiona, please forgive me.*

"They won't bite," said Tommo.

I walked towards the girls. They lay on their fronts with their bikini straps undone and read a magazine between them. My mouth dried up, and I'd no idea how I'd be able to speak. I was about to step right past them and pretend to be doing something else, when they spoke to each other in an Eastern European language.

I turned on my heels and marched back.

"How d'you go?" asked Tommo.

"They don't speak any English; they're Russian or something. Sorry." I shrugged and held my palms up.

"Damn, we struck out this afternoon. Maybe we'll have better luck in Byron."

I lay down and experienced the odd combination of the warm air and the shade from the buildings. The last time I'd tanned on a skyscraper-backed beach was with Fiona in Waikiki, on the way to Tonga.

Hawaii. The mopeds. The snorkelling. The *luau*.

Fiona running into the sea in her bikini.

I miss you so much.

≈ ≈ ≈

Tommo prodded me. "No time for napping on the job. Time to head to our next destination."

I sat up and rubbed my eyes. "How long until we reach Byron?"

"About an hour. We'll arrive in time for something to eat."

A brief image of yet another Big Mac crossed my mind, and I hoped McDonald's hadn't reached Byron Bay yet.

"Okay. Could I look in that gift shop before we go?"

I entered the store and browsed the displays. Should I have desired, I could've bought Fiona a necklace with a silver outline of Australia, a bracelet engraved with the word 'Queensland' or earrings with kangaroos dangling from them.

A salesman approached me. "Yes, mate. Can I help you find anything in particular?"

"Something for my girlfriend. D'you have any normal jewellery?"

He tilted his head and frowned. "Normal jewellery?"

"I'm not looking for souvenirs. Something more classic."

"Is your girlfriend into surfing? We have bracelets with wave designs." He indicated a small display on a shelf.

"I don't think she's ever surfed. D'you have anything plainer? Not with Australia on it?"

He pointed at a sign behind the till. "This shop's called Down Under Jewellery and Gifts."

"Ah. I didn't notice. Thank you."

I stepped back outside and joined Tommo.

"Did you find anything?" he asked.

"No, just looking."

We stood on the pavement and waited for a gap in the traffic. Tommo nudged me and pointed at his parked truck. "Here we go. Have a look at these two beauties. What d'ya reckon?"

A pair of young ladies sporting gold bikinis stood by his car. One giraffed on tiptoes and slid a piece of paper under the passenger-side windscreen wiper.

"Bloody hell," said Tommo. "That girl's leaving you her phone number. Looks like you've pulled."

My cheeks flushed. "Hilarious. Are those the meter maids?"

"Yep," said Tommo. "D'you want a photo with them?"

We crossed the road as the girls moved onto the next car.

"Ladies," called Tommo.

They pivoted on their heels, grinned with identical, perfect, white teeth and, in a well-rehearsed move, posed like Linda Evangelista on the cover of *Cosmopolitan*.

"Could we take a photo? My friend's from England and wants a souvenir to make his girlfriend jealous."

I hid behind him and inspected the pavement.

"Of course," said one of the golden twins. "Stand between us, in front of the world famous Surfers Paradise beach."

They'd clearly shared the same tanning lotion, the same bottle of bleach to colour their hair and each one wore a prom queen-sash which read *Surfers Paradise Meter Maid*.

Tommo unlocked his car. "Grab your camera."

I tugged out my Olympus, switched it on and passed it to him.

The girls stood on either side of me and draped their arms around my shoulders. They crouched slightly. Not only were they both taller than me, they also wore sparkly, gold platform shoes, which added another six inches to their height and reminded me of costumes in *Priscilla, Queen of the Desert*. I rested my arms on their hips, and my hands touched their sun-warmed skin. I hadn't felt a bare, female body except Fiona's for years and I wasn't sure if I should do this, plus my face was at the same level as their boobs and I didn't want to turn too far to the left or right in case they jabbed me in the eye.

CLICK

"I'll snap another one. Can you both shuffle closer to Simon?"
They squished against me, and I realised how a hot dog sausage feels in a bun.

CLICK

The meter maids elevated to their full height of two feet taller than me.
"Thanks, ladies," said Tommo.
"No worries. Could we have a donation, for the photo?"
Australian accents. Similar, yet different to New Zealand ones. More like Home and Away.
I reached into my denim shorts, gave them a $5 note, stood back and slipped my hands in my pockets. Paying to pose with naked, female flesh didn't feel right, and I relaxed as they continued down the street, attending to their customers.
We pulled our bags from the front seats, threw them in the tray and climbed into the ute.
I cupped my chin and watched the meter maids' rears saunter along the parked cars. "They walk up and down the esplanade all day, feeding parking meters?"
"Yep. It's organised by the local traders. The public can enjoy a day out, buy from the shops, eat in the restaurants, drink in the bars and not worry about parking tickets. I'm surprised you haven't heard of them."

The smell of eucalyptus filled the air, and the sun lowered in the sky as we rejoined the highway and headed south. Above the sound of the ute's engine, I heard the loud scraping calls of ten thousand cockatoos in the trees fringing the road.

"It gets dark early, doesn't it?" I asked. "It's six o'clock and the sun's setting already."

Tommo looked at his watch. "In one minute, it'll be seven o'clock."

"Sorry?" I shrugged and frowned.

Tommo pointed at a sign which said 'State Border—New South Wales'. "We're in another state now. They have daylight saving; we don't subscribe to it in Queensland. So now it's seven o'clock."

"Oh wow. Sydney's in New South Wales, right? Could we visit? I'd love to see the Opera House and the Harbour Bridge."

"Only another twelve hours' solid drive." He grinned. "I don't think we'll make it tonight."

The scenery became more rural in the dusk. Tommo indicated, and we exited onto a smaller main road. Vast flocks of white birds launched from trees as we slowed for a roundabout.

"We're almost at Byron Bay," he said. "Chilled-out, laid back, hippy town. Let's find somewhere to stay, eat at Macca's and then chat up some girls over a few beers. Then tomorrow, are you still up for a dive? See the manta rays?"

"Sounds good."

Tommo swung the wheel violently across the road, and I grabbed the door handle as the car swerved so hard, I worried it'd tip on its side.

"Shit!" he said. "Did you see that?"

6. BIERFEST

LATITUDE: 28° 38' 28" S
LONGITUDE: 153° 36' 22" E

I gripped the dash, and my heart thumped against the inside of my chest.

"Was that a kangaroo?"

"Yep," said Tommo. "A massive grey. Keep your eyes peeled. They feed in the evening, so they'll be everywhere."

"There." I pointed at the side of the road where two adults and a joey munched dinner and ignored the traffic. "What are all these kangaroos doing here? Have they escaped from a zoo?"

Tommo slowed and peered into the dusk. "They're wild. And you don't want to hit one. It'd be fatal for the roo, and serious for us and the car."

I leant forward and scanned the bushes. The last thing I wanted to do was kill Skippy.

≈ ≈ ≈

I loved feeling warm at night wearing only a T-shirt. Groups of young people strolled along Byron Bay's streets as we cruised through the town. Light spilt from shops displaying tie-dye clothes, long flowery dresses, flowing scarves and strings of beads. I heard surf, but I couldn't see the ocean in the darkness.

"Main Beach Backpackers." Tommo pointed. "This'll do."

Four wooden steps led up to a reception area, tastefully decorated in the style of Bob Dylan's living room. A joss-stick mounted in a small, glass bottle wisped smoke. The man standing behind the counter had long, white hair and an impressive long, white beard.

"G'day, guys. Welcome to Byron, the most chilled-out town in Australia. You here for long?"

He wore a style of tunic made fashionable by biblical prophets, garnished by a collection of dangly neck ornaments.

Tommo gazed around and sniffed. "One night. D'you have two beds in a dorm?"

"No problem, man. I'll put you in number three. Four beds and its own bathroom. Here's the key. That'll be forty bucks, please."

Tommo and I both pulled out twenty-dollar notes. I heaved my dive gear onto my shoulder, and we headed through a door behind reception.

≈ ≈ ≈

"Here we are," I said. "Number three. The door's already open."

We entered a cramped space which smelt of my grandmother's sparsely-used guest bedroom. Paint flaked off light-blue walls which had four single beds shoved against them, and a high, frosted window provided a convenient gallery for an exhibition of spiders' webs. Tommo threw his gear on one of the less stained beds, and I dumped my dive bag in a corner.

"This place stinks," I said. "Fiona wouldn't sleep in it."

"Good job she's not here, then. You hungry?"

"Yep, sure. I could eat something."

"All right, we'll find Macca's and then head to the pub. Sound good?"

I sighed, and my tastebuds paused at the thought of Big Macs and fries. We locked the door and returned to Moses in reception.

"Excuse me," said Tommo. "Which way's McDonald's?"

"No McDonald's in Byron, man. No fast food at all in Byron. We didn't allow it."

I hid a grin behind my hand.

Tommo's face paled. "What d'ya mean, no McDonald's?"

"Byron people don't need fast food. We like our healthy lifestyle, untouched by American multinationals. All those places do is breed antisocial, modern behaviour. And litter."

I observed a half-finished can of 7up at his elbow and figured his sentiment might be selective.

Tommo darted a wide-eyed glance at me and gripped the reception counter. "Where's the nearest Macca's, then?"

The receptionist's Gandalf-like sleeve drooped from his tunic as he pointed. "Half-hour drive to Ballina. That's as close as we allowed it to come." He unfolded a pamphlet displaying pictures of cooked meals. "They serve burgers at the pub."

Tommo ran his hand through his hair. "Jeez, I hope they're as good as Macca's. I bet they don't have the special sauce. Which way's the pub?"

"Just on the corner by the roundabout, man. The Beach Hotel."

≈ ≈ ≈

Young people crammed the pub tables, and a fog of blue-grey smoke hung in the air, not all of which smelt like tobacco. A bearded man tuned a guitar in the corner, and a girl wearing a flowing, colourful dress and one thousand kilos of cheap jewellery danced by herself to background music. I reckoned she was on drugs.

A waitress negotiated the crowd with two plates.

"Those burgers look pretty good," I said. "I'll buy the food; you grab the drinks."

Tommo gazed at the waitress and the burgers but didn't distinguish which one he appreciated more. "I'll try them. Not sure about bloody salad, though. Why the hell would you stuff vegetables in a burger?"

I leant against the bar.

"Yes, mate," said the long-haired, Jesus-bearded barman.

"Two burgers and chips, please."

"No salad on mine," said Tommo, behind my shoulder.

The barman wrote on a pad. "Drinks? It's happy hour for another fifteen minutes. Beer and house wine's half price."

Tommo yanked a wodge of cash from his back pocket. "I'll tell you what, Simon. Let's buy all our drinks while it's cheap. Then we can spend the whole evening drinking them."

"Okay." I sucked in a breath through clenched teeth.

"How many beers can you down in a night?" he asked. "We're diving tomorrow, so we should limit ourselves. If we buy four jugs between us, we only pay for two."

Two jugs each? I'm out of Tommo drinking-session practice.

"D'you want to grab that table near the band before someone pinches it? I'll bring the beers. Take two glasses with you."

"Sure."

I collected two pint tumblers from a pile on the bar, jostled through groups of people drinking, chatting and smoking, and annexed the small, round table.

Tommo dumped two jugs of beer on the little table, then returned to the bar and fetched the other two. He plonked them down and poured.

"Cheers, Simon. None of your warm English bitter here. Welcome to 'Straya."

He gulped his drink. I slurped from my glass and licked my upper lip.

"'Straya?"

"Australia. Jeez, we'll have to train you to speak 'strine."

"'Strine?"

"Never mind."

"Excuse me," said a voice behind us.

The waitress splayed four jugs of beer in front of her chest like a Munich Bierfest Fraulein. She rearranged our existing drinks and slotted the new ones between them.

"What's this?" asked Tommo. "We didn't order these."

The waitress finished burying the table under gallons of beer. "It's happy hour. You bought four jugs, so you've four more, free. Enjoy."

My eyebrows raised at her, then at Tommo.

"Ah," he said. "I thought the drinks were expensive, but I didn't say anything. I meant to buy four jugs, including the free ones." He clinked his glass against mine. "Cheers, cobber."

I sighed and, as the flowery-dressed girl crooned *San Francisco (Be Sure to Wear Flowers in Your Hair)*, we completed jug number one.

≈ ≈ ≈

Thirty minutes later, the band had progressed to *California Dreamin'* and we'd progressed to jug number three.

The waitress hovered over us. "Two burgers? One without salad?"

"Thanks, love," said Tommo. "I'm starving. Hang on." He rearranged several jugs, belched spectacularly and inserted an extra crotchet into the third verse.

"The chips are salty," I said. "They make me thirsty." I tipped back the contents of jug number three and added it to the empty glassware under the table. Tommo topped me up from jug number four.

I stood, grabbed the back of my chair, wobbled to the toilets and leant against the wall with both hands to ensure it didn't collapse.

Thank goodness Fiona wasn't here. I could almost hear her voice from New Zealand saying, "Far out, Simon. You can sleep on the couch tonight."

We still had four jugs to drink.

≈ ≈ ≈

9:30. Jug number six had emptied, and I couldn't swallow any more.

"I'm done. I feel like the European beer lake's sloshing around inside me and it's working its way back up. Anyway, don't we have diving tomorrow? What time's that?"

"Shit, I forgot about diving," said Tommo. "We need to be at the shop by 10:30 a.m."

"10:30. Okay. I've time to sober up."

I pushed myself to my feet. "At least I can stand. I'll be fine."

Tommo swigged from jug seven. We abandoned number eight.

≈ ≈ ≈

I spent a minute attempting to push the exit door before Tommo grabbed it and pulled. The warm night air disorientated me; I wasn't accustomed to leaving air-conditioned premises and feeling hotter outside.

We staggered along the beach road. Voices from the sand and the flickers of fires betrayed nocturnal beach activities.

A police car cruised slowly.

"Simon," whispered Tommo. "It's the cops. Walk as straight as you can."

I bent double with laughter at this observation and hid behind a palm tree.

The hippy had closed reception for the night, and we spent several minutes trying to insert the key into the exterior door before it swung open by itself. Tommo had a similar challenge unlocking the room.

I held my hand over my mouth. "Hurry. I'm not feeling great."

Tommo rolled his eyes and clicked the door open. "What happened to party Simon? You held your drink better in the old days."

I knelt and gripped the toilet. The refreshing, cold porcelain caressed my cheek, and my eyelids closed.

Tommo knocked. "You all right? Can I come in? I need a pee."

I opened my eyes. The room centrifuged around me like a particularly exciting fairground ride, although the toilet stayed still. I hugged it to prevent it from waltzing across the floor and taking me with it.

Tommo opened the bathroom door.

"Go away," I said. "Let me die in peace."

He pushed me aside, and I heard the tinkly sound of peeing, followed by water cascading. The flush sprinkled my face with delicious, cold water.

I lay down beside the bowl.

≈ ≈ ≈

The unexpected sensation of being dragged by my legs across the bathroom floor woke me abruptly. My eyelids unstuck, and I scrabbled at the tiles.

"Comfortable night?" said Tommo's voice. "Don't forget, we're scuba diving in three hours."

"Fetch me some water. I knew I shouldn't have drunk all that beer."

I rose to my knees and paused over the toilet.

Breathe, Simon. Breathe. You're going diving. You're going to be okay.

The face of a 100-year-old Simon reflected in the mirror. "I'm never drinking again. This time, I mean it."

"You said that every Sunday morning in London. Let's find a chemist on the way to the dive shop. We should ask if they've anything to make you better." Tommo threw a towel at me. "Have a cold shower and chuck your swimmers on."

≈ ≈ ≈

The clinical odour caused my stomach contents to somersault, as I gripped a shop display and bent double. A middle-aged pharmacist leant on the counter with both hands and inspected me. I figured, given the party reputation of Byron Bay, this scene was commonplace. Maybe a daily occurrence.

"May I help you?"

I shuffled towards him, leant on one elbow and held my forehead.

"D'you have anything to prevent vomiting? I overdid it last night and I'm scuba diving in one hour. This is an emergency."

The pharmacist crossed his arms. "Are you still vomiting? Have you kept anything down today?"

"I haven't dared eat today."

He sucked in a breath through his teeth and shook his head. "There's no point taking tablets if you're going to bring them up again. Sorry. Maybe reschedule your diving?"

I glanced at Tommo. "We can't reschedule diving. I'll have to risk it."

I turned away and wondered whether he'd refused to prescribe anything to teach me a lesson. In Fiona's absence, someone had to.

≈ ≈ ≈

"G'day, guys, welcome to Ocean Divers. Are you here for the Julian Rocks trip?"

Tommo gave him two thumbs-up. "Yep, we booked yesterday."

"Fantastic. I'm Chris, one of the instructors."

He wore a white T-shirt displaying his dive school logo. Someone seemed to have hacked the sleeves off using garden shears.

"You've picked a great day. There's a breeze, though; might be bumpy on the ride out."

I held my stomach and blew my cheeks out. "Erm, how long's the boat trip?"

"About ten minutes on one of our IRBs." Chris pointed at two grey, inflatable boats balanced on trailers behind four-wheel drive vehicles.

"D'you suffer from seasickness?" He plucked a tiny cardboard box from the counter and held it up. "I have some Kwells. Would you like one?"

"What are they?"

"Seasickness tablets. They prevent nausea."

"Prevent nausea? Yes, please. How many can I swallow at once?"

"I'm no doctor, but I usually take a single one. That's what it says on the packet."

He handed over a silver blister pack, and I popped out a small white pill.

Tommo frowned. "I wonder why the chemist didn't suggest these?"

"No idea. Maybe he'd run out."

Chris passed a clipboard. "Could you guys complete your details on the dive log? You're both experienced divers, right? You're not one of today's students?"

"Yep, we're qualified." I managed to stand upright. "I'm a Rescue Diver."

"And I have my Advanced PADI," said Tommo.

"Great," said Chris. "Were you the guys who dropped off your kit last night?"

"Yep. That's us."

"It's over there." He pointed. "James already assembled it; you've a full tank of air and weights. Short wetsuits'll be fine. The water's around 27 degrees centigrade today."

A row of tanks stood against a wall, and I identified my kit among them.

"Could I buddy both of you with another diver?" asked Chris. "He's by himself, and it's better if he goes with you than with me and the students."

"Sure. No problem."

He called over to a man sitting on a bench. "Excuse me, Richard? These guys'll dive with you."

Richard stood and walked towards us.

I opened my eyes wide and gaped up at him.

---

7. WOBBEGONGS

LATITUDE: 28° 36' 35" S
LONGITUDE: 153° 37' 50" E

Richard's tanned biceps threatened to rip the sleeves of his red T-shirt, which advertised Rocky's Gym, Pasadena, CA. This guy had muscles in places where most people didn't have places. He wore dark, formal shorts and had a small, black belt bag with a white insignia strapped around his waist.

"Hey, guys. Thanks for letting me tag along."

His sunglasses stretched around his shiny, shaved head.

"I'm on vacation with my wife, but she ain't no diver. She prefers to pose on the sand in a tiny bikini."

We laughed.

Tommo shook his hand. "I'm Tommo. Whereabouts are you from?" He winced and waggled his fingers as Richard released his grip.

"From the City of Angels. Los Angeles, Cal-i-forn-i-a. We're in Australia celebrating my fiftieth birthday. I've never left the US before. You folks sure have a swell country. We drove up from Sydney yesterday, heading for Brisbane, and misjudged the distance, so we stopped for the night."

"Yep," said Tommo, "that old Sydney-to-Brisbane-in-a-day thing catches out several tourists. You need over twelve hours, with stops."

"So we discovered. Anyway, when I found out you could see manta rays, I booked a dive immediately. I've rented an underwater video camera so I can show my dive buddies back home. I've always wanted to see a manta."

He pointed at us with a forefinger the size of a cricket stump. "You guys both Australian?"

"I am," said Tommo, "and Simon's visiting from London."

Richard turned to me and grinned. "London, England?"

I wiggled my eyebrows. "Yep. The very same."

"Wow. Have you met the Queen?"

"I glimpsed her in the distance once, at a parade."

"I'd love to meet her," said Richard. "Seems like a fine lady."

"We'd better pull on our wetsuits," I said. "They're about to start."

I stripped down to my swimmers, tugged on the neoprene and reached out to grab hold of Tommo as I pulled the wetsuit over my head.

He grabbed me as I doubled over. "Are you all right?"

I took a deep breath. "I hope I can complete this dive without spewing."

Chris stood in the door and circled his hands around his mouth. "Guys, listen up. I'll brief you before we leave."

General chatter died down.

"Good morning, everyone. Welcome to Ocean Divers. Today, we'll take a trip to Julian Rocks, renowned as one of the best dive spots in the whole of Australia. Over one thousand marine species call this site their home, thanks to the unique convergence of warm and cold water. You'll not only see thousands of colourful fish; if you're lucky, you'll encounter turtles, octopus and even mantas."

Tommo and I turned to each other, smiled and nodded. Richard familiarised himself with the controls on the rented video camera. The buttons seemed small for his huge hands.

Chris continued. "The group who completed the beginner course in the swimming pool yesterday should ride in the brown truck. You'll be diving with me and Tyler here." He pointed at a young man with long, bleached hair. "We'll take you out in the boat; we'll drop over the side and kneel on the sand where you'll demonstrate the skills you learnt in the pool, then we'll take a guided tour around the rocks. On the second dive this afternoon, we'll complete the assessment, and you'll be fully qualified divers able to dive by yourselves." He turned to Tyler. "Anything else you want to add?"

Tyler grinned. "Nah, mate. I think you covered it. Pretty good for your first day on the job."

I watched the students exchange worried glances as Chris punched Tyler's arm.

"That joke never gets old." He turned to us. "You three experienced divers, hop in the blue truck towing the smaller IRB with James." He indicated an older man standing at the rear of the group, who lifted his hand and waved. "James'll anchor at the entry point, give you some tips on where to find the best sea life, and remain in the boat. Does anyone have questions?"

Richard raised an arm the size of a backhoe. "Will there definitely be manta rays?"

"Unfortunately," said Chris, "the mantas declined my invitation to this briefing, so they're not clear what's expected of them."

He raised his voice above the laughter. "I've seen them on half of the dives this summer, so you're in with a good chance. Okay, everybody ready? Throw your gear in the boats, and let's go."

Tommo turned to me. "Are you feeling better?"

"Still queasy. The fresh air helps. Don't buy me eight jugs of beer tonight. Or talk about beer. Or take me anywhere with a beer smell."

≈ ≈ ≈

Tommo climbed into the boat as it floated in the shallow water. I hesitated, took a deep breath and pulled myself in.

"Not like the dive boats we have in the US," said Richard, as he passed up the video camera. "For the Catalina Island trip, there's a gangplank and everything. This is more like the navy seals." He launched himself into the bow.

Are you a navy seal?

I groped for the straps and buckles of my gear and found I couldn't look down without feeling nauseous.

James turned us head-on into the waves. "Sorry guys, it's a lumpy one today. Five minutes, and we'll be in the lee of the rocks. Hang on to something."

He pushed the throttle forward; we bounced into the swell, and I tried to watch the horizon and simultaneously contain my stomach inside my body. Richard braced himself and allowed the spray to splash over his tanned, shiny face.

BOUNCE

BOUNCE

BOUNCE

James steered the boat in a dramatic semi-circle and stopped. He tossed a weight over the side on the end of a line and switched the engine off.

I panted, rinsed my mask in the sea and splashed cool, salt water over my face. "I can see the bottom. How deep is it?"

"Around ten metres," said James. "It's a shallow dive, which is why it's great for beginners." He pointed at the larger boat, which had followed us and anchored nearby. "You don't want to dive near the students; they'll be on the bottom demonstrating skills, and they'll stir up the sand. I recommend you swim between the two main rocks; there's a trench where the depth reaches eighteen metres. It's home to turtles, rays and sharks."

I narrowed my eyes, then wished I hadn't, and opened them to study the horizon again. "What type of sharks?"

"Wobbegongs, mainly. Native species. They'll leave you alone."

"Wow, I've never heard of them."

"Once you reach the ocean side of the trench, that's where the mantas congregate."

Richard pumped the air. "Yes!"

"And look out for a tame blue grouper. You can stroke him, like a dog."

I puffed and tried to replace the nausea with excitement.

James continued. "Once you're done searching for mantas, swim around the rocks and surface here."

Richard made final adjustments to his video camera.

I stared across the water and recalled the last time I'd dived with Jan in the Pacific islands of Tonga, surrounded by flying fish.

Tonga.

Travelling with Fiona.

I wish you were here.

SPLASH

Water sluiced over us as if we'd chosen to sit in the front row during the Orca show at Sea World.

"Shit," called Tommo. "Richard jumped in without us. Come on."

We stuffed our air regulators in our mouths and dropped backward over the side of the boat.

Richard showed me the okay sign, a closed thumb and forefinger. He pointed and motioned for us to swim beneath.

We obliged, as he descended and filmed us swimming towards the trench.

My medical problems became less significant as I listened to my bubbles and tasted the salt. A small, flat-headed, brown shark flipped away under a rock as I approached. Ahead of me, a turtle ascended to breathe at the surface. The surge rocking me back and forward in front of the trench restarted my nausea, and I had this horrible feeling I was about to throw up underwater, so I turned around and watched Richard film Tommo. We gave each other the 'okay' sign and swam towards the dark-blue, deep sea.

I paused at the opposite end of the trench and waited. An enormous fish hovered a metre above the sea floor close to an outcrop.

I bit down on my air regulator.

That must be the grouper.

The fish floated motionless. I reached out and touched its cold, slimy skin. Richard filmed me stroking the grouper, then Tommo patted it like a pet poodle. I motioned for Richard to pass me the video camera, but he didn't want to.

Richard escorted a turtle, then we swam above him, and he lay on the sea floor and filmed our James Bond antics.

I raised my eyebrows and looked up, as three massive shadows blocked the sun and drifted above us like *Independence Day* spacecraft.

Manta rays!

I waved both hands to attract Tommo's attention, jabbed my finger and made flying bird motions. Tommo glanced up and gave me the 'okay' sign. He pointed upwards, as Richard filmed through his video camera.

The mantas headed to deeper water, and we circumnavigated the rocks.

I pulled off my mask at the surface.

Tommo swam away. "You look like shit. If you're gonna chuck up in the sea, you're on your own."

Too late.

A slick of yellow bile spread away from me.

James shouted over the side of the boat. "Poor chap. Seasickness?"

Waves splashed my face, and I swam towards him. "Yep, that's it. Seasickness." I pulled myself up the ladder and collapsed in the boat.

"How was the dive, guys?" asked James. "Did you see any manta rays?"

"Yep," said Tommo. "They drifted directly above us. Three, maybe four."

"You serious?" said Richard. "I came all this way, and I was metres from manta rays, and never saw them. Damn. I guess I was too busy looking through the lens."

"Shame," said James. "You could come for another dive this afternoon?"

"I can't. My wife's booked a sunset cruise in Brisbane. I'm lucky she let me do this one."

≈ ≈ ≈

Richard shook our hands as we packed our gear away. "Thanks for being my dive buddies today." He grabbed a pad and paper from his black belt bag. "Write your addresses, and I'll mail you copies of the video from Los Angeles."

"Sure," I said. "In fact, I'm visiting Los Angeles next month. I could pop around and collect it."

"You are? Where are you staying?"

"I haven't booked anywhere; I'm only stopping for two nights. Maybe I'll find a backpackers."

"Come stay with me," said Richard. "I'll write my phone number here; call me a day or two before you arrive. I'd be happy to accommodate you."

He tore off a piece of paper.

"Wow, really?" I said. "That's very kind. Thank you."

"No problem," said Richard. "Thanks for a great dive. Shame I didn't see the mantas."

≈ ≈ ≈

Tommo and I lugged our gear to his car.

"Great job feeding the fish," he said. "I'm sure they appreciated the meal."

"No idea how I held on until we surfaced. I've never spewed underwater, and I don't intend to start."

I patted his shoulder. "Thanks for bringing me here. So cool we saw the manta rays."

"That Richard chap was gutted he missed them. At least you found somewhere to bunker down in Los Angeles. That's kinda handy."

"Yeah, I prefer to stay with a local resident in any country, then you see the way real people live, not some plastic tourist land."

If I'd known the trouble staying with Richard would cause me, I'd have chosen the plastic tourist land any day.

≈ ≈ ≈

I'd almost completed the ascent into Tommo's passenger seat when I spotted a jewellery store.

"Do I have time to pop in there? I might buy something for Fiona."

"No worries. I'll wait here and enjoy the scenery."

I crossed the road, pushed open the wooden-latticed, glass door and immediately recoiled from the spice of incense. On both sides of the entrance, multiple burners produced a weaving, ecclesiastical fog. A small wind chime tinkled, then stopped when I closed the door.

I'd entered the opening scene of a Stephen King book.

8. WITCHCRAFT

LATITUDE: 27° 30' 1" S
LONGITUDE: 153° 2' 2" E

I pushed aside dangling dream catchers and fluffy feathers on string and headed for the back of the shop, where a lady with dyed jet-black hair stood behind a counter. She wore a black velvet shirt covered with a thin, purple cape. Her claw-like hands ended in obsidian fingernails, and the number of bangles on her wrists made me wonder how she ever managed to lift her arms. Rainbow-coloured displays of necklaces and brooches sat alongside pewter earrings, nose rings and unidentifiable-body-part rings. As I snorted more incense and approached her, I realised she was at least eighty years old.

She gazed at my white surf-logo T-shirt and ripped denim shorts as if I wasn't approved to enter her emporium of valuable rubbish.

"Are you looking for something, sonny?"

Her long nose finished at an impressively sharp point. If this had been sixteenth century England, she would've been sent straight to the ducking-stool.

I glanced around the shop. "Erm, I'm not sure if this is the right place? I want to buy a ring for my girlfriend."

"Getting married, are we, sonny?"

I tilted my head from side to side and shrugged. "I don't know. Maybe."

She presented a tray of pewter-coloured items. "Is the young lady in question a witch?"

I recalled several times Fiona had asked me to hang out the laundry when it clearly wasn't my turn. Or stolen the duvet during the night. Or finished the last drop of Sauvignon Blanc.

"She has her moments."

"I mean, is she into witchcraft? Does she follow Wicca? Here's one she might like."

She plucked a heavy-set ring with a pagan symbol from the board and held it out.

"I'm not sure this is the kind of shop I need. I thought you were a jeweller's store, with all the trinkets in the window. D'you have anything more, um, normal?"

"How about this one?" She produced a further dull-metal band. "It has the slithering serpent on it, which druids believe to be a symbol of virility. It'd be an appropriate commitment ceremony artefact, don't you think?"

I hesitated and shook my head.

"I had something more traditional in mind."

"Ah, well, if it's traditional you want, this ring here"—she prised a further item out—"has an image of the phallus on it, which is of course the ultimate traditional fertility symbol, wouldn't you agree?"

I recoiled and stepped back as I imagined Fiona's reaction to being presented with a ring featuring a giant penis.

"Thanks, anyway. I don't think these are what I want."

"Suit yourself." She tidied away her assorted snakes and phalluses and muttered under her breath.

"What's that smell?" asked Tommo, as I climbed into the car. "You stink like you've been in Janis Joplin's boudoir."

"I visited that jewellery shop. They didn't have anything I liked, though."

"Not surprised. It looks like they hold seances. Let's find a McDonald's for lunch."

He sounded the dixie horn, spun the wheel and we headed to the highway.

≈ ≈ ≈

Tommo overtook a progression of trucks tailing each other along the inside lane.

"This is an emergency," he shouted, above the rushing wind through the open windows.

"It is?"

"Yep. Where the hell's the next McDonald's? At this rate, we'll be back at my local one before dinner. Could you eat any food yet?"

"I'm still queasy. Getting better. Let's pick up a takeaway and head to your place."

"Okay. And a six-pack of beer?"

My head leant into the slipstream as the thought of more alcohol made my stomach react again.

"I don't think I'll be drinking beer for a while."

≈ ≈ ≈

I slurped the end of a cola, stuffed in leftover cold chips and watched Tommo lean back on a sofa, bare-chested and shoeless in his board shorts. He cracked open his third bottle. Two beers had evaporated from the six-pack and none of the remainders had my name on them.

"That was such a great dive," I said. "I can't believe we saw those sharks and turtles, and then the mantas. I reckon it could've been the best I've ever done."

Tommo sipped his beer. "That Richard guy was a mystery. D'you reckon he's a bodybuilder, or maybe a retired American football player?"

"He said something about navy seals. I wonder if he's in the forces?"

The hot breeze blew through the fly screens, and Australian rock music on the radio reminded me I was in a land of constant sun, sea and surf, where every man had a blonde mullet, every woman wore a string bikini over a deep-brown tan and the entire population lived on the beach in brightly painted wooden houses. Further slurps of cola negated the salty meal.

I smiled and stared out of the window.

I wondered if Fiona would enjoy the Queensland lifestyle.

I wondered what she was doing right now.

I wondered if she was thinking of me.

My hand flew to my ear as a sudden, stabbing pain pierced my skull. "Shit, Tommo, I'm in agony."

He clonked down his beer and stared at me. "What's wrong? Why are you holding your ear?"

"It's like someone's jabbing a six-foot red-hot knife into my head. Oww."

"When did this come on?"

"Right now. I reckon it's an infection from diving. I've had this happen before. The doctor gave me prescriptions for antibiotics and ear drops. Aaaah, shit."

I lay on Tommo's couch and pushed a cushion to my head.

He stood over me and pursed his lips. "What d'you want me to do?"

"Take me to a bloody doctor."

"It's 8:30 p.m. The doctors aren't open."

"I need medical help. I need antibiotics. Oww."

"D'you want painkillers?"

"I have some in my washbag. By the sink. Aah."

Tommo found my container of Nurofen Plus, and I washed two down with the end of the cola.

"Aah. This is horrible."

"I could take you to accident and emergency? To the hospital? You could see a doctor there."

I wrapped the cushion around the side of my head and pushed my face into it.

"If there are no medical centres open, definitely. This is life or death."

"All right. Hang on, I'll chuck some clothes on. Bloody hell. Good job I hadn't finished my third beer."

I squeezed the cushion against my face.

"Shit, shit, shit. This is absolute agony. How far's the hospital?"

"Ten minutes. The Princess Alexandra. There'll be a queue, though. I waited three hours to be seen last year when I nailed through my big finger. Come on, in the truck."

I stumbled downstairs holding the cushion, and we climbed into Tommo's car.

"Please don't sound the dixie horn," I said. "I don't think my ears can handle it."

≈ ≈ ≈

56

Tommo spun around the hospital car park in circles and failed to find a space. There were none in the outdoor area, and his truck's height prevented him from entering the undercover section.

I shoved the cushion into my ear and tapped my hand on the dashboard. "Drop me off. Pick me up later."

"All right. D'you have my number?"

"Write it down."

Tommo found a pen and an old McDonald's fries carton in the footwell of his car.

I jumped out, strode through the sliding glass doors and wondered why, wherever they were in the world, all hospitals stank of the same disinfectant. And it wasn't a fragrance to make you feel better. They should produce cleaning fluid that smelt of roses, or chocolate cake or something happy. And why such stark, white lighting? Surely a soft, dim glow would help sick people.

I approached a middle-aged lady seated behind a window and spoke through a slit in the glass.

"Hi. Could I see a doctor immediately, please?"

She turned from her computer screen and tugged her glasses down her nose.

"What's the problem?"

"It's an emergency. Severe earache. I need antibiotics."

Her eyebrows raised, and she puffed. "Earache. Right." She slid over a clipboard with a ball-point pen on string Sellotaped to the top. "Take a seat, fill in your details and bring them back." She looked behind me. "Next, please."

"Please can I see a doctor immediately? I'm in agony."

"You won't see a doctor at all if you don't fill the form in."

I held the cushion and completed my name in spidery, wrong-handed scribble, made up Tommo's address as I couldn't remember it and copied his phone number from the chip carton. I returned it to the lady and waited while she dealt with another casualty.

She raised her eyebrows at my scrawly clipboard offering as if I'd presented her with a note saying, 'Put the money in the bag and nobody gets hurt'.

"Your Medicare card, please?"

"I'm not sure what that is. I'm from England."

"D'you have your passport with you?"

"No. I can ask someone to bring it."

The lady's mouth straightened as she annotated ticks on my sheet and tapped on her computer.

"How long have you suffered from earache?"

"For a couple of hours. I think it's an infection caused by scuba diving. Aaah. I'm in real pain."

"We'll attend to you as soon as we can. There's a queue."

"How long?"

"Hopefully, you'll see a doctor tonight."

I squished into my cushion. "Oww. Tonight? I need help now."

The lady pointed behind me and swung her arm from left to right at rows of chairs filled with people in various degrees of discomfort. "So does everyone. Sorry, you'll have to wait."

I breathed out, took my cushion and slumped in a seat beside a man with a crutch and his leg in a bandage. Opposite me, a young lady wearing one shoe occupied a wheelchair. Next to her, a scruffy-looking man gurgled throatily.

A woman wearing jeans and a checked shirt exited a side room, holding a clipboard.

Is she a doctor? I thought they wore white coats.

I tried to make eye contact.

Please ask for me. Please ask for me.

"Mrs Holden? Mrs Holden?"

A large lady pushed herself up and wobbled towards her, leaning on a metal walking stick.

I squashed my ear back into Tommo's cushion.

A young man wearing casual trousers and rolled-up sleeves entered. A stethoscope hung around his neck, and I permitted myself a brief smile as I remembered Fiona struggled to pronounce that word.

I suppose these must be doctors. But he doesn't look old enough.

"Mr Brand? Mr Brand?"

Nobody responded. The doctor walked through to another area, and I heard him call again.

"Mr Brand?"

I sat up and stretched my neck to see where he'd gone.

There are more people next door? I'm going to be waiting forever.

Pain stabbed into me, and I shut my eyes.

About an hour later, I opened them to a female voice, close to my face.

"Simon? Is that you? What are you doing here?"

9. ANGELS

LATITUDE: 27° 29' 59" S
LONGITUDE: 153° 1' 55" E

I winced as the imaginary blade stabbed my ear. A young lady stared in my face.

"Oww," I said. "Are you the doctor?"

"Simon, it's Kylie. We met on the plane from New Zealand, remember? Why are you here?"

I squished the cushion to my ear. "Sorry, I didn't recognise you. I've got severe earache. Is this where you work? Um, how's the new job?"

She crouched down, set her hand on my knee and looked me in the eyes. "How long have you been waiting?"

"No idea. Maybe an hour? Aaah." I squirmed into my cushion.

"Stay there. I'll find someone."

"I'm not going anywhere. Owww."

I folded my head against the wall and hugged myself.

I wish Fiona were here. She'd look after me.

The background noise of a wall-mounted television blended with patients' chatter.

≈ ≈ ≈

"Mr Prior? Mr Prior?"

The lady doctor in the checked shirt grasped a clipboard and glanced around the room. She turned away and headed for the second seating area.

I stood and waved after her. "Hi! Over here. That's me. Oww."

She turned and smiled. "There you are. Come through."

She led me to a small office with a brown, metal-legged table and three black chairs.

60

Posters on the walls advertised various attractive-looking M&M-coloured drugs, and a life-size plastic model of a leg was propped up in a corner as if someone had rescued it from a nasty industrial accident.

The lady motioned for me to sit. "Sorry for the wait. We're unusually busy for a weeknight. I'm Emma Walsh, one of the doctors here. How can I help?"

Dark rings under her eyes made me wonder how many hours she'd been at work.

"Severe earache. I think it's caused by an infection I picked up while scuba diving. I've suffered from this before, and the doctor prescribed antibiotics. Oww."

Emma opened a drawer and unboxed an instrument for looking in ears.

"Which ear is it?"

"My right one."

"Okay. We'll look in the good one first." She poked the otoscope in my left ear. "Now the other one."

I removed the cushion, and she inserted her tool.

"Owww. Shit."

"Sorry." She wiggled it around and I felt her breath on my cheek. "Okay, you've acute otitis externa and otitis media. Probably labyrinthitis too. What are you taking for the pain?"

"These." I showed her the painkillers I'd brought from New Zealand. She read the label, turned the box over and raised her eyebrows.

"Gosh. Ibuprofen and codeine in the same tablet. Well, if they work, keep taking them. I'll prescribe you Amoxycillin. Three per day, for seven days. And Ciprofloxacin and Dexamethasone. Four drops in the ear, twice a day. Lie on your side and massage them in. Is anyone at home who can help you with this?"

Tommo was a good friend, but I reckoned asking him to put drops in my ear and massage it twice a day might traverse a line two unrelated males shouldn't cross.

"I can do it myself. This isn't the first time I've been in this condition." I winced and grasped the cushion.

"And you know not to get the ear wet, such as in the shower? Are you planning on travelling by plane?"

"To Hong Kong, next week. Then on to London."

"Let's hope the swelling's reduced by then. I don't recommend flying with an ear infection. Once you've finished the course of antibiotics, I advise you to visit another doctor. The drum's not visible at present, and you may have perforated it."

"I'll be in London by then, so I'll see Doctor Atkins, my family GP."

"Anything else I can help you with?"

"That's all, thank you. D'you know where I'd find Kylie? The nurse?"

"I don't know her, sorry. Try the nurses' station." She glanced at a clock. "It's the 10:00 p.m. shift change now, so they should all be there."

"Thank you, Doctor." I clutched my prescription, opened her door and found Kylie waiting outside.

"Are you okay?" She placed a hand on my shoulder. "You don't look too well. D'you want to lie down in the nurses' accommodation? I've finished work."

"I'd love to. All I want to do is sleep."

$$\approx \approx \approx$$

Kylie led me out of the emergency department through the warm night, across a hospital service road and a car park. The Doppler of an ambulance siren made me wince as it exited the hospital, and I pushed the cushion firmly to my ear. I knew I should be sociable with Kylie and ask her about her new job and her new life, but the pain saturated my conversation capability.

"This way," she said. "Nearly there."

We walked through another section of the hospital, then into a brown, utilitarian, two-storey brick building. Kylie led me up a flight of stairs, then held a door into a corridor.

"Wait a mo. I need to find my friend."

She left through a side passage. A young man exited and furrowed his brow as he passed. I leant against the wall on the cushion and closed my eyes.

Voices approached.

"… and it's late, so I wondered if he could stay in the guest room tonight?"

Kylie strode towards me, accompanied by a tiny, young, Asian lady.

"Simon, this is Leanne, my friend I told you about."

Leanne wore a white uniform identical to Kylie's, and she displayed a gold badge which advertised 'Leanne Cheng: RN'.

I lifted my head from the cushion. "Hi, Leanne. Sorry for the trouble."

She frowned. "You look terrible. It's no trouble; I know how debilitating earache is. There's no-one in the guest suite tonight."

Despite her complexion, she had a strong New Zealand accent.

Leanne opened a door and led me into a room, which reminded me of the accommodation I'd stayed in during my student years at North London University. A single bed stood under a window, made up with white sheets and a blue blanket, and a light-coloured Ikea-wood desk, cupboard and bedside cabinet completed the furnishing. A tiny bathroom showed through a sliding door.

I slumped on the bed and held the cushion to my ear.

Leanne lowered her voice and conversed with Kylie. "He looks hot. I'll fetch my thermometer. Could you find cold flannels?"

The nurses departed, and I closed my eyes.

I opened them again when someone sat on the bed next to me.

"Stay there. I'm taking your temperature." Leanne pulled the lobe of my good ear and stuffed something pointy and hard into it.

BEEEP

"Thirty-nine. He's running a fever. Pass me a flannel."

A cold cloth covered my forehead. It quickly warmed and was replaced by a second one.

Leanne spoke to me in her professional voice. "Simon, you're staying here tonight. We'll look after you. Is there anyone you'd like us to call?"

"Yes, please."

I sat up, reached into my pocket and tugged out the McDonald's chip scoop and the prescription. Kylie raised her eyebrows. I handed them to her.

"Could you call my friend, Tommo? Here's the number. Please ask him to bring some clean clothes. And my wash bag. Oh, and don't be surprised if he asks you out on a date or something. That's him."

I managed a small smile before collapsing.

I woke for the first time, panting and needing the toilet. Gallons of sweat soaked the pillow as if I'd slept in a Byron Bay rock pool. I stumbled to the bathroom and pa-dinged the light cord. The bright, clinical beam hurt my eyes, and I closed them. I turned it off and collapsed back into the saturated sheets.

I woke for the second time as light spilt from the corridor; the thermometer poked my ear and a new, cold flannel wiped my face. I wasn't sure which of the nurses attended to me, and I mumbled, "Thank you."

I woke for the third time and found Kylie seated at the end of the bed. Sun streamed in through the window. I sat up gingerly. The stabbing pain had morphed into a dull ache.

She offered me a tablet and a glass of water. "Here. I fetched your prescription once the pharmacy opened this morning."

I took the tablet and chugged the water.

"Temperature?" She brandished the thermometer, and I offered my good ear to poke it in.

BEEEP

"Thirty-seven point six. Headed in the right direction. Lie down, and I'll administer your ear drops."

I shook my head and reached for the tiny bottle.

"It's okay, I can do it myself."

"It's better if someone else does. Rest your head on the pillow."

I lay down, felt a wet sensation in my ear and experienced it being blocked by the liquid entering. Kylie massaged around my ear, and I heard the inside of it crackle.

"You, Kylie, are an angel." My voice sounded funny with clogged ears. "You're all angels, you nurses."

Kylie smiled. "Are you feeling better after your rest?"

"I think so, but my ear hurts still."

I sat up, felt the liquid roll out and perched on the edge of the bed with my head on an angle as if my brain were too heavy.

Kylie glanced into her lap. "Your friend dropped off your bag last night. And you were right, he asked me for a date."

I covered my eyes with my hand. "Oh, no. Did you say 'yes'?"

Kylie giggled. "I did, kind of. I suggested you and Leanne join us and make up a foursome. She knows a Thai restaurant called the Siam Surprise. We could go on Friday? Hopefully, you'll feel better by then. Leanne and I are rostered on a late shift the day after, so we can have a few drinks and enjoy the night."

My face prickled as I thought about Fiona, and how she'd have no idea two nurses were caring for me at their accommodation and kidnapping me for a double date.

"Um, I don't know if I should cramp Tommo's style."

Kylie laughed. "We'll see. Stay here and rest today. I'm starting my shift now, but I'll check on you during my break."

I lay down again and closed my eyes.

≈ ≈ ≈

Kylie returned several hours later and presented me with a ham sandwich in triangular packaging. I sat up.

"How are you feeling?" she asked.

"My ear's blocked, but the painkillers help. I'm so pleased you found me in A&E. I'm like the wounded guy in *The English Patient*."

She smiled. "Take your next antibiotic. Here."

She opened the box, popped another pill from the blister pack and passed me a cup of water. "How d'you know Tommo?"

I sipped the water and swallowed.

"We met in England when we both drank in the same bar. I hooked up with my girlfriend, Fiona, there too."

Kylie lifted her chin. "Tommo doesn't have a girlfriend, does he?"

10. SIAM SURPRISE

LATITUDE: 27° 30' 10" S
LONGITUDE: 152° 58' 5" E

I shrugged. "I don't think Tommo has a girlfriend today. He hadn't when I saw him yesterday."

We both laughed at this, but only I realised how true this statement could've been.

"He's a good guy," I said. "Heart of gold. Listen, you've been so kind to me. I think I feel well enough to return to his house. D'you mind if I call and ask him to collect me?"

"Sure. There's a payphone in the common room. It's the end of my break, so I'll head back to work. But I'll see you on Friday night for our double date?"

I cracked my knuckles, smiled and shrugged.

"I guess so. Thanks again, for everything."

≈ ≈ ≈

Tommo's truck screeched around the central flower border as if he drove the getaway car in a bank robbery.

Please don't sound the dixie horn outside the hospital.

I clambered into the passenger seat and slammed the door.

Tommo grinned and shook his head. "You're a dark horse. I leave you at accident and emergency with a sore ear and, next thing, I receive a call from a cute-sounding nurse saying you're asleep in her bed. That's the sort of thing which happens to me, not you."

My cheeks reddened. "I wasn't asleep in her bed; I stayed in the guest room."

"It's all right, I won't tell Fiona." He punched my arm playfully.

67

"Anyway," I said, "I hear you asked her on a date."

"Yep. You know me, never one to let an opportunity slip. What's she called again?"

"You don't remember her name? It's Kylie."

"Kylie, as in Kylie Minogue?"

"Yes, but don't say that to her; she doesn't appreciate it. And please don't hurt her. She's a sweet girl, and she's arrived in Australia after breaking up with some loser in New Zealand. She doesn't need mistreatment."

"It's all good. If things become serious too quickly, I'll cut and run."

"Exactly. That's what I'm afraid of. You know what? Kylie wants me to come out with you and her. And she wants to bring her friend, Leanne, to make up a foursome."

Tommo nodded. "Sounds interesting. Two nurses for the price of one."

I shook my head and puffed. "You're too much. I definitely need to ride shotgun."

≈ ≈ ≈

The hot water of Tommo's shower sluiced down my body the next Friday evening, and I angled my head to ensure no water entered my ear. The pain had gone, but I still couldn't hear properly.

A musky fragrance filled the living room as Tommo clicked the lid off a can of Lynx and sprayed most of it over his clothes. I coughed and flapped my hand in front of my face. He handed me the can, and I aerosoled a few squirts.

"This Leanne girl," said Tommo, "she's from China, right? I've never dated an Asian girl."

He poked out his bottom lip, frowned and tilted his head.

"At least, I don't think I have." He shrugged. "Can't remember."

I handed back the deodorant. "She looks Chinese, but her voice sounds as Kiwi as anything. I thought you liked Kylie?"

He grinned. "I do, but I need to keep my options open."

I tugged on a shirt and shorts, rubbed a splodge of gel through my hair and sat down to tie up my shoes. "D'you know where this Thai restaurant is?"

"The Siam Surprise? About halfway between here and the hospital. I've been before. It's more of a cocktail bar."

"Cocktail bar? That's posh, isn't it?"

"Wait until you see it. We'll take a cab."

≈ ≈ ≈

Tommo handed the driver ten dollars and shut the taxi door. I checked my hair in the cab's window, placed my hands on my hips and inspected the evening's location.

We grinned at each other.

Tonight's venue didn't resemble any restaurant I'd seen before.

Multi-coloured lights flashed through wide wall-hatches propped open by poles. Under the tropical palm tree-frond roof, an open area at the front of the building enclosed small chest-height tables where groups of young people smoked, chatted, and grasped glasses of steaming liquid in assorted primary colours like a space bar in *Star Trek*. Pumping music competed well with the volume of shouting between staff and patrons. Guys wearing shirts and shorts chatted with girls barely covered with summer skirts and strapless dresses. The air temperature, coupled with the beach-bar ambience, made me feel like Roger Moore on a Caribbean island at sunset.

This was no restaurant.

It possibly wasn't a cocktail bar.

This bordered on a nightclub.

"D'you think the girls are here yet?" I yelled at Tommo, as we pushed our way through the reverberations.

He surveyed the crowd and his eyes settled on three young ladies with identical, blonde-streaked hair, drinking cocktails.

"Well, if they're not, we've plenty of other options."

I rolled my eyes and followed him to the bar.

≈ ≈ ≈

Tommo slipped a wad of folded banknotes from his back pocket. "What'll you have? It's happy hour until eight."

I had a terrible flashback to eight jugs of beer sitting on a table in front of me and a night spent French-kissing a Byron Bay toilet bowl.

"A beer, please. Whatever's on special. And one beer. Not a bloody jug or anything."

Tommo laughed. "I thought you were never drinking again. D'you want a pot, or a schooner?"

"Remind me which is bigger?"

"Schooner. Bit smaller than a pint."

"I guess I'll manage one of those."

Someone poked me in the back.

"Hey, Simon. Did you just arrive?"

I swivelled to find Kylie clad in a short, black dress, clutching an empty glass containing a pink straw and a broken cocktail umbrella.

"Hi, Kylie." I kissed her cheek and glanced behind her. "Are you by yourself? Where's Leanne?"

"She's saying goodbye to her boyfriend. He's here with his pals, but they're moving on to some cricket function. D'you like this bar? This is what I emigrated to Australia for; feel the heat in the night air. I love it. There's no way I'd have ventured out for drinks in New Zealand without a cardigan."

Tommo turned around with the beers.

"G'day, Kylie." He thrust out his chest and leant in her direction. "You look lovely."

"Hey, Tommo." Kylie ducked her chin, smiled and touched her lips. She tossed her long, black hair over her pale shoulders and it cascaded down her halter-neck outfit. She'd clearly invested a significant amount of time in applying her makeup, an activity completely wasted on Tommo who merely required ladies to be upright and breathing. This new subtropical lifestyle suited her well.

"Are you okay for a drink?" Tommo asked her.

"Could I have another Pina Colada? Are they still on two-for-one?"

"Yep."

"Great. Leanne'll have the same. I'll buy the next round."

Kylie rubbed my shoulder. "Are you feeling better now? You were in a real state with that ear infection."

"I am, thanks. The pain's gone, although I can't hear on this side." I tapped my skull twice. "Thank you for your care. I don't know what I'd have done if you hadn't found me in A & E."

"I'm sure Tommo would've looked after you."

"He's a nice guy, but he's no nurse."

Tommo passed Kylie two identical glasses containing opaque, white liquid, more straws, further cocktail umbrellas and glacé cherries speared on wooden skewers.

Their hands touched as she accepted the drinks, and she glanced at him and smiled with her lips closed.

"Thanks," said Kylie. She sipped one of the cocktails. "Just what I needed. Let's find Leanne. We've scored a table outside."

We followed Kylie through the throng. Someone bumped me and I spilt beer on my shoe. I lifted my schooner higher to avoid a reoccurrence. We exited the noise of the main bar and entered a large courtyard where small groups of people sat at metal outdoor chairs and tables, and strings of white fairy lights criss-crossed. I smelt a potpourri of aftershaves and perfumes as we weaved through the crowd and found Leanne sitting by herself near the back.

"That's better," said Kylie. "We don't have to yell at each other here."

She turned to Tommo and held out her arm. "Tommo, this is my friend from the hospital, Leanne. Leanne, this is Simon's friend, Tommo."

Leanne shook Tommo's hand, then turned to me.

"How are you, Simon? Recovered?"

She grinned and I realised Asian girls needed no makeup; her unblemished skin shone.

"I'll live." I sat down next to her. "Thanks for looking after me and for allowing me to stay. I've said it before; you nurses are angels."

Leanne sucked the straw of her Pina Colada. "This is my third. If I have too many more, I mightn't be so angelic."

We all laughed. I watched a waitress shoulder a tray of nibbles and park it on an adjacent table. The smells of coconut and coriander wafted in our direction, and the diners oohed and aahed at the dishes.

A small, laminated menu poked from a holder. I picked it up. "Are you guys hungry? We should ask for some food."

"Let's order the combo platter," said Leanne. "We can share it."

Tommo craned his neck and inspected the adjacent table's dinner.

"Are they eating one of those? We'll need two. I reckon Simon and I could polish one off by ourselves." He pulled cash from his back pocket. "I'll order at the bar."

Kylie pushed herself to her feet. "I'll come with you."

She followed him inside.

"Kylie's so excited about partying with you guys tonight," said Leanne. "I reckon she's pretty keen on your friend."

I clenched my teeth and sucked in a breath. "Yep. Tommo has that effect on girls. So long as Kylie doesn't think he's the one. He, um, has a lot of girlfriends."

"All good. She's out to have fun and meet new people. I'm so pleased she's away from New Zealand and her dropkick ex-boyfriend." She slurped her cocktail. "What brings you to Brisbane?"

"I've lived in New Zealand for the last year with my Kiwi girlfriend, Fiona. But my visa expired, and I had to leave. I'm heading back to England to have a new visa stamped at the High Commission in London, and then I'll return to New Zealand with permanent residency, so I can stay forever. Only..."—I paused and bit my lip—"I'm not sure if Fiona wants to stay there forever. I think she misses London. We'll have to see when I return."

I took a sip of beer. "What about you? Where are you from, originally?"

"I'm from Christchurch," said Leanne. "Born and bred." She smiled. "But you mean, where does my complexion come from?"

"Yes. I figured you'd been in New Zealand a long time, because of your accent."

"My dad's Cambodian Chinese, but he lived all his adult life in Hong Kong. My mum's a Kiwi who worked there in the 1960s and that's where they met. They returned to New Zealand and had me and my two younger sisters. My grandmother still lives in Hong Kong; we visit her most years."

"Wow. I'm travelling to Hong Kong next week. Any tips on accommodation?"

"When we visit, we stop with her, so we don't do touristy things. I think most people on a budget stay in Kowloon at one of the backpacker-type places in Tsim Sha Tsui."

"How do I spell that?"

Leanne pulled a pen and paper from her bag. "Here. I'll write it in English and Cantonese, in case you have to show anyone."

Her pen stroked black calligraphy across the page like Tony Hart's *Vision On* logo.

"Thank you. And what about the sights? I'm staying for two days, so I want to cram in the principal attractions. But I'd like to get a feel for the place. Not visit museums."

"Okay. You must take the tram up Victoria Peak. On a clear day, you see the most amazing view of the entire city. And go to Aberdeen Harbour. They have these incredible floating restaurants which seat thousands."

"Those sound great as tourist attractions. But where would I find the real Hong Kong? Where would I walk alongside the residents living their daily lives?"

Leanne sucked the end of her drink.

"Are you there midweek? You could stroll around the skyscrapers in the city; watch the workers in the financial district. You can enter the lobbies of some of them and study the amazing architecture. I used to visit my grandfather at his office for lunch as a little girl. Then, the night markets in Kowloon. You can buy anything you want. Clothes, food, even puppies."

"I'm not sure I need a puppy. Er, can you buy jewellery?"

"Of course you can buy jewellery in Hong Kong. Why? Are you thinking of finding something for your girlfriend?"

"Yes." I glanced in my lap and twisted my fingers together. "I want to surprise her when I return to New Zealand."

"Wow," said Leanne.

She wagged her finger.

"Be careful, Simon. Hong Kong jewellery comes with a warning."

11. FIVE-STOREY PINEAPPLE

LATITUDE: 26° 40' 24" S
LONGITUDE: 152° 59' 28" E

"A warning?" I asked.

"Yes," said Leanne. "Be careful of the quality. There's a lot of Chinese fake rubbish sold as high-quality gems."

I ruminated on her disdain for Chinese-made items, given her ancestry.

Tommo and Kylie returned, arm-in-arm and laughing.

"You guys took your time ordering food," said Leanne.

Kylie giggled and made eyes at Tommo. Her arm snaked around his belt and pulled him towards her. "Can you believe it? Tommo's travelled to twenty countries. He told me all about Thailand. It sounds so exotic. He said he'll take me one day."

I rolled my eyes and shook my head minutely.

Another one falls under Tommo's magic spell.

Tommo, Leanne and I compared overseas cities we'd visited, while Kylie stirred her cocktail and listened. The conversation steered to New Zealand, where three of us had lived, but Tommo had never been. I shared stories of the South Island's West Coast; driving tractors, helping cows give birth, playing rock music to adoring crowds. My eyebrows raised as I discovered that, despite living three hours away, neither Kylie nor Leanne had ever seen it.

"My dad won't drive over the mountain pass," said Kylie. "He says it's too dangerous."

Leanne nodded. "Yeah, my parents said the one time they visited the West Coast, it bucketed with rain the whole week."

I blinked rapidly and began to explain how Fiona had been driving across the pass since she was fifteen years old, and how the rain came all at once, and the number of clear, still, sunny days exceeded those in Christchurch, when a server dressed in a white T-shirt and denim shorts stood over us.

"Two combo plates?"

She dumped bin-lid sized oval dishes of Thai canapés and swept away empty glasses.

"Anyone need another drink?" I asked. "My round."

≈ ≈ ≈

Midnight.

The creak-creak-creak of insects accompanied the commingled perfumes of tree-flowers and spilt beer. I kissed Leanne's cheek. "Thanks for your company tonight, and thanks for all the tips about Hong Kong."

"No problem. I enjoyed our chat."

Kylie and Tommo's mouths limpeted together like fingers welded with spilt superglue.

"Come on," said Leanne. She tugged Kylie's elbow. "Even though we're on lates tomorrow, we still have to wake up by ten."

Kylie surrendered Tommo. She raised her palm to her cheek and made a phone handset symbol at him. "Call me, okay?"

Tommo grinned and nodded.

"Bye, Kylie," I said. "I'm so glad we met on the plane. I had a lovely evening."

She hugged me and spoke in my ear. "Thanks for introducing me to Tommo. I can't wait for our next date."

I nodded and pursed my lips. "My pleasure. I hope it works out for you." I kissed her cheek.

"Make sure you keep in touch," she said. "You know the number? The one I gave you on the plane."

"Yep. Will do."

≈ ≈ ≈

The sun's 6:00 a.m. heat baked the Venetian slats as I pulled them aside and gazed down at the street outside Tommo's house. Joggers ran past, pensioners exercised dogs, couples speed-walked along the streets. The curtains flapped gently. I smiled and inhaled the warm air. I'd only slept a few hours, but the perfect, exciting weather destroyed any tiredness.

A kettle bubbled in the kitchen, and I opened my bedroom door.

"G'day, mate," said Tommo. He stood bare-chested at the counter. "Coffee?"

"Thanks, I'd love one." I pointed out of the window. "How come everyone's active so early? I've noticed it every morning."

"Queensland. We're all awake before five so we complete our exercise and outdoor chores before the sun's too hot." He pointed behind him with his thumb. "Look out of the kitchen window."

In the next door back yard, an older man snipped tomatoes, and an elderly lady plucked oranges, dropping them in a bag around her shoulder.

"See, my neighbours are gardening." He smiled. "Then everyone's in bed by 8:30 in the evening. It'll be a hot one today."

He poured my coffee and pointed at a muted television, where a weather presenter indicated a symbol of a yellow sun with the number 39 beside it.

"Wow, so everyone has their evening in the morning, so to speak."

"Yep." He laughed. "Everything's upside down in Australia."

"What are the plans for today?"

He slid my coffee across the kitchen worktop.

"I thought we could drive north to the Sunshine Coast, stay the night in Maroochydore, check out the nightlife and cruise back tomorrow. What d'ya reckon?"

I glanced down. "So long as we take it easy on the beer. I don't want a hangover like Byron Bay ever again."

Tommo tipped back his coffee, then grinned. "Where's your sense of adventure?"

"Hmm. What's at Maroochydore?"

"The three B's. Beach, bars and babes."

"Right. Sounds good. I'll partake of the first two."

"But first, we'll grab breakfast at Macca's."

I shrugged and smiled thinly. "McDonald's. Can't wait."

≈ ≈ ≈

We queued behind a couple with a spherical boy of about four years old. The child wasn't yet at a stage where he could legally cover himself in tattoos, but judging by the state of his parents, I figured this event featured somewhere in his future.

The father parked his belly on the McDonald's counter and scratched his unkempt beard.

"May I take your order, please, sir?" asked the server.

"Three bacon and egg McMuffins. And three portions of fries."

He hitched up his ragged shorts.

"Sorry, sir," said the server. "We don't sell fries until 10:30 a.m. We have hash browns?"

"Right-o. Three McMuffins, three hash browns and three coffees."

The server pushed till buttons.

"Three McMuffins, three hash browns and three coffees. Is that all, sir?"

"You're bloody joking, aren't you? That's just for me."

He turned to his well-inked partner.

"Jolene, what are you having?"

Her selection of chins oscillated like a serving of my grandmother's blancmange. I grimaced as she bent over, and her short, blue singlet exposed a butt crack so deep it deserved its own visitors' centre.

"I'll have the hotcakes and sausage. Make it two. One's never enough. And two hash browns. And a chocolate milkshake. Two chocolate milkshakes."

The server pressed buttons.

"Okay, I've three bacon and egg McMuffins, two hotcakes and sausage, five hash browns, three coffees and two chocolate milkshakes. Anything else?"

"Jolene, what does Mitch want?"

The child looked up at his mother and pouted.

"I wanna Happy Meal."

"He wants a Happy Meal, Kev."

"A Happy Meal, please."

"Sorry, sir, we don't serve Happy Meals until 10:30 a.m."

"They don't serve Happy Meals until 10:30, Jolene."

The mother addressed the boy.

"You can't have a Happy Meal."

His demeanour switched instantly. He flailed his arms and whacked his mother's legs with both hands.

"I wanna Happy Meal, I wanna Happy Meal. Gimme a Happy Meal."

She clipped him around the head.

"I said, you can't have a Happy Meal."

The boy lay on the floor, thumped the lino, kicked his legs and let out a series of high-pitched screams, the volume and variety of which I'd previously only thought possible on a Mariah Carey record.

"Kev, ask them to stuff a McMuffin in a Happy Meal box. That's what they did last week."

She grabbed her offspring and yanked him off the floor.

"All right, we're buying you a Happy Meal. And when you eat it, you'd better be bloody happy."

I gazed around the restaurant to see if anyone else observed the performance and vowed if Fiona and I ever had children, this scene would never feature in our repertoire.

≈ ≈ ≈

Tommo's pickup truck swung onto the road, and I held his coffee as he bit into his breakfast. The heat of the cup caused me to alternate which fingers I rostered to touch it.

"How long does it take to drive to Maroochydore?"

"About an hour. Straight up the freeway."

Large trucks sped past as we headed north, and Tommo's vehicle drifted in the slipstream. He drove with one hand and took the coffee from me. I applied cream to my window arm as the sun rose higher. I'd never seen a sky this blue in my life, so uniform, so undeviating, so reliable.

Australian songs I didn't recognise played on the radio, and I tapped my hand on the outside of the car door. I was singing loudly to the chorus of one about a working-class man, when Tommo pulled off the road and parked beside a five-storey plastic pineapple.

"Won't be a minute. I'm busting for a pee." He opened the driver's door.

I stared up at the pineapple. The sun reflected from its golden sides and lit up the green tufts forming its top.

"What is this place?" I asked.

"I'll tell you when I come back," shouted Tommo over his shoulder as he ran through the side door of a visitors' centre.

A sign advertised that, for a fee of $10.50, I could ascend stairs inside the giant, fibreglass structure and also experience an exciting train ride through a sugar cane plantation.

Tommo returned from the gents. "Ready to keep moving?"

I placed my hand on my chin and looked up.

"Hang on. Why's there a gigantic, fibreglass pineapple here?"

"It's one of Australia's big things. There are loads of them, scattered around the country."

"Big things?"

"Yep, there's the Big Banana at Coffs Harbour, the Big Prawn at Ballina, there's even a Big Mosquito somewhere. Grey nomads make it their life's mission to drive around the whole of Aussie, visiting all of them."

"What's a grey nomad?"

I had a vision of a wizened, bearded, old man leaning on a staff tugging a donkey through a desert.

"It's our name for retired people towing caravans gazillions of miles around the country, dodging their next heart attack. Please shoot me if it ever gets to that."

We switched highways, then Tommo swung the truck into a petrol station.

I pulled twenty dollars out of my wallet and held it out. "Here, let me pay for this."

"Thanks," said Tommo. "D'you want anything from the shop?"

"All good. I'll stretch my legs."

I hopped down from the truck and wandered to the rear of the petrol station car park. The heat reflected from the asphalt and melted the soles of my shoes, which stuck to the ground and peeled off as I walked.

I paused. From the top of a rubbish bin, something I'd never seen before gawked at me.

12. PSYCHO

LATITUDE: 26° 39' 15" S
LONGITUDE: 153° 5' 45" E

Two pink-and-grey parrots looked up at me from the lid of the rubbish bin, as if they hoped I'd dispose of something tasty, like a McDonald's wrapper.

Stay there, stay there. Don't fly away. I'll grab my camera.

As the birds scrapped over a food container, I crouched down and snapped a photo. One inspected me with its head on one side. I clicked another photo of it engaged in this activity.

"Are you taking pictures of rubbish bins?" said Tommo, behind me.

The birds flapped away.

"I was taking a photo for Fiona of those pink-and-grey parrots."

Tommo blew a raspberry and waved the back of one hand. "Galahs? Bloody pests. Common as pigeons."

"They're not where I come from."

"I'm sure you'll find some in nicer settings than next to a rubbish bin. C'mon."

I replaced my camera in its pouch, and we climbed into the car.

≈ ≈ ≈

Tommo pointed. "Driftwood Backpackers. Right next to the beach."

We parked outside a green-and-white building secreted behind tall palm trees. A rain gutter dangled from the roof, and one window exhibited a yellowing newspaper stuck across a cricket ball-sized hole.

"At least it should be cheap," I said. I tapped my fingers together.

Five wooden steps creaked alarmingly as we climbed to reception, and the air stank of rotting rubbish. I wrinkled my nose. An unshaven, fat man wearing a red singlet sat behind the counter, and I watched smoke curl up from an ashtray by his elbow.

"G'day, guys. Two of you? How many nights?"

He tipped his head back, swigged a beer and flung the bottle into a corner bin, where it clinked against previously jettisoned glass.

"Just one, thanks," said Tommo.

The man relieved us of thirty dollars and handed us a key attached by thin rope to a broken piece of wood. We stumped through a passageway behind him.

"Here we are," said Tommo. "Number two."

The door creaked open like a scene from *Psycho* to reveal a cramped space with two sets of bunk beds pushed against each other. I dumped my bag in a corner, and Tommo shoved his gear under a bottom bunk.

He pointed at the upper bed. "I made the mistake of sleeping on the top once after a few beers, woke up in the night busting for the toilet, swung my legs over the side and cracked my head open on the floor. Never again."

I laughed. "Yep, good idea. I'll sleep on the bottom too."

"D'you wanna head down the beach? Check out the babes?"

"Sure."

I tugged on my swimmers and grabbed a towel.

≈ ≈ ≈

Miles of white sand stretched in both directions, and gigantic waves crashed on the beach, but, as at the Gold Coast, the lifeguards supervised a fifty-metre-wide strip of sand between two flags. I left Tommo talking to a girl he'd met three seconds previously and waded into the surf. I stopped as the water reached my thighs, as I didn't want to get water in my ear, but the waves immediately rolled me over like wet towels in a spin dryer and spat me back at the beach. I hit my head and saw stars, so I left the least relaxing swim I'd ever had and rejoined Tommo.

He watched me exit, grinned and pointed at my midriff.

I looked down. "What?"

His glance darted to the left and right. "We'll have to do something about those budgie smugglers of yours."

My ears tingled, and I wrapped my towel around my waist.

"Where did the girl go who you were talking to?"

"Turns out she's an off-duty lifeguard. Unfortunately, her boyfriend's an on-duty lifeguard. We'll find some chicks at the pub tonight. What d'ya reckon?"

"What about Kylie?"

"Kylie?"

"The nurse from the Thai place the other night? My friend?"

"Oh, that Kylie. I'll see her when we return to Brisbane."

"She likes you, y'know. Please don't break her heart."

"Since when did you become my relationship counsellor?"

"Sorry. I'll keep quiet. What she doesn't know won't hurt her."

"Remember, the same applies to Fiona."

"That's different. We've been together for years."

"Just because you're getting married doesn't mean I have to."

I shook my head. "I'm not getting married. Not yet anyway."

Tommo lay back and closed his eyes. I studied the sand between my legs. If Tommo found a girl to talk to, I'd have to make my own entertainment for the evening. I stared at the surf and thought of Fiona. People such as Kylie and Leanne were fun to chat with, but I wanted someone to cuddle.

I stood. "Hey, Tommo, I'll check out the shops. Back shortly."

≈ ≈ ≈

Vintage surf boards decorated the window of one store, which contained a backdrop of a sunny beach and real sand sprinkled on the floor of the display. I peered closely to see if they'd included any discarded soft drink cans to complete the realism. One mannequin posing on the fake beach wore a blue dress with a white dolphin design.

The young, blonde shop assistant read a magazine behind the counter. I figured she'd prefer to be outside enjoying the sunshine than waiting in an empty shop in case someone like me strolled in.

"Hi," I said. "I'm looking for something for my girlfriend."

The assistant stuffed her magazine in a bag at her feet. "No problem. Is she into surfing?"

"No. But could I look at the dress in the window? The one with dolphins?"

"Sure. That's a popular design. Now we're coming to the end of summer, we're almost sold out. What size is she?"

"Eight? Maybe a six?"

"Wow, she's tiny. I don't know if we ever stocked it in a six. Let's look."

She led me to a rack where three blue dresses coathangered. "Two fourteens, and a twelve. That's all we have left." She unhooked one and held it up.

I rubbed the thin material. I reckoned it would suit Fiona perfectly. "How much are they?"

The assistant unravelled a label. "Thirty dollars. Down from sixty. End of season sale."

"Okay, I'll take the size twelve. Hopefully, she can alter it."

"All right. Anything else I can help you with?"

"D'you have any boardies?"

"Board shorts? In ladies' size six? I'm not sure we've any so small."

"They're for me. I take a men's medium."

"Oh, no problem, we've loads." She led me to the other side of the shop and stroked her hands over two long racks. "The ones on this rail"—she tapped her left hand—"are in the sale; the others are full price. The fitting room's at the back."

"Thanks."

I slid the hangers back and forth and selected two pairs of shorts, one with a cartoon of a bronzed surfer wearing sunglasses, another decorated with a beach and palm trees.

The door of the plywood cupboard which passed for a fitting room banged open. As soon as I closed it, I found a third pair of board shorts hanging on the back which another occupant had discarded.

I immediately rejected my previous two choices, lifted down my new discovery and peeked at the label.

Medium. Perfect.

The full-length mirror reflected my fashion success.

Now I look like an Aussie. No more budgie smugglers. These'll impress Tommo so much.

I abandoned the other two pairs and marched back to the counter.

"I'll take these, thanks. Can I wear them now?"

"Of course. They're in the sale too. With the dolphin dress, that'll be sixty dollars, please."

I tugged out notes from my wallet as the assistant folded the dress and slid it into a bag.

She brandished a pair of scissors and pointed at my new shorts as if she were about to perform a vasectomy. "Would you like me to remove the label?"

"Oh, yes, please. Should I take them off?"

"Nah." She grinned. "I promise I'll be careful."

She snipped and extracted the tag. "There we go. Your receipt's in the bag. Thank you."

I strode out of the shop, crossed the esplanade and glanced down at my new shorts.

I can't wait to see what Tommo says. With this design, I'll really fit in with the locals.

Tommo sat with his hands clasped around his knees and stared at the ocean. He turned to me, covered his mouth and snorted.

I frowned and held my palms upwards. "What? You said I should buy board shorts, so I bought board shorts. What's wrong now?"

Tommo threw his head back and laughed. "Nothing shouts 'tourist' louder than a pair of bright-blue boardies with the Australian flag design blaring from them." He shook his head. "They're an improvement on the budgie smugglers, I suppose."

I folded my arms. "I like them. Sorry you don't."

≈ ≈ ≈

The lifeguards packed away their flags as the shadows on the beach lengthened.

"You hungry?" asked Tommo.

"Yep, sure. I could eat something."

"Okay. Let's change for dinner."

He made it sound like his valet was about to attire him in a set of white tails. In reality, he'd swap his board shorts for different ones and wear thongs on his feet.

We entered our room. No-one else had claimed the top bunks, and we splashed our sunburnt faces and pulled on clean clothes.

"I checked," said Tommo, "and they have Macca's here. We'll find it and then head to the pub. Sounds good?"

My insides paused at the thought of a further meal of McDonald's.

"Umm, sure. Although, on the way into town, I noticed a couple of other places that… what are you looking at?"

13. INFERNO

LATITUDE: 26° 40' 48" S
LONGITUDE: 153° 7' 15" E

Tommo stared behind me. I swivelled and met eyes with a petite, brown-haired Mediterranean girl.

"Hi-ya, guys. This is room two?" An identical key to ours dangled from her hand.

Tommo stood with his mouth open, as she indicated a young, blonde lady behind her.

The brunette raised her eyebrows. "My friend and me, we stay here?"

Tommo grinned and nodded. "Sure." He pointed at the bunk beds and winked. "But only if you're happy to go on top."

I covered my face with my hand. Tommo had some cringey lines. Fortunately, the girls didn't understand his double entendre.

The dark-haired one turned to her taller companion and spoke a language I recognised as Italian. They threw their packs onto the top bunks.

"We were about to buy food," said Tommo. "Would you like to come with us?"

"Okay," said the blonde. "We saw a pizza shop. They have two-for-one."

"Pizzas," said Tommo. "That's exactly what we were thinking of. Wasn't it, Simon?"

Yes! Saved from the third McDonald's in a day.

She pulled a hairbrush from her bag. "We go to the bathroom."

They shut the door, and the lock clicked.

Tommo angled towards me. "You don't think they're a couple, d'you? Why are they both in the dunny?"

"Dunny?"

"The toilet."

"Girls often use the facilities together, don't they?"

"Which one d'you fancy?"

I folded my arms across my chest.

"Neither. Bloody hell. I have a girlfriend."

Tommo grinned and nodded towards the bathroom. "I reckon you might have another one. She likes you."

I unfolded my arms and wrinkled my forehead at the closed door.

"Which one?"

"See, you're interested."

I narrowed my eyes and shook my head rapidly. "Stop it; I'm not. Anyway, how can you tell she likes me?"

Tommo pointed at his chest. "You, my friend, are looking at an expert in woman-ology. I can read girls' body language like a magazine."

"I'm happy to chat with them. You can do what you like."

Tommo rummaged in his bag, found a can of Lynx underarm deodorant and sprayed it over himself as if he were a beekeeper about to harvest a hive.

We heard a toilet flush, and the door opened.

"We go now?" said the blonde.

"Yep," said Tommo. "We go now."

He winked at me as we exited.

The girls walked between us as we strolled into town.

Tommo cleared his throat. "Anyway, I'm Tommo, and this is my mate, Simon."

I nodded and smiled.

The blonde girl pointed at herself. "I am Fran, and this is Veronica."

"We are from Italy," said Veronica. "I am from Napoli, and Fran is from Milano. Where are you from?"

I found her accent intriguing, and anticipated chatting with her. Just chatting.

"I'm from London," I said, "and Tommo's a local Aussie."

"Oh," said Fran, "Australian, hey?" She turned towards him and flicked back her peroxide hair. "I like Australian men."

Tommo grinned. "And I like Italian ladies."

You like any ladies, Tommo. Nationality isn't a determining factor.

"How do you know each other?" asked Veronica.

"I used to live in London," said Tommo, "and Simon and I drank at the same pub. The Redback Tavern. Shit, we had some good times, didn't we? Cheap beer, a live band every night, and the floor packed with people; everyone became instant best friends. You met your girlfriend there, didn't you, Simon?"

I grimaced at a sudden thought of Fiona sitting alone on the farm and wondered whether enjoying myself with two attractive Italian girls who were sharing a room with me was an activity I should make her aware of.

"We met on the dance floor. We've hardly spent any time apart since then. Until now."

"Where is she today?" asked Veronica.

"In New Zealand. We live there."

"We go to New Zealand next," said Fran. "After three months in Australia. You holiday with Tommo?"

"I'm taking a round-the-world trip. After this, I'm travelling to Hong Kong, then England, Los Angeles and back to New Zealand."

"We stay in Hong Kong last month," said Veronica. She puffed and shuddered.

I furrowed my brow. "What was wrong with Hong Kong?"

"Nothing. Hong Kong is amazing. But where will you sleep? Because do not stay in Chungking Mansions. It is, how you say in English? A sheety-hole."

"Okay, I'll remember not to stay in Chungking Mansions. Thanks for the tip."

Tommo held a door. "After you."

≈ ≈ ≈

I realised that no matter where in the world I entered a pizza take away, they all smelt identically of baked oregano. The pizza shop lady addressed a telephone handset cradled between her ear and her shoulder.

"Right. I'll say this back to you slowly. One family-size Meatlovers. One family-size Vegetarian. One large Hawaiian and one large Inferno. Is that everything? What d'ya mean, is the Inferno spicy? Of course it's spicy, it's an Inferno."

She concealed the mouthpiece and rolled her eyes at us. "Won't be a minute."

She returned to educating her customer.

"Yes, mate. You want the Inferno, but not too much chilli? Right-o. With the two-for-one offer, that'll be twenty-five dollars for the four pizzas. Pick up in fifteen minutes. Thank you. Bye." She passed a piece of paper to a stout man in a dirty-white apron who pasted tomato sauce onto flat, round dough.

The Italian girls leant on the counter and studied the process. I suspected this was unlike any pizza preparation they'd seen in Italy.

The lady picked up her pad. "Yes, love."

Fran turned to Veronica. "*Prosciutto e funghi?*"

"*Si.*"

"Hello. Can you make one small ham and mushroom and one small *Vegetariana?*"

"Vegeteriana? A vegetarian pizza?" asked the pizza-shop lady.

"*Si.* And a ham and mushroom."

"No problem. And for the lads?" She glanced up at Tommo.

"A large Inferno," he said. "And I'll have all the chilli the other guy didn't want."

The pizza lady laughed. I figured Tommo might be happier with his pizza than the Italians were going to be.

"I'll have a large Supreme," I said. "But no pineapple."

"Is that all? Eighteen dollars, please. It'll be fifteen minutes."

I tugged out a twenty-dollar note. "I'll pay for these. It's cheaper than pizza in London."

"Shall I pop next door to the bottle shop and buy some drinks?" asked Tommo.

I grimaced. "Only one beer for me, please."

"There are pizza flavours we do not know," said Veronica. "Inferno is spicy, yes? We call it *Diavola*. And they say the same here for *Margherita*, but they do not spell it right. But what is Supreme?"

"Supreme is everything," I said. "Every topping on one pizza."

"Like *Quattro Stagioni*? That has ham, mushrooms, olives, maybe little fish."

"I think Supreme contains every ingredient. They try to put pineapple on. I don't think pineapple should be allowed on pizza."

Fran shook her head. "I have not heard of this before."

The door bumped open and a fat, long-bearded man dressed in a singlet and shorts entered. His bare feet thudded across the tiles.

"Four pizzas for Wayne?"

"Yep. Here you go." The lady passed the boxes over. I enjoyed the brief fragrance of pepperoni as they sat on the counter while the customer paid.

The fat man balanced the boxes on his tummy and departed. I watched the cook slide our pizzas from metal trays into open cardboard boxes, lacerate them with a pizza wheel and close the lids.

"Shall we eat them on the beach?" I said. "It's a hot evening."

We bounced down the wooden steps, and I kicked off my shoes, so the warm sand squished between my toes. We gathered in a circle and opened our pizza boxes as 547,000 seagulls circled and eyed us hopefully. Tommo passed around beers from his six-pack.

Fran rotated her bottle and studied the label. "XXXX?"

"Yep," said Tommo. "Four X. 'Cos Queenslanders can't spell beer."

We all laughed. I looked at my drink. "Damn. We didn't bring a bottle opener."

"Chuck me your beer," said Tommo.

I expected him to perform a *Crocodile Dundee* act and open it with his teeth, but he grabbed the top and turned his wrist. With a brief *pfp* the lid popped off. He passed it back to me.

"Twist top. Incredible inventions we have here."

We laughed again, picked up pizza slices and chatted about travelling.

We discovered we'd all stayed in Paris.

We discovered Queensland pizza wasn't as good as Italian pizza.

We discovered Queensland seagulls were as annoyingly persistent as Italian ones. Tommo threw a crust at them. One grabbed it, and several hundred others pursued it down the beach.

We discovered six beers didn't last long between four people. Tommo and Fran shared a beer, then Veronica disappeared to the bottle shop and returned with a further six-pack of XXXX.

"Aie!" shouted Fran. "Something eat me." She slapped at her ankles.

"And me," said Veronica, rubbing her bare legs. "We go inside. There are bitey things."

≈ ≈ ≈

The reception area stank of stale smoke. Groups of young people crowded around the desk and chattered in English and North American accents.

The receptionist raised his hands to his mouth and shouted, "The shuttle bus for Candyshack Nightclub leaves at 8:30 p.m. Twenty dollars including entry fee. Nineteen seats on the bus. First come, first served."

Tommo turned to the Italian girls. "D'you want to go nightclubbing tonight?"

My insides wavered at the thought of further jugs of beer.

"Si," said Fran. "But we don't have nice clothes with us."

"That won't matter," said Tommo. He pointed at the queue of young people receiving tickets from the receptionist. "Look at these guys. They'll be going as they are."

"I think," said Veronica, as she studied the ripped denim shorts and scruffy T-shirts, "that the nightcloob here will be different from Napoli."

≈ ≈ ≈

I perched on the bus seat next to a young man with a shaved head.

"All right?" he said. "I'm Paul. Where are you from?"

A large tattoo crawled up his neck, and another on his arm advertised he supported Liverpool Football Club.

"My name's Simon. I'm from London, originally, but I've been living in New Zealand for over a year with my girlfriend. Are you from Liverpool?"

"Close. The Wirral. I've been in Australia for a week. I'm here for a year, travelling around. Might pick up a fruit picking job."

"Fruit picking? Sounds hard. I've worked on a farm, milking cows and helping them give birth."

He glanced at the two seats across the aisle, where Fran and Veronica sat. Tommo chatted with them from a seat in front.

Paul nodded his head twice to the side.

"Are those foreign girls with you? Very nice."

My arms folded across my chest. I felt possessive and protective of Fran and Veronica, which didn't seem right as I'd met them three hours ago and they probably didn't need protecting and certainly didn't need possessing.

"They're staying in the same room as me and my friend. But they're not really with us." I unfolded my arms. "One of them has a boyfriend back in Italy."

You made that up, Simon.

"Oh, right," said Paul. "Which one?"

I shrugged and waved the back of one hand.

"I can't remember. Maybe they both do." I glanced over my shoulder. "There are plenty of other girls on the bus. And I'm sure there'll be loads at the nightclub."

The bus braked opposite a long row of shops, bars and cafes facing the beach. The surf crashed to my left, although I couldn't see it in the dark.

"Candyshack Nightclub," announced the driver. "Show your white tickets to enter for free."

We trooped off the bus. I noticed Tommo take Fran's hand to help her down the two steps. Once she'd reached the bottom, they didn't let go.

Okay, that's how it's going to be.

Paul stepped down and inclined his head to my ear.

"Is your friend with the blondie? I like the dark-haired one."

I wanted to say, "Leave her alone," but I knew I had no right to.

We crossed the road and queued up to enter.

≈ ≈ ≈

Paul leered at Veronica as we showed the King Kong doorman our tickets.

"All right, love? I'm Paul. Are you up for a big night? What can I buy you to drink?"

Veronica glanced around to find Fran, but she'd disappeared into the club with Tommo. I stood closer to her.

"It is okay, thank you," she said. "I do not want a drink."

Paul made to put his arm around her. She clasped her bare arms and shrank back.

I pushed between them. "Hey, she's not interested in you. Find someone else to bother."

Paul stood tall and raised himself up on his toes. "Why the hell d'you care? You told me you had a girlfriend in New Zealand."

I faced him front on. "You're not getting the message. She doesn't want to be with you tonight. Leave her alone."

Paul extended his neck forward, so I smelt his breath. His lips curled back, and he bared his teeth.

"Why don't you let her say so herself, you little shit? You and me, outside, now."

14. SOMEBODY ELSE'S GUY

LATITUDE: 26° 40' 10" S
LONGITUDE: 153° 6' 29" E

Paul shoved his hands against my chest. I stepped backward and accidentally squashed Veronica against the wall.

Suddenly, he kicked his legs in the air, waved his arms and flew upward as the doorman lifted him by his shorts, which wedgied him severely and may have permanently curtailed his reproductive ability. King Kong carried him out of the club, dumped him on the pavement and pushed him away.

"Out. Get out. Don't think about trying to come back in. Ever."

The doorman returned and poked his finger in my chest.

"And you. Time to go."

I blinked rapidly and panted as I held the wall.

Veronica pushed in front of me and jammed her hands on her hips. "He did nothing. The other man push him. Please let him stay. He is good guy."

I tried to appear as gentle and weak as I could, incapable of fighting my way out of a soap bubble.

The doorman jabbed his finger at me. "Any trouble with anyone else, and you're out as well. Final warning. Understand?"

I nodded meekly as King Kong returned to his vitally important job of inspecting tickets.

Veronica took my arm. "Thank you. I did not like this man. I think, we are together tonight. You have girlfriend and I have boyfriend, so we dance and no-one else trouble us, yes?"

We descended the stairs into the bright-pink neon, which glowed like Debbie Harry's lipstick.

"You said you have a boyfriend?" I asked.

She closed her eyes and took a deep breath. "Yes, I have Fabio. Fabio in Napoli. He typical Italian boy. But I love him. When I go back to Italy, we marry and have lots of *bambinos* and make his mama happy. Will you marry your girlfriend?"

"She's only 24. But I've thought about it."

"I am 23. But when you find the one, it does not matter how old you are. What is her name?"

I pictured Fiona, climbing into bed by herself, with no idea her boyfriend was discussing his life plans in a Sunshine Coast nightclub with a pretty Italian girl he'd met that evening.

"She's called Fiona. We've been together two years."

"Fee-oh-naa. Is same in Italian. I have friend in Napoli called Fiona. It means *bellissimo*, um, beautiful. You are lucky guy. Come, we dance. I love this song. And then we buy a drink."

She pulled me onto the dance floor, where we boogied under the flashing disco lights to Jocelyn Brown's *Somebody Else's Guy*.

≈ ≈ ≈

2:00 a.m.

Closing time.

Sweat discoloured my shirt and shone on Veronica's forehead. We'd danced all night and consumed nothing but water. The music stopped, and white ceiling lights extinguished the neon.

She stood on tiptoe and glanced around. "Do you see Fran? And your friend?"

I watched people's backs ascend the stairs to the street.

"Maybe they left already?"

"All right. We go home. We find them."

A gentle breeze rustled the palm trees as we stepped out of the club into the warm, night air.

I gazed left and right along the esplanade. "How do we return to the backpackers? I thought there'd be taxis, but everything's closed."

"Then we walk," said Veronica.

"But which way is it?"

"Is easy. The nightcloob is on the beach. The place we stay is on the beach. If we walk along the beach, we find it."

She held out her hand. I took it and followed her.

≈ ≈ ≈

The beach path curved gently along the sea. Veronica and I strolled.

I let go of her. I knew Mediterranean people were more tactile than the British, but it didn't feel right when we both had partners.

We discussed travel. She asked me about New Zealand.

We discussed our homes. I asked her about Naples.

We discussed our relationships. I asked her about Fabio. She wanted to know all about Fiona and our lives in New Zealand.

She stopped, turned and pointed. "Look at the light on the water."

We stood at the top of wooden steps leading down to smooth sand stretching into the darkness. The rising full moon shimmered a cream fan from the horizon across the ocean towards us.

Veronica pulled my hand. "Come, we touch the sea." She removed her sandals and sprinted down the stairs. I followed her and watched her splash her ankles. She laughed and spun in the shallows with her head tipped back and her arms outstretched.

I squished sand between my toes.

We sat on the beach in the warm breeze and listened to the swish swish swish of the wavelets.

It reminded me of Tonga, sitting on a desert island in the dark, huddled up to Fiona, terrified of the wild pigs in the jungle behind us.

"I wish Fabio could see this," said Veronica. "He does not like to travel. He need his mama's cooking."

I laughed.

"I wish Fiona could be here too. Sorry, I mean, I enjoy talking to you, but it's not the same."

Veronica placed her hand on my shoulder.

"I know what you are saying. When you go back to New Zealand, I think you have to ask her to marry you, yes?"

I drew patterns in the sand with a shell. "I suppose so."

"Of course you must. Listen, I will tell you how."

I shrugged. "Okay."

"First, you buy a ring."

"I've been looking in shops for jewellery, as a present for her."

"Yes, but Simon, this is not any ring. This is ring for marry."

"Engagement ring? Okay. If Fabio bought you a ring, what'd impress you?"

"Diamond. Has to be diamond." She spread her arms wide and grinned. "Beeg, beeg diamond."

I rubbed my chin.

"I'm not sure I've the money for a big diamond. Maybe several small diamonds?"

"No. Is better if you buy the biggest diamond. And gold ring. Must be gold ring. Like this." She engraved a circle in the sand with an Egyptian pyramid-sized upside down triangle on top of it.

"All right. I'll look in more jewellery shops and see what I can afford. Rings may be cheaper in Hong Kong."

"They might be, but be careful of things which are not real. I do not know how to say in English."

"Fake? Another girl also told me that. Thanks for the tip."

Veronica nodded. "Okay. You have ring. Then you land at New Zealand airport. She come to meet you, yes?"

"Yes, I'm sure she'll pick me up."

"Perfect. When you see her, you walk to her, you go down on one knee, you open the ring box and you say, 'Fee-oh-naa, I have missed you so much. I want to be with you forever. Please, will you marry me?'"

I frowned. "What, in front of all the other people in arrivals?"

Veronica threw her hands up. "Of course, then she has to say yes. Here, we practise it. I pretend to be her."

She picked up a seashell and handed it to me.

"This shell is the ring. You walk away with it, then come back and say what I told you."

"Um, okay." I took the shell and walked back to the steps.

Veronica stood by the water, silhouetted in the bright moonlight. I watched her untie her hair, flick it forward over her face and then back again. There couldn't be a more romantic setting for a proposal. I wished Fiona were with me, and this moment was real.

I passed the shell from hand to hand, as a night-bird called above me.

Practise, Simon. Practise.

"Fiona, I have missed you so much," I whispered to myself. "I want to be with you forever. Please, will you marry me?"

Veronica faced away, as if she didn't expect to see me. I walked across the beach towards her. The sultry night breeze swished in the palm trees, and waves splashed rhythmically.

I glanced left and right, approached her and knelt on one knee. The sand scratched my bare skin, and my leg sank into it. She turned around.

I cleared my throat and held up the shell.

"Fiona, I have missed you so much. I want to be with you forever. Please, will you marry me?"

Veronica reached out and touched the seashell.

I paused, and our eyes met in the moonlight.

"Shit!" shouted someone behind me. "What the bloody hell are you guys doing?"

15. MR FRIENDLY

LATITUDE: 2° 44' 20" N
LONGITUDE: 122° 43' 45" E

I scrambled to my feet and hid the shell in my hands as Tommo and Fran crashed from bushes at the back of the beach.

Tommo's teeth gleamed in the moonlight. "What's going on, you two? Is there something you need to announce?"

My feet shuffled and buried in the sand.

Veronica planted her hands on her hips. "Nothing is going on. We talk about Simon asking to marry."

Tommo laughed and punched my arm. "I told you she liked you, but this is very sudden."

I threw my arms up. "I'm not asking Veronica; I'm practising proposing to Fiona. Anyway, what were you two doing in the bushes?"

Fran took Tommo's hand, met eyes with him, then concealed her face behind her hair.

Tommo grinned. "C'mon, guys, let's return to the backpackers."

≈ ≈ ≈

I awoke to the sound of frantic crashing, as if there was about to be a natural disaster and we'd have to evacuate immediately.

Fran and Veronica bumped into each other, swept makeup and bangles off a table and jammed clothes into backpacks.

I sat up, rubbed my eyes and looked for a clock. "Are you leaving?"

"Yes," said Fran. "We catch bus to next place. But it go in five minutes. We sleep too long."

Veronica zipped her pack and threw it over her shoulder. She bent over and kissed my forehead.

"*Arrivederci*, Simon. Thank you for a lovely evening. And don't forget. Big diamond. The biggest you can buy. And practise the words I told you."

"Thanks for the advice. And the rehearsal. Have a great trip."

"Say goodbye to Tommo for me," said Fran. "He sleep like *bambino*."

They threw open the door and were gone from our lives forever.

I reflected on the previous evening. My conversation with Veronica on the beach at three o'clock in the morning, in the warm breeze, under the moonlight. Rehearsing my proposal to Fiona. Dancing in Candyshack nightclub. The unpleasant scene with Paul, the tattooed skinhead from England.

The tattooed skinhead from England.

Shit.

I poked Tommo.

"Wake up. I need your help."

Tommo pulled his sleeping bag over his head. "What? Whadyawant?"

I found my watch. "It's midday. We should've checked out by now, but I can't leave the room."

He sat up. "Where's the girls?"

"Gone. Fran says goodbye. They had to catch a bus."

He ran his hands through his hair and looked at me. "Why can't you leave the room?"

"Last night, when we entered the club, some idiot tried to hit on Veronica. She wasn't interested, and I told him that. Then he started shoving me, and he wanted to take me outside and beat me up."

Tommo's mouth fell open. "Shit. Why didn't you call out to me?"

"You'd already disappeared downstairs with Fran. Anyway, this gigantic bouncer threw him out."

Tommo ruffled his hair. "Great. Problem solved."

"Not quite. He's staying here, at the backpackers."

"How d'you know?"

"He rode with us on the bus. Could you open the door and check the coast's clear? Then we'll make a run for it."

≈ ≈ ≈

Tommo kerbed two wheels outside Brisbane airport's terminal, hopped out and reached into the tray to unload my bag.

Idling engines and slamming doors of taxis surrounded our goodbye.

He studied his shoes.

I reached out and shook his hand, which felt stupidly formal, then met eyes with him.

"Thanks for showing me around Queensland. We had the best time."

"No worries. I'll see you sometime."

My eyes looked down at the ground, then back up again. "I'd better catch the plane. Thanks again."

Tommo punched me playfully, then climbed up into his car. I flinched as the dixie horn sounded, then his arm waved from the window, and I watched the tall, white ute drive away until it turned the corner. I wondered whether he'd ever call Kylie, or whether his relationship with Sweetykins the spider would continue to be his most enduring love affair.

I shouldered my pack and lifted my hand luggage bag.

The time had come to tackle the Orient.

≈ ≈ ≈

Hot, Queensland air abruptly transformed to cold, artificial-tasting air-conditioning as I checked in my backpack and negotiated passport control.

My guidebook's cover featured an image of a Chinese junk, and I sat at the gate and riffled through the pages.

In my childhood, an elderly neighbour's grandson had played at my house during the boarding school holidays. His parents lived as expats in Hong Kong, and he related extraordinary tales of hot, humid camps on deserted islands, hornets as big as your hand which could kill a child with one bite and opulent parties in extensive, swimming-pooled residences.

I wished I'd stayed in touch with him.

I didn't think I'd be sleeping in an immense house with a swimming pool tonight.

But I had remembered not to stay in Chungking Mansions.

The British had recently returned Hong Kong to China, but they hadn't seen fit to consult me before the handover. I'd be arriving a few months after Chris Patten had accepted the folded Union Jack and sailed away with Prince Charles on the Royal Yacht Britannia while, behind them, Chinese armoured vehicles crossed the border and entered the city.

I hoped it hadn't changed yet.

Passengers queued for the plane, and I decided everyone else must be from Hong Kong, and I was the sole tourist.

This didn't bother me at all. I loved striking up conversations with people from different countries and cultures. Tommo and I became friends at the Redback Tavern in London by discussing a band. I'd met Kylie the nurse by talking to my seat neighbour. Gosh, I'd hooked up with Fiona in this fashion by chatting to a cute-looking Kiwi girl about travelling. Most people loved to talk about their lives and hometowns.

Unfortunately, the man in seat 34A was about to be the exception.

I squeezed my hand luggage into the overhead compartment; grabbed the guidebook and plopped in the aisle seat.

"Hi," I said to the plump, middle-aged man in the neighbouring seat. "I'm your new best friend for the next ten hours."

He turned away to face the window, so I didn't continue our conversation.

As usual, I watched the safety demonstration intently, out of respect for the cabin crew's training, and out of a deep fear one day I might need to remember the exact location of my light and whistle for attracting attention. The man in seat 34A ignored their presentation and emitted occasional grunting noises.

I relaxed as the tractor reversed the plane, and we taxied and took off. Hong Kong would be not only a new country for me, but a new continent and a new culture, and I was determined to absorb it as fully as possible.

Hong Kong, explained the guidebook, was an enigma; a city balanced on a knife-edge of Chinese culture and western colonialism. British street names, afternoon scones and cars driving on the left side of the road sat alongside gigantic Buddhas, sailing junks, dragon festivals and stilt houses. It was perfectly possible to eat hot buttered toast for breakfast, McDonald's hamburgers for lunch and snake soup for dinner.

A voice to my right. "Excuse me, sir? Could I offer you the roast chicken with vegetables, or the Szechuan pork with rice?"

I inhaled the exotic fragrance of Asian spices which radiated from her trolley. "The Szechuan pork, please. My taste buds should prepare for our destination."

The flight attendant smiled, removed a tray from her trolley, added the expected foil-covered, rectangular dish and tonged a bread roll on top of it, which wasn't a usual feature of an oriental cooking experience.

She glanced past me at Mr Friendly.

"And for you, sir?"

"Pork," he said, in the one word I heard him utter during our ten-hour relationship.

She passed his tray over and continued her service on the opposite side of the aisle, while the man in seat 34A glanced at his food, dismissed it, leant back and closed his eyes.

I rubbed my hands and unfolded my paper napkin.

One of my greatest flying pleasures is to unwrap all the little plastic dishes of airline food and discover what goodies await me. I opened the entrée of mixed salad and tore the sachet of accompanying dressing. I peeked under the cover of the dessert and smiled as I discovered the hidden surprise was a chocolate brownie. My utensils crinkled from their plastic wrapping, and I'd begun intense preparation for arrival in the land of the chopstick, when the man next to me issued the loudest, lengthiest, most pungent fart my nostrils had ever consumed.

I shielded my mouth and nose and slanted away from the stink. His rear end appended another brief *thhhpp*, like a punctuation mark after its earlier prolonged statement. The stench reeked as if something had died under our seats. I picked at my food and desperately hoped the other passengers wouldn't imagine the smell came from me, but I'd lost my appetite; everything tasted of fart.

I flipped up my tray table and evacuated to the bathroom, hoping if I hid inside for a while, the smell would die down. After five minutes in the toilet, five minutes watching the ocean from the small, oval window in the plane's rear door and five minutes queueing behind the drinks trolley, I slid back into my seat.

His fart had dissipated, but the memory lingered, and I didn't feel like eating. As I'd failed to achieve the desired chopstick practice, I wrapped the airline blanket around myself and slept.

≈ ≈ ≈

"Ladies and gentlemen, this is First Officer Clement Wu, speaking to you from the flight deck. I trust you've enjoyed your flight with us today, and you've managed to get some sleep. Shortly, we'll begin our descent into Hong Kong, where the weather this evening is clear, about 22 degrees, with a light breeze from the south. We should have you on the ground slightly ahead of schedule, just before 6:00 p.m."

I opened my eyes and peered out of the window, but I couldn't see any land or any sea. The man in seat 34A read a magazine with Chinese characters, and the photographs showed Asian people wearing western clothes.

"Cabin crew, please prepare the cabin for landing."

I fidgeted in my seat and tugged my guidebook from the pocket. A more modern facility on an island some distance from the centre of Hong Kong would soon replace Kai Tak airport, but until then, it remained one of the most hazardous commercial landings in the world. Pilots needed to line up visual markers, complete a low-altitude sharp right-hand turn and weave between residential skyscrapers to land successfully. It was normal for passengers to look from a plane window and observe upper storey residents hanging out their washing. Terrifyingly, the guide imparted that accidents occurring during this manoeuvre had killed over two hundred people.

The plane circled slowly while the cabin crew inspected tray tables and seatbelts, and I glimpsed land in the distance.

"Cabin crew, please take your seats."

The wheels extended below me, and I drummed my feet on the aircraft floor.

A new country and a new culture.

Hong Kong.

Asia.

I might find a ring for Fiona. But not a fake.

Green mountains filled the opposite window, then the plane turned sharply and straightened up as we bisected the high-rises like Luke Skywalker piloting his X-wing fighter through the Death Star. Multiple balconies garnished the buildings, and I peered past my seat neighbour but, disappointingly, I couldn't see anyone hanging out laundry.

The plane landed without incident. I wondered if I should stand up and applaud, but I guessed all the locals on the flight experienced this journey regularly.

I realised this time I was completely by myself.

No Fiona.

No Tommo.

No Kylie, or Leanne or Veronica.

My survival depended on my wits and a slightly dog-eared Lonely Planet guide to Hong Kong.

≈ ≈ ≈

Ceiling fans whoomp-whoomped overhead as other passengers shoved and jostled their bags away from the carousel. I stood back and flicked through the where-to-stay section of the guide.

Hong Kong, it imparted, possessed no mid-level accommodation. Every option was either luxurious and expensive, such as the Peninsula Hotel, or seedy and cheap, such as Chungking Mansions, a complex of several blocks of guest houses, ethnic bistros and money changers. A bed could be had for US$10 per night, but it boasted a dubious history of fatal fires, drug deals and murders.

I had a vision of Veronica walking to the pizza shop with me, saying, *"How you say in English? It is sheety-hole."*

Fortunately, the guide continued, other cheap options existed along Nathan Road, in an area called Tsim Sha Tsui. I remembered Leanne had mentioned it, and I tugged the piece of paper she'd inscribed from my pocket.

My bag bumped along the carousel, and I marched out to the public bus area.

Despite the cool, winter, late afternoon temperature, my T-shirt immediately dampened with sweat. An exotic, not unpleasant smell permeated the air; the combination of swarms of people and wok-fried Chinese food, backdropped by fragrances of wet, tropical plants.

A bus marked 'Kowloon' sneezed at me and opened its doors. I shoved my way through passengers standing in every available space.

"Excuse me," I said to the driver. "Tsim Sha Tsui?" I showed him the piece of paper with Leanne's Cantonese calligraphy.

"Yessir, Kowloon, Kowloon."

I brandished the note at him and spoke slower. "Do you go to Tsim Sha Tsui?"

The doors closed behind me, and I grabbed a handrail as we swung away from the kerb.

"Yessir. Bus go Nathan Road."

I remembered stern instructional signs on the red London buses: 'Do not speak to the driver while the bus is in motion' and I hoped I'd boarded the correct one.

Regardless of whether a terminal was in London, Los Angeles or even Tonga, as soon as any bus departed an airport, it began a main-road journey of various distances towards the city it served.

Not this bus.

Immediately we left the boundaries of Kai Tak, it was as if we'd entered London's Oxford Street. The pavements thronged with men, women, children and dogs; the streets thronged with cars, buses, small trucks and bikes. Shouts alternated with screeching tyres and dinging bicycle bells. Motorbikes dodged between the other traffic, many with couples and families balanced on them.

I'd never seen so many people packed into such a small space. Not in London, not in Paris, not in Los Angeles. I'd no idea how the cars didn't all crash into each other. The transition was immediate. One minute normal, sedate, anywhere-in-the-world airport movements, the next complete chaos.

The crowds didn't abate. Ever. There were no quiet streets. The bus cruised through the traffic while we all gripped handles and rails as it swung around corners and came to abrupt halts.

I peeked between other travellers out of the windscreen.

Neon.

So much neon.

Neon everywhere.

My eyes widened at the assault of Smarties-packet illuminations.

I heard the driver call, "Nathan Road," and I leant forward. "Is this Tsim Sha Tsui?"

"Soon, soon."

We careered on through infinite neon. Flashes of blue, red, green, pink and purple lit up the bus interior each time we stopped. Finally, the bus paused at a phenomenally crowded section of the street, and the door behind me creaked open.

"This Tsim Sha Tsui, sir. You get out now."

"Thank you."

I turned around, descended one step onto the pavement, and a baying mob of Chinese teenage boys thrust out their arms and grabbed at my bags.

16. THE LUXURY ROOM

LATITUDE: 22° 17' 47" N,
LONGITUDE: 114° 10' 23" E

I tugged my bag away from multiple Chinese arms and attempted to step backward into the safety of the bus, but people disembarking behind me prevented this.

"What d'you want?" I shouted. "Get off me."

"You need place to stay?" asked the owner of one pair of arms.

"You come with me. I have bed," said another.

"You sleep with me?" inquired a third, slightly more ambitiously.

I selected the cleanest looking arms' owner, and we carried my bag between us. The remaining accommodation vendors attacked the passengers behind me like seagulls fighting over discarded chips.

My new, wiry, bespectacled porter scraped my bag along the pavement.

"My name Ignatius. I take you nice place."

I ruminated on the likelihood of a Hong Kong couple waking up sixteen years ago and deciding to christen their first-born Ignatius.

Lights emanated from the tower block above me and I studied the silhouettes of bicycles and laundry visible in the windows. Yells and shouts drifted down from the upper floors. "It's not in Chungking Mansions, is it? I don't want to stay in Chungking Mansions."

"No Chungking Mansions. I take you Mirador Mansions," said Ignatius.

"Um, okay. Mirador Mansions."

I'd heard nothing negative about Mirador Mansions, so I gave him the benefit of the doubt.

We entered a dimly lit, ground floor foyer, bereft of anything except a three-wheeled pram in the corner, which looked like it had been there long enough for its former occupant to have children of their own, and a kiosk covered in photos of various items it may have sold decades in the past. The regulation aroma of stale uric acid filled my nostrils. Ignatius pressed a lift button, and we waited in awkward silence until the doors opened. He pushed level eight. I tensed, and figured if anyone attempted to mug me, the chances were I was bigger than them.

I jammed myself against the lift wall as the doors creaked closed.

They ground apart so slowly at level eight I wanted to prise them open with my hands. A filthy corridor smelt of old food and, at the end, an elderly Chinese lady sat at a cheap, plastic, outdoor table on a cheap, plastic, outdoor chair. She watched a small, portable, black-and-white television.

I stared at her and bit the inside of my cheek.

Ignatius rested my bag on the ground.

The Chinese lady looked me up and down. She held up one stubby, plump, index finger.

"One person? How many night?"

I pointed two fingers in a Winston Churchill V-sign, unintentionally copying her.

"Two nights, please."

She bashed buttons on a pocket calculator and turned it around.

"You pay me one hundred dollar."

I glanced at Ignatius, then back at her.

"Could I see the room?"

The lady spoke to Ignatius in Cantonese. He beckoned me down the corridor, back towards the lift. I squinted over my shoulder at my bag resting next to the Chinese lady, who'd returned to her black-and-white television.

"I show you best room," said Ignatius. We passed rows of identical, brown doors, without numbers or any differentiating characteristics.

Ignatius stopped, pulled open a door and showed me a cupboard with a single bed in it. I'd have to store my bag under the bed, and then open the door to retrieve it.

111

If this is the best room, which is the worst room?

"D'you have a bigger room? For fifty dollars per night, it seems small."

We returned to the lady, who focussed on her television and seemed incredibly annoyed my visit was interrupting her Chinese soap opera. Ignatius spoke to her.

She punched her calculator again and scowled. "Bigger room, two night; one hundred-fifty dollar."

One hundred and fifty dollars. Goodness knows what the Peninsula Hotel charged. I pulled out one hundred and fifty dollars and offered it to her.

She looked at the money, frowned and shook her head.

"Hong Kong dollar only."

Of course. Hong Kong Dollars. About five to the New Zealand Dollar. This room's cheap.

I shoved the Kiwi money in my pocket and tugged Hong Kong currency from my bag.

She grunted, took the cash, folded it up and added it to a clear, plastic sleeve full of notes in a drawer.

Ignatius picked up my bag again, and we re-entered the lift.

I glanced up at the lift numbers and frowned. "Is the room on a different floor?"

He smiled, but he'd forgotten how to speak English. The lift reached the ground floor, and we exited into the busy street. He led me across a courtyard and towards an entrance populated by the type of people who I didn't think I'd want to socialise with.

A hollow-cheeked man with lank, greasy hair who suffered from a nervous affliction.

A lady in the shortest leather skirt and tallest high heels I'd ever seen, who licked her top lip and beckoned.

A skinny, heavily tattooed, bald-headed man, who slid down a wall and collapsed on the pavement as we approached.

I wiped sweat from my palms, glanced up, and read the words above the entrance.

Chungking Mansions.

≈ ≈ ≈

I drew myself up to my full height and grabbed Ignatius by the shoulder.

"No!" He swivelled, and I pointed at the sign. "No. Not Chungking Mansions."

I had the terrible thought I'd have to chase him into this den of iniquity to retrieve my bag and run the gauntlet of the druggies and hookers, but he accepted my outburst and led me back to the lifts.

The Chinese lady was phenomenally pissed off to see me a third time. I'd no idea how good her English was, but I was about to test its extremes.

I thumped my fist and leant over her table. "Not Chungking Mansions. I want to stay here, in Mirador Mansions. Can I have the room you showed me?"

She shook her head without removing her gaze from the television. "No."

I threw my hands in the air. "Why not?"

"A man take it."

I considered the likelihood of someone having rented the tiny room during the ten minutes while I had been reconnoitering the piss-stained, needle-strewn entrance to Chungking Mansions and my cheeks tingled. "D'you have another room? Here, in Mirador Mansions?"

"Only luxury room. Eighty dollar more." She faced the calculator to me again. Her prices fluctuated more than the New York Stock Exchange.

I sighed, peeled off more Hong Kong dollars, examined the denominations and handed them over. She stuffed them in the same plastic sack which bulged with paper money and nodded at Ignatius. The sixteen-year-old lifted my bag for the fourth time and led me back down the corridor, then we turned right, and he opened a door.

The room was identical to the first one. A single bed in a cupboard.

I tilted my head. "I thought you were taking me to the luxury room?"

Ignatius dumped my bag on the bed and pointed to where a ceiling fan gently rotated.

"This luxury room."

I sighed and watched him amble back down the corridor.

≈ ≈ ≈

Nathan Road by night shone as brightly as Nathan Road by day.

I stood still on the pavement and stared above heads.

Squishing amongst this many people wasn't an experience I enjoyed, and I clutched the pocket concealing my wallet. The roar of voices competed with an English football match where Manchester United were 2-1 down, five minutes before full time. People pushed past me; I had to push past them.

Smells emanating from all angles assaulted my nostrils. Steam poured from vents in the sides of buildings and dissipated the scent of fried food, steamed food, boiled food, discarded food.

Neon covered both sides of the street, with advertisements in Cantonese script and English.

Bright-yellow.

Bright-red.

Bright-blue, green, pink, white.

Despite the late hour, everything was open and trading and, encouragingly, several of the shops sold jewellery.

Maybe I can find Fiona a ring?

I looked in the window of Yue Hwa—Chinese Products.

I inspected the offerings in Emperor—Watch and Jewellery.

I pressed my nose against the window of Rolex—Zurich Watch Company.

I had a sudden flashback to standing on Mooloolaba beach with Veronica.

"Simon, be careful of things that are not real."

These shops all looked genuine. They had uniformed staff, tidy displays, professional-looking branding.

Are they all a scam? How will I ever know?

There was one thing to do—consider it over dinner.

The bright lights of McDonald's enticed me in various languages to consume one of their internationally homogeneous offerings. I pushed the door, witnessed the usual behind-the-counter chaos, smelt the universal eau-de-French fry and concluded I'd eaten enough McDonald's with Tommo potentially for the rest of my life.

I wanted to eat like the locals, not a western translation.

A side-alley offered a view of shops and eateries. I took a quick breath and ducked down it.

Maybe I can find a locals' restaurant here?

The window of the first establishment contained faded, laminated pictures of identical-looking dishes. Diners poked chopsticks and scooped small spoons to half-eat, half-drink from large, white bowls. This didn't resemble Mr Wong's in London's Chinatown.

Where was the crispy fried beef?

Where was the sweet and sour pork?

And where, most importantly, were the prawn crackers?

I'd no idea what I'd order.

The next restaurant offered a similar view. Crucially, there didn't appear to be any menus either in Cantonese or, more usefully, English.

I entered another, narrower side-alley. The buildings crowded closer, and above me, acres of sheets draped from racks hanging out of upper-floor windows.

I briefly considered returning to McDonald's in all its westernised reliability when a tiny, human hand grabbed my finger.

17. CANTONESE PAVAROTTI

LATITUDE: 22° 17' 54" N
LONGITUDE: 114° 10' 17" E

I froze, and glanced down at a smiling, black-haired girl of about seven years old.

She yanked my hand. "You want eat? Come."

She wore a grubby, faded dress, no shoes and grinned yellow teeth at me.

I rubbed my chin and peered ahead, then behind.

The little hand tugged harder, and she dragged me farther along the narrow alleyway. I wrestled my finger from her grasp and squinted into the darkness.

Is this a trap?

Will all her relatives set upon me in the shadows, come at me with knives in their teeth, stab me, steal my wallet and leave me lying among the rubbish bins?

Is this where it ends?

"Come." She grabbed my hand again and hastened me into the alleyway. The neon lights and busy restaurants faded.

Laundry hung lower and lower until I could reach up and touch the sheets. The slender alley bisected a similar one at a junction. Small, dim lamps dangled from strings above us and four cheap, plastic chairs surrounded a white, plastic table.

The girl pulled a chair out. The smile never left her face.

"Sit."

She walked further into the alleyway and vanished.

I sat, obediently, conflicted between fear of the unknown and curiosity of what would happen next. My eyes peered along the four exits of this crossroads. A stale smell hung throughout the alleyway, which reminded me of wet clothes someone's left in the washing machine and forgotten about.

116

Behind me, I could see the distant hubbub of the shops and restaurants.

To the right, the alleyway ended in laundry and darkness.

To the left, the dim passage stretched miles into the unknown. I made out an elderly man crouching in the corner, smoking a long pipe. He didn't look my way. Doorways faced onto the alleyway, and the ever-present laundry hung everywhere and added to the humidity.

I'd no idea where the girl had gone, but I could hear voices and the sounds and smells of a kitchen.

I waited.

Insects buzzed around the dim lights.

The laundry continued to steam.

The old man continued to smoke his pipe.

I wondered if I should leave quietly, but my inquisitiveness prevented my departure.

A voice behind me. "Eat."

I jumped and turned around as, like the magic shopkeeper in the *Mr Benn* cartoon, the young girl reappeared. She placed a dark, steaming bowl on the table and handed me chopsticks and a white, plastic spoon. The bowl wasn't the same shape as the ones I'd seen in the restaurants behind me, nor as big. It resembled a large ramekin.

I smiled at the girl. "Thank you."

"Chicken," she said, "Eat." She ran back into the shadows.

I picked up the spoon and scooped some liquid from the bowl, then immediately winced as it burnt my mouth. I blew on the food.

The child returned with a plate of plain, white rice and a small pile of white paper napkins. She placed them in front of me, bowed slightly and skipped away.

I looked around at the dark, dirty alleyways, the swaying laundry, the old man with the pipe, and decided I couldn't have found a more authentic experience.

Fiona would've loved this.

I scooped rice and took a tiny sip from the bowl. All I could taste was hot water. I spooned a bigger portion. A mild taste of Chinese spices.

I peered ahead and realised the girl watched me from the shadows, with an older lady. Much older. I smiled at them and waved, in what I hoped passed for an international gesture of friendship.

The young girl waved back.

I finished my meal, sat back in my chair and patted my stomach. The food didn't have strong flavours, and the liquid consistency didn't seem to contain any chicken. I concluded this constituted the usual daily fare for a Hong Kong resident, a far cry from the westernised buffets of London's Chinatown.

The seven-year-old cleared my plates and held up ten fingers. "Ten dollar."

Ten dollars. That's about a British pound. One pound for a meal.

I gave ten Hong Kong dollars to the girl. She made to go away, and I called her back. "Wait." I reached into my wallet and found a five-dollar note. "Here. For you." Her eyes gleamed, and she stuffed the tip inside her dress. The old lady looked up at me, nodded and returned to the shadows.

Was I being condescending to this young girl who clearly lived in extreme poverty? Where were her parents? Did she attend school? I wondered if she wanted to spend her evenings doing something more fun than waiting for tourists to come by and enticing them to eat in her grandmother's kitchen.

I stood, stuffed the leftover napkins in my pocket, pushed the white plastic chair under the table and retreated down the alleyway. As I rejoined the neon of Nathan Road, the world of the young girl and her grandmother seemed like a dream which had never happened.

I wished Fiona could've seen it.

≈ ≈ ≈

The clattering of the windowless luxury room's ceiling fan woke me. My body clock told me the time had the potential to be morning, but it could've been midnight.

It didn't matter what time it was; my bowels were about to explode.

I tilted my head on one side and angled it towards the door.

In the distance, I heard singing.

118

At least, it sounded like it might've been singing.

Or someone was experiencing pain. Bad pain.

Is this a country they practise torture in? Have I accidentally checked into an interrogation facility?

I opened my door a crack and disturbed a large gecko, which slithered into a vent.

AIIIIIEEEEE AIIIEEEEE AIE AIE AIE AIIIIIII

My body stiffened as I peeked into the corridor.

What the hell's that din?

I rescued my bag from under the bed, closed the door again and yanked out clothes. My watch said 6:00 a.m.

The noise continued.

AAAA AWWW EEEEE AIEEE

I pulled on trousers as fast as I could. Whatever I'd eaten last night in the alleyway had disagreed with me in a big way.

I slid off the bed, opened the door, padded along the corridor and hesitated.

AW AW AW AW EEEEEEE AWOOOOOO

If I hadn't needed the toilet so urgently, I would've run in the opposite direction.

I rattled the bathroom door handle.

Locked.

The screeching stopped.

I jammed my ear to the door and heard a shower running.

The contralto aria restarted.

EEEE EEEE OOOO AWWWWWW AWW

I wasn't proficient in Cantonese, but the shower's occupant clearly enjoyed participating in this production.

We reached a quieter movement during the concert.

Haw haw haw hee, haw haw haw hee, hu hu hu hu hu hu haw haw haw heeeeeee

I held my stomach and wondered whether latecomers would be admitted at a suitable interval in the performance.

The *adagio* section continued.

A-hoo, a-hoo, he he he heee. A-hoo, a-hoo, he he he heee

The shower's torrent and the singing both ceased.
I clutched my stomach and crossed my legs.
Yes! He'll come out soon, and I can use the toilet.
Pause.
I paced in a tight circle outside the bathroom door. Despite the humidity, a cold sweat ran across my forehead and down my face.
Come on, come on, please.
I stuck my ear on the keyhole to hear the latest developments.
Silence.
I squashed my ear right up against the door.
Come on. You must be finished. Hurry, I'm desperate.
Pause.
Nothing.

Pat pat pat pat pat

Rustle rustle rustle

What are you doing? For goodness' sake.
Silence.
More silence.
I wondered if he'd gone to sleep.
Pause.

AIIIIIEEEEE AIIIEEEEE AIE AIE AIE AIIIIIII

The shower restarted, and we continued with the third act of the concerto, a lively *forte* movement.

120

I couldn't wait any longer without a lively forte movement of my own.

Further down the corridor, I glimpsed a shirtless, young, Asian male exit from one of many similar doors and close it behind him.

Maybe that's another bathroom?

I took deep breaths, held my stomach and galloped along the corridor.

Which door did he come from?

I tried the first one.

Locked.

I tried the next one, which opened into a cupboard containing several old mattresses stacked against a wall.

I doubled over in pain. At this point, I would've given up all my life's possessions to find a toilet.

I opened the adjacent door and reeled from the smell of stale sweat and sleeping humans. Lots of them. A corridor-narrow room full of half-naked, young, Asian men lying on triple bunks stretched out in front of me. There must've been fifty of them, and they all slept.

It resembled an opium den in a *Tintin* book. I held my stomach and stared into the dormitory.

These guys must have a toilet somewhere. They can't all use the opera singer's bathroom.

At the far end of the row of bunks, another door offered potential relief. I tiptoed in as quietly as I could, stepping over bags, bowls and chopsticks and navigating naked limbs poking from under sheets. I pushed the door open and witnessed the most beautiful sight in any desperate human's life.

The toilet stood in the corner of a minuscule room, which also contained a small shower and a basin. The door had no lock, and the bowl had no seat, but I didn't care; I slumped on the porcelain and rested my elbows on my legs.

I hoped nobody'd heard me.

I hoped nobody entered.

I hoped there was toilet paper.

There wasn't.

I searched the room, on top of the cistern, next to the shower, under the basin.

Nothing in the bathroom could be considered toilet paper.

121

Every resident of the dormitory must bring their own, and as I wasn't a resident of the dormitory, and I wasn't familiar with the opium den-etiquette, I hadn't.

What to do, what to do?

I perched on the toilet bowl and considered my options.

I could wait until someone entered and ask them for toilet paper. But I wasn't supposed to be here, the Cantonese word for toilet paper wasn't in my vocabulary and I didn't relish explaining with hand signals.

I could slip outside and pinch some toilet paper from a sleeping resident of the opium den. This wouldn't be a good idea; they might all wake up and attack me.

I could pull up my underwear and trousers, leave, and deal with the subsequent mess in the shower. I hoped the Cantonese Pavarotti had completed his arias.

Someone stirred in the opium den.

I needed to make a decision, now.

18. PUSHMI-PULLYU

LATITUDE: 22° 17' 2" N
LONGITUDE: 114° 9' 2" E

Option three seemed the least worst, so I pulled up my trousers and felt a lump in the pocket.

The napkins from last night's dinner.

"Yes!" I threw back my head and laughed.

Disaster averted.

I used the serviettes, flushed and exited as quickly as I could. One shirtless, Cantonese teenager sat upright on a middle bunk and watched me, bleary-eyed. By the time he'd had a chance to say anything, I'd gone.

≈ ≈ ≈

Leaving the Chinese dawn chorus in Mirador Mansions, I elbowed through the constantly crowded streets to the equally jam-packed boat harbour, where I watched one of the iconic green-and-white, open-sided Star Ferries dock.

I couldn't tell which was the bow and which was the stern. Like Doctor Dolittle's mythical, double-ended beast the pushmi-pullyu, the Star Ferry was identical from both ends. White on the top deck and green on the bottom, it resembled a giant, floating, liquorice allsort. I read the name 'Solar Star' in gold and bounced on my tiptoes.

Nowhere else in the entire world offered the chance to take a boat ride in a rusty ferry with rows of black car tyres hanging from the side for the equivalent of 10p, so I paid my fare, queued with the throng to enter the lower deck and ran to secure a seat on the stark, wooden bench.

I gazed at the dark-green water as the engine revved up, the smell of diesel filled the cabin and, accompanied by two hundred smartly dressed, oriental commuters, I set off across the water towards Hong Kong Island and Victoria Peak.

The ferry swayed as we crossed. My seat neighbour read a newspaper in Chinese script, and my eyes boggled as he turned the page from right to left. The engine vibrated, and the splash-splash of the salty-smelling water against the bow invigorated me. I raised my camera to snap pictures of the skyscrapers with Victoria Peak in the background. Another ferry passed us, and I snapped it too. I waved at the passengers, but they didn't return the gesture.

The centre of Hong Kong appeared as if a celestial Roy Rogers had lassoed the whole of it and pulled the rope tight, cramming all the buildings together. Several of the skyscrapers butted up against each other and I couldn't see daylight between them. The modern, quirky architecture enthralled me; piercing spiked towers, vast curvy roofs and huge, glass triangular monoliths.

Fiona would've loved this sight.

I'd never visited a Buddhist place of worship, but my guidebook informed me in the event I wished to do so, Man Mo temple was the one. Its joint dedication to the Gods of literature and war seemed an odd combination, and I wondered if Hong Kong had suffered a shortage of temples at the time of construction, so these two deities had to share premises.

I smelt it before I reached it. A pungent odour of incense filled the street as if there'd been a recent Woodstock reunion. I heard tiny bells tinkle, which immediately reminded me of the little wind chimes in the Byron Bay jewellers where one of Macbeth's nemeses had tried to sell me a phallus.

Man Mo temple seemed lost and out of place, a tiny, single-storey building enveloped by soaring, modern architecture which suffocated it on all sides, a forgotten relic of another dynasty, trampled by the affluence of the 1990s.

Near the temple entrance, an elderly lady lay on the ground at the foot of a pillar topped with a terrifying stone dragon. I put her age at about three hundred. She'd discarded a crutch by her side and fussed with belongings in a plastic carrier bag. She took no notice of me.

I climbed the steps towards the main entrance and stared at the delicately painted murals on the walls under the lean-to roof. They reminded me of scenes displayed in every Chinese restaurant found on every English High Street: willow trees, sparse plant cover, tiny figures in open boats and grey mountains in the background.

Hong Kong must've resembled this scene at the time of the temple's construction, before Norman Foster and his glass, steel and concrete vandals arrived and dumped architecture all over it. A sign requested silence, which I had expected, and another sign requested I refrain from entering the central area if I was a menstruating woman, which I hadn't expected.

I breathed in the deep, ventolin-powerful incense which curtained the temple entrance and stepped inside. Huge, spiral burners resembling overgrown mosquito coils hung from the ceiling and competed with smoke issuing from yellow candles in tall, gold, urns. The fog was so thick, I expected Jack the Ripper to emerge at any point clutching a knife. Instead, a tiny, elderly man swept the floor and tended to the smog. Like an entertainer spinning plates, he ensured none of the smoking burners extinguished and reduced the smoke level from London fog to merely English mist.

I snapped a few photos and realised my lungs couldn't cope with any more burnt offerings. The three-hundred-year-old lady at the entrance had transferred to a squatting position. She leant on her crutch and held out her hand, so I crouched and pressed a few dollars into her palm. Though she didn't acknowledge me or make eye contact, it seemed the right thing to do.

≈ ≈ ≈

The bright-yellow, modern double-decker buses entered and exited Exchange Square bus station in a well-choreographed, efficient ballet. They advertised their destinations both in Cantonese and English, so I could easily identify which one to board. I stood at what I believed to be the correct stop for the number 70 and waited with several locals.

I was the only tourist, which didn't bother me at all, but it clearly bothered a middle-aged, bespectacled lady who marched in my direction and brandished a folded umbrella above her head.

"I say, you there."

I turned around to see who she shouted at.

"You there. Ahoy."

She trotted towards me in a headscarf, tweed skirt and green jacket of the kind the Queen might have worn at Badminton horse trials.

I furrowed my brow and pointed at myself, although I was certain in a heart-sinking way I was her target, and she was about to score a bullseye.

"Yes, you. Is this the right stop for the bus to Aberdeen Harbour?"

She spoke at me in the way the headmistress of Roedean might address morning assembly.

"I hope so," I said. "That's where I'm headed."

"Good. We will go together."

"We will?" My shoulders slumped and my mouth formed a straight line as my visions of spending a productive day exploring Hong Kong Island and searching for Fiona's ring evaporated.

"My husband's in Hong Kong for a conference. You may have heard of him? James Urquhart. Director of private clients at the Standard Chartered Bank."

I confessed Mr Urquhart's name had escaped my attention, but then the likelihood of me being a public client of the Standard Chartered Bank, let alone a private one, was remoter than the far side of Pluto.

She gripped her handbag and drew herself up to her full height, which I estimated at around four feet ten in her heels.

"I," she inspected me over her glasses, "I decided to accompany him, despite my extreme misgivings about"—her voice dropped to a stage whisper—"mixing with the natives."

I glanced around and clenched my teeth.

"Which is why," she continued, "I will visit Aberdeen Harbour with you. Better if we Westerners stick together, wouldn't you agree?"

I didn't have an answer for this. The trap had been sprung. The bus pulled up, and I politely allowed this lady to board first.

She stepped through the doors as they opened.

"Driver," she barked at the man behind the wheel. "Driver, do you go to Aberdeen Harbour?"

She threatened him with the curved handle of her umbrella.

"Aberdeen Harbour, yes, lady, bus go there. Two dollar."

Everybody's aptitude at speaking English impressed me, and I wasn't proud of my inability to converse in Cantonese.

She tapped on the Perspex separating them. "Driver, do not refer to me as 'Lady'. You are permitted to call me Mrs Urquhart. My husband's a director of the Standard Chartered Bank."

I reckoned the chances of the bus operator fathoming the correct etiquette to deal with this situation were minimal, so I coughed and assisted him.

"Mrs Urquhart? He's asking you for two dollars."

"Two dollars? I can't give him two dollars. I never carry cash. Would you pay him two dollars for me?"

Somehow, I found myself pulling out a five-dollar note and asking for two singles to Aberdeen Harbour.

Mrs Urquhart brushed her gloved hand over the bus seat. She sat bolt upright, stared straight ahead and spoke without looking my way.

"Well, what d'you call yourself, young man?"

"Simon's my name."

"Very good. A strong name. I approve. Where are you from?"

"London, originally. But I've been living in New Zealand with my girlfriend on the family farm."

"New Zealand? How exotic. My local butcher in Surrey sells New Zealand lamb. It probably comes from your farm."

I withheld the temptation to tell her Fiona's parents dealt in beef and dairy.

"And what, pray, have you planned in Aberdeen Harbour?"

"I haven't booked anything, but I intend to take a sampan boat ride and see the floating restaurants."

"Very well. I will accompany you. It would be quite unnecessary for us to requisition more than one boat. I can devote an hour to this activity before attending a function with my husband."

My mind see-sawed between the horrible thought of sharing my experiences with Mrs Urquhart and the anticipation that, if she lowered herself to using an ATM, we could split the cost of the sampan.

I pressed my nose to the window and hoped she'd change her mind.

The driver semicircled around the bus station, then swept along a busy main road which pierced the central business district. The glass and steel skyscrapers stood like contemporary chess pieces sentried in rows, ready for a giant's game to start. Palm trees planted in the central reservation gave a tropical feel. Small red taxis with white roofs zipped past as the bus pulled into lay-bys where the road had not only been marked in the local language but also helpfully said BUS STOP for the benefit of Mrs Urquhart. Everything looked so clean: the streets, the pavements, the buildings.

Mrs Urquhart sat tight-lipped. I wondered if she'd ever taken public transport.

The road headed inland through an area where gangs of tower blocks punctuated tropical-smelling, verdant hills, then abruptly dived into a two-lane tunnel. The bus was obviously far too large to fit through it, and I expected to hear a horrible scraping sound. We sped straight past a toll booth, scorning lesser mortals who queued up to pay, and then entered another area of massively tall buildings.

I was busy wondering if any part of Hong Kong hadn't been skyscrapered over when the bus pulled off the main road and stopped opposite a shopping mall, which for some reason had been named after Sweden's most famous musical export.

"This Aberdeen Harbour, lady," said the driver.

Mrs Urquhart gave him a look which could've demolished a few of the taller buildings and stood. "Come on, Simon," she said, "we have one hour."

I stepped off the bus and wondered how my itinerary had become so intertwined with this woman's schedule in such a brief space of time.

The unexpected smell of chlorine filled my nostrils as I ran to catch up with my newly appointed tour guide. Mayan pyramid-shaped fountains tumbled into shallow, rectangular pools in a waterside plaza with the backdrop of the ever-present monoliths.

Mrs Urquhart marched towards the water's edge and waved theatrically. "I say, my good man." I held back as she flapped her hand at an elderly Chinaman sitting in one end of a small, canvas-roofed boat, smoking a cigarette. The vessel contained an unnecessary number of blue plastic barrels, and coils of rope and old car tyres dangled from both sides.

He looked up.

"Sampan? Sampan?"

"Yes, sampan."

She jabbed her finger at his boat to ensure he was completely aware he sat in a sampan.

He threw the end of his cigarette in the water. "I take you see floating village and Jumbo. Forty dollar."

Mrs Urquhart accepted the man's hand and permitted him to help her board the small vessel. She sat in the centre and leant on her upright umbrella with two hands. The boatman assisted me, and I squatted in the front.

He repeated his financial request.

"Floating village and Jumbo. Forty dollar."

Mrs Urquhart opened her handbag and made a big show of rummaging through its infinite depths. The sampan driver and I waited. I wondered if she'd turn it upside down and shake it out in the bottom of the boat.

She extracted a gold fountain pen and exclaimed, "Traveller's cheque okay?"

He shook his head. "Forty dollar. Cash."

Mrs Urquhart replaced the cheque in her bag and closed it with a loud click, like a crocodile consuming a chicken.

"Oh dear, how frightfully inconvenient."

I sucked in a long, slow breath. I knew what would come next.

19. JUMBO

LATITUDE: 22° 16' 32" N
LONGITUDE: 114° 8' 44" E

"Simon, could you give this man forty dollars?" Mrs Urquhart addressed me as if I were her lady-in-waiting.

I rolled my eyes and puffed through thin lips. "Okay, but d'you think..?"

Mrs Urquhart cut me off and turned back to the sampan captain. "My companion will pay you the requested funds."

I pulled out my wallet and handed over forty dollars. I considered I wasn't out of pocket; the ride would've cost the same if I'd been alone.

Mrs Urquhart jerked her head left and right like a bird of prey sitting on a perch. She turned around and looked over her shoulder as dark smoke rose from the engine. My stomach was still queasy after last night's dinner, and I wasn't entirely sure this voyage was a good idea.

"I say." Mrs Urquhart flapped her hands at the driver. "Lifejackets? You must have lifejackets?"

The sampan operator shook his head and pulled a lever. The boat completed its departure manoeuvre and headed out into the harbour. I couldn't discern whether his head shake meant he didn't have lifejackets, he didn't understand her request, or he'd chosen not to answer her question. I considered whether I should employ this approach.

Mrs Urquhart coughed melodramatically and called to me above the noise of the engine. "This is extraordinary. There must be regulations about lifejackets. I shall report him to the relevant authorities." She grasped her umbrella and handbag as if they'd save her in the event we capsized.

We passed similar sampans of assorted sizes cruising up and down the harbour. Some carried cargo, some were tourist shuttles like ours, some were employed as fishing boats. They all chugged black smoke from their engines, and the taste of diesel permeated everywhere.

I wished Fiona could've magically replaced Mrs Urquhart. She would've appreciated this experience.

"Look!" My mouth fell open. "People live on these boats." I breathed in the smell of wok-cooking and domesticity.

Mrs Urquhart pointed her nose in the air and inspected the homes of people who couldn't afford to reside on the land. Several generations of families crammed into vessels clearly too small to accommodate them. Some were seaworthy, some were a few repairs off taking on significant amounts of water. Laundry strung along ropes criss-crossing the top deck of each boat. I wondered how many people lived on board to generate this quantity of dirty clothes.

The sampan operator steered the tiller and pointed at a family sitting inside their floating home. I looked away and wondered how these people felt about wealthy foreigners poking their cameras at their kitchens and their washing.

Mrs Urquhart submitted a different point of view.

"How utterly wonderful, to live on the water. What a marvellous lifestyle these people enjoy. My husband occasionally invites me to one of his champagne and canapé functions on the company yacht, but living on board must be tremendous. I must say I'm very envious."

I shook my head at her callousness and glanced at the cramped conditions; row upon row of wooden boats tied to each other, tarpaulins draped over them, tyres hanging over the side. I smiled and waved at a young boy in a filthy T-shirt sitting on a boat's stern. He jumped up, turned away and ran into the darkness of the vessel's innards. My eyes moistened, and I wondered if he ever played in a park or attended any formal school. A lady washed something in the harbour water from the edge of her boat, a kitchen utensil or clothing. These dwellings couldn't be referred to as anything but slums.

Our sampan threaded through the channels between the vessels. I realised we'd completed a half-circle and were returning past the point where we'd started from. Car engines rumbled across a bridge above us, and I glanced upwards at the source of the noise, then gazed ahead and my jaw dropped.

Ahead, two towering, monolithic, Chinese-style vessels floated in the centre of the harbour. The driver slowed the engine as we approached, and the sampan drifted slowly.

One word.

Jumbo.

As if someone had constructed an industrial complex with a complete disregard for the laws of physics, the office block-sized barges loomed over our microscopic sampan. Water splop-splop-splopped along their sides and shouts and clangs from their interiors indicated staff were preparing for their twice-daily biblical miracle of feeding the five thousand.

I stood up in the sampan as we glided past the first barge and took a photograph of the vast sign above the entrance; giant, gold, Cantonese writing and the English translation underneath: 'Jumbo Floating Restaurant'. The word JUMBO in lettering as tall as a three-storey house stood on the roof. Between the two barges, the word 'Welcome' flashed in green neon, with the equivalent red Chinese translation above.

Mrs Urquhart pulled down her spectacles and stared over the rims. "I can't imagine anything more dreadful, dining with the masses. It reminds me of the time I visited some awful factory my husband's bank had financed, and the management thought it'd be a good idea if we joined the workers in their refectory." She lifted her chest and jabbed herself with one finger. "Honestly, imagine me in a canteen."

We curled around the end of the floating restaurants and entered a harbour of vast, sleek yachts. Men in white *Love Boat* uniforms scrubbed decks, and I watched a lady with gold braid on her shoulders instructing three deckhands who polished brass. The sampan had intruded on the world of the rich and famous, a far cry from the little boy in the filthy T-shirt's home in the poverty tourism segment of our itinerary. No-one here had any cognisance of his family's daily struggle.

Mrs Urquhart pushed up her perm and adjusted her neck scarf as we passed close to one immaculate white-and-brass gin palace. I wondered if she expected to see someone she knew.

A sign ahead announced, 'Aberdeen Marina Club'. Mrs Urquhart turned around and waved her arm at our boat driver. "Hello, hello. I want to get orf. Yes, me. Orf. Here." She directed the boat driver to nudge the sampan against a wharf, gathered her handbag and umbrella and stood.

"Are you leaving?" I asked.

"Yes. I'm meeting my husband here for the Standard Chartered Bank function. Thank you for your company. Good day to you."

And with that, she stepped off the sampan and marched up the jetty.

The boat driver gestured with his right arm and waited for me to follow.

"No, no." I shook my head. "I'm not going. We're not together."

I watched the rear of Mrs Urquhart disappear into the yacht club and realised she'd left without donating any money towards her bus or boat fare, which may have been her intention all along.

The boat driver pulled a lever, and the vessel reversed. We chugged past shiny, chrome fittings and scrubbed, wooden decks. I wondered if these yachts ever sailed anywhere. Some of them must have belonged to Mrs Urquhart's cronies.

I motioned the universal sign for a camera clicking and passed my Olympus to the driver. He snapped me riding in the sampan's bow.

I turned around, gazed up at the hills and remembered Leanne's other recommendation.

It was time to tackle Victoria Peak.

≈ ≈ ≈

The Peak Tram journey commenced from a small underground platform accessed from a street called Garden Road; a misnomer as it didn't contain any gardens, only lanes of traffic leading to flyovers flowing with other lanes of traffic.

I waited at the tram stop. There didn't seem to be any Mrs Urquhart-equivalents waving umbrellas at me, so I relaxed.

A squeaking noise and an essence of burnt brake pads heralded the tram's arrival. I boarded it and stepped back in time fifty years to an experience unlike the tall, slim trams that plied the streets of Hong Kong city, trundling between the lanes of non-stop traffic. These two old-fashioned, dark-red carriages contained wooden seats which reminded me of park benches in Kensington Gardens, and the floor ascended in steps, as did the platform.

Every tourist in Hong Kong boarded the tram with me, and we set off at such a steep angle I braced myself for a snapping sound followed by a reverse hurtling down the hill. The tram climbed through lush, green jungle, and the skyscrapers and water fell away beneath us. I craned my neck to see the view behind, then my stomach informed me that wasn't such a good idea so I looked straight ahead to relieve motion sickness.

Despite the large contingent of tram passengers, when I alighted, I had the paved area at the top to myself, and I leant on the balustrade and ogled Hong Kong in all its Oriental glory. A cool, less humid breeze blew and, below me, an extraordinary delineation between the tropical greenery and the stark city skyscrapers betrayed where our journey had originated. I held my hand to my eyes and tracked the double-ended Star Ferry chugging across the harbour, criss-crossed by the white wakes of other commercial vessels. To my left, a large, baby-pink mansion poked from the trees lining the perpendicular hill. I remembered Leanne in Australia telling me her grandmother lived on Victoria Peak, and wondered if this was her house.

But watching all this without Fiona meant nothing. I stared into the distance, smiled and sighed.

I was about to leave the viewing platform and set foot on the tram for the return journey when my eyes were drawn to an art stall with a striking, orange painting of Victoria Peak at sunset. The direction of the sun in real life didn't set in the location depicted, but I smiled and forgave the artistic licence. In the picture's foreground, old Chinese junks floated on Hong Kong harbour in place of modern container ships.

I knew Fiona would love this painting. I also knew in the open air, outside a major tourist attraction, the price would be vastly inflated, and I'd need to barter.

The art vendor approached me.

"You like? One thousand dollar."

He wore a flat cap, and yellow pointed teeth showed from under his thin moustache.

I paused and tilted my head.

One thousand dollars. I should be able to buy this for two hundred. But we both have to play a little game first.

"One thousand dollars?" I shook my head. "Sorry, no way."

I walked away.

He called after me. "How much you want to pay?"

I turned around. "One hundred dollars."

"No," said the vendor. "For one hundred dollars I cannot sell. But for you, my good friend, I make special offer. Five hundred dollars."

Fifty pounds. Still too much.

"I can't pay five hundred dollars. I'll give you one hundred and fifty. That's all I have."

This wasn't a correct statement. Unfortunately, we both knew that.

"Because you are my very good friend, three hundred and fifty," said the vendor. "My final offer. It is less than it costs me."

This was another untrue statement. We both knew that too.

"One hundred and fifty."

"Two hundred and seventy-five. I give it away. How will I feed my children? You are breaking me."

I studied the print with my head on one side and imagined it on a future living room wall. I really wanted it. But I couldn't let the vendor know that.

I held my chin high. "All right, two hundred. But no more."

"Two hundred and fifty. You give me two hundred and fifty; I give it to you now."

The game neared conclusion. And in a perfect world, we were both going to win.

"Two hundred." I feigned disinterest and turned my back in the sure knowledge he'd shout after me and tell me I could have it.

Instead, something unexpected happened.

20. VIRGIN TERRITORY

LATITUDE: 51° 28' 14" N
LONGITUDE: 0° 27' 32" W

I stepped away and waited for a shout to tell me the vendor had accepted my price.

Come on, come on.

Silence.

I slowed down.

Nothing.

I glanced subtly over my shoulder. The vendor had turned his back to me and rearranged paintings.

Now what do I do? I really want this print.

I pretended to take a photo and darted glances at the vendor from the corner of my eye. He spoke to an older couple who'd stopped to admire my painting.

My painting. Please don't buy it. It's mine.

I briefly considered going back and offering two hundred and fifty. But I needed to save face. And so did he.

The older couple walked on.

Phew.

The vendor glanced up. We met eyes, and I knew the print was mine.

He took one step towards me.

I took one step towards him.

I cleared my throat. "Two hundred and twenty."

He held out his hand, and we shook.

Yes! Fiona's going to love this on our wall.

He tugged a copy of my print from a pile, showed it to me, rolled it up and twanged an elastic band around it.

I peeled off two hundred and twenty Hong Kong dollars.

"A tip," he said. "You give me a tip. Fifty dollars."

Nice try.

The tram carried me back down to the humidity.

≈ ≈ ≈

I'd seen security guards in London. Representatives of Securicor or Group 4; heavy, middle-aged people dressed in ill-fitting suits who didn't look like they'd be able to tackle a great-grandparent, let alone an armed robber.

Things were different in Hong Kong.

The young, fit sentry stood fully dressed in black with a shrapnel vest, helmet and enormous boots. He held a rifle across his body and immediately reminded me of a scene from *The Terminator*. I stood back and pretended to read my guidebook while two other men in white shirts carried steel boxes into a large jewellery shop under his supervision.

T H C, followed by white, illuminated Chinese characters.

Tse Ho Chuen Jewellery Co. Ltd.

Everything looked so enticing.

So sparkly.

So glittery.

A photo depicted a stunning, black-haired lady modelling a necklace and staring into the camera.

The opposite life-sized poster advertised a couple standing next to a cream-coloured classic car with whitewall tyres. The lady's hand prominently showcased a vast, solitaire diamond ring.

I pursed my lips.

How will I ever know if these are real or fake? I can't afford to be ripped off.

I took a deep breath and entered the store.

Horizontal glass counters flashed tray after tray of rings, necklaces, earrings and bangles. About twenty staff wearing baby-blue T-shirts under navy suit jackets watched me as I ran my finger along the counter. One of them broke free and breathed over my shoulder.

I glanced out of the entrance and watched the security guard click his heels, present his rifle vertically and march to the front of the truck. My new companion stood beside me and blocked the door.

"Hello, friend. You buy bangle?"

I smiled politely.

"You buy necklace? Best price here."

"I'm just looking." I tried to shake him off and migrated to the adjacent display. He followed behind me like a pickpocket.

"You buy ring? These rings very beautiful."

"I don't know. Maybe."

"How much money you have? I give you best price in whole of Hong Kong."

I pointed. "What does this one cost?"

He grinned and nodded at a colleague, who slid the tray out in a joint pageant of brainwashing.

"This one nice, sir. Very popular."

"Are these genuine diamonds?"

"Everything made in our factory, sir. Best quality."

"Yes, but are these genuine diamonds?"

"Diamonds, yes, sir. We have diamonds. This one special offer." He held up a gold band with sparkly jewels. The store lights refracted rainbows through the translucent stones.

He slid a calculator from an inside pocket, pressed keys and turned it to face me.

I'd forgotten where the decimal point belonged in the exchange rate, and I wasn't sure if he was asking me for one hundred pounds or one thousand.

He still hadn't answered my question.

"Are these genuine diamonds?"

He avoided my eyes, and I knew the answer. I pushed past him out of the store.

$$\approx \approx \approx$$

My mind was filled with Fiona and my planned proposal.

I wished she were with me, riding the longest escalator in the world, which transports commuters one mile down the hills into the centre of Hong Kong in the morning, then reverses to take them back up in the evening.

I wished she were with me, clunking along on the thin tram, which took me away from Central to Wan Chai ferry terminal.

I wished she were with me, sailing on the slow, rocking Star Ferry across the water, back to Kowloon.

I sat at the harbour's edge in Tsim Sha Tsui and watched the sunset.

A junk sailed past, crowded with tourists.

Couples cuddled up to each other and enjoyed the last rays of sun.

People everywhere, but no-one to share with, no-one to talk to.

I rested my chin in my hands, then hugged myself and slumped.

Surrounded by humanity, yet completely alone.

I stood and set my jaw. It was time to board another plane.

≈ ≈ ≈

"Excuse me, is this the gate for the Virgin flight to London?"

The scarlet-uniformed lady behind the desk at Kai Tak airport looked up at me.

"Yes, sir. Are you travelling with us today?"

"I am." I glanced around at the empty rows of seats. "Where is everybody? Am I late?"

"No, sir. There's still an hour before we depart. It's not a full flight. May I see your boarding pass, please?"

I handed her the rectangular piece of thin card they'd given me at check-in.

She tapped her computer. "D'you definitely want a window seat? Because if you don't mind being in the centre of the plane, I can give you four seats to yourself, and you can stretch out and sleep."

"Thank you. That'd be wonderful."

She printed me a new document, and I paced up and down while I inspected it.

Hong Kong to London.

I wandered to the plate-glass windows and stared down at the asphalt, past the air bridge, to where a petrol wagon filled the plane, and a cantilevered catering truck kissed the door. Workers conveyor-belted bags into the hold, and I unsuccessfully searched for my dark-green backpack among their collection.

Virgin.

The emblem of the blonde, red-swimsuited lady soared along the plane's nose, a British flag flying in the breeze behind her.

She'd take me somewhere I hadn't been in eighteen months.

England.

Home.

But I wasn't sure where home was.

Was home in London?

Would Fiona live there? I knew she missed the city life, but when it came down to it, would she want to leave her family and friends again?

I pressed my hands and nose against the window and stared at the Union Flag.

"Ladies and gentlemen, welcome to Virgin flight VS239 to London. May I invite all passengers to board through gate number seven."

The flight attendant had been right. This flight would have a sparse number of people.

I handed my boarding pass to a smartly dressed steward at the plane's door.

"Good evening, Mr Prior. 42D? Straight down this aisle, please."

I paused. "Excuse me, am I now on British territory?"

He raised his eyebrows and one side of his mouth turned up.

"Not yet, sir. But you are on Virgin territory."

≈ ≈ ≈

England in February.

Dark.

Very, very dark.

The Virgin plane had touched down at 5:00 a.m., forty minutes early; we'd whisked through customs and immigration instantly and I stood outside arrivals waiting for my father to turn up.

We swerved out of the car park in his Austin Maestro and hurtled down the Heathrow M4 spur road into the rain.

And the dark.

I couldn't believe the size of the motorways, the volumes of flat-fronted articulated lorries swishing water across the carriageways, the black taxis everywhere.

I'd forgotten so much.

I couldn't decide what was new and what I'd forgotten.

I'd forgotten what I'd forgotten.

I stared open-mouthed at the five lanes of traffic and wondered how there could be so many trucks in the entire world.

"How was your flight, Simon?"

I glanced at my father as oncoming headlights illuminated his heavy-framed Ronnie Barker spectacles. Since I'd last seen him, he'd abandoned his age-denying comb-over hairstyle and the bald-head-with-white-fluffy-border gave the impression of an elderly university professor.

"The plane was good, thanks. I had four seats to myself, so I slept all the way."

"Goodness. That's not usual, is it?"

"It isn't. How are you? What's changed since I've been away?"

My father indicated and swerved across three streams of traffic to join the M25 motorway. I listened to a symphony of car horns behind us, then we slowed down and merged into four lanes of near-stationary morning commute.

"What's changed? The Prime Minister, for starters. Britain has a labour government now."

I had a distant childhood recollection of a raincoat-clad man with a grey quiff called James Callaghan.

"Yes, I saw the news. I barely remember the last time we weren't under the rule of the Conservatives. Anything else?"

"The fifty pence piece is smaller."

I shrugged.

"That's it?"

"It's annoying. I keep confusing it with the ten pence. Or the twenty."

"Um, okay. What else has changed?"

"You have," said Dad. "You're different."

I folded my arms. "How am I different?"

"It's like you're not English any more. You've become a world traveller, or a nomad, or whatever young people are called these days. And you have an accent."

142

I considered my father's words.

I stared blankly at cars in the neighbouring lanes.

I didn't think I'd changed.

But I felt like a visitor.

An alien.

A tourist in my own country.

I watched the drizzle, which didn't seem to have altered in my absence.

My father's cold, brass doorknob led me into a world of central heating and damp laundry.

I hadn't slept in my boyhood bedroom for years. Like a sealed-off time capsule, it was as if I'd never left. Paintings of Beatrix Potter characters gazed down as I sat on my single bed and immediately stood again as a hard lump under the covers poked into my bottom.

Winnie-the-Pooh had waited patiently all these years for his little boy to return. I pulled the teddy out of the sheets and held him.

Fiona loved you, Pooh. I should've taken you travelling with me.

My father's voice and the smell of burnt toast heralded breakfast, so I tucked Pooh back into bed.

≈ ≈ ≈

"Tea?"

Dad opened the fridge. "Sorry, I only have skimmed milk. The milkman hasn't delivered yet."

"Skimmed's fine. Gosh, I remember waiting for the milkman. How ironic. I've been living on a dairy farm, but we drove twenty minutes into town to buy milk; nobody brought it."

I unfolded yesterday's news.

The papers were obsessed with minor celebrities; people I'd never heard of who were marrying, splitting up, having babies, having dogs. Colour supplements showed advertisements for products I couldn't imagine anyone having any use for. Ever.

My father inhabited a different world, far away from the mountains of South Island New Zealand, the vast plains of Canterbury, the beaches of Queensland.

A world I used to be a part of.

143

And there's a good chance I'll be a part of again.

"Dad, could I call Fiona quickly? It's bedtime in New Zealand and I'd like to catch her before she goes to sleep. I haven't spoken to her for two weeks."

"Of course. You know where the phone is; in the hall."

"I won't be long; I know how expensive it is."

My finger pushed in the '0' hole of his rotary dial phone and hesitated.

"How do I dial an international call? I've forgotten."

"Zero-zero and then six-four for New Zealand."

"Got it, thanks."

I heard the different tone of the New Zealand exchange.

"Hi, Linda. It's Simon."

Pause.

Did she hear me?

"Hi, Linda." "Hi, Simon," we said simultaneously, as the electrical signals bypassed each other around twenty thousand kilometres of globe.

"Did you want Fiona? She's here. Hang on."

I heard shouts, followed by footsteps.

"Hello?"

My chest tingled as I heard her voice.

"Hi, it's me," I said. "How are you?"

"Good, thanks. I'm in my pyjamas, about to go to bed. Where are you?"

I imagined hugging her tightly and burying my face in the smell of her conditioner.

"I'm at Dad's. Just landed. Sorry I haven't rung. It's been hard to find anywhere to make an international call."

"Have you had a good trip so far?"

"Amazing, thanks. Australia was full on; d'you remember Tommo? He still lives life in the fast lane, never sure which day it is or which girl it is. We drove all around South East Queensland and as far down as Byron Bay—have you heard of that? We went diving and saw manta rays."

"Yep, I remember Tommo. Sounds like he's still the same. What else have you been up to?"

"Hong Kong's incredible. I travelled by tram up Victoria Peak and rode a sampan around Aberdeen Harbour. It's so crowded, though. People everywhere."

"Did you do any shopping?"

I mustn't let slip about the search for the ring.

"Maybe." I grinned. "I might surprise you."

"Sounds intriguing. And how's London?"

I looked out of the window.

"Wet. It's not yet seven o'clock. The sun hasn't come up. And strange. It feels like I don't belong. Dad says I speak with an accent."

"I'll bet you can't wait to go to the West End and see all the shops and sights."

"Yes, but I miss you like crazy. I wish you'd been with me on this journey. You'd have loved seeing the beaches in Australia."

"I miss you too."

"And in Hong Kong, you would've been so proud of me; I had a meal at a tiny place down a back street which most tourists would never have known existed. I wish you'd seen it."

"You'll be back in two weeks, and you can tell me all about it. Especially about London. I can't wait to hear all about London."

"I'd better talk to Dad. I miss you and I love you."

"I love you too. Bye."

I replaced the receiver, stood still and stared at it. I couldn't believe how far away she was. This whole experience didn't seem real at all.

I returned to the kitchen and spread New Zealand Anchor butter on my toast. At least it formed a tiny connection.

≈ ≈ ≈

"The next station is Embankment. Change here for the Bakerloo, District and Circle lines. Please mind the gap between the train and the platform."

I'd left Dad's house in the suburbs with a list of tasks to do in Central London longer than a phone book and not enough time to accomplish them.

Come on, train, come on. So much to do.

I mentally ticked off my jobs.

Pick up my new permanent visa at New Zealand House, which was, after all, the entire crux of this trip.

Pop into my old work. Have a chat with my former boss, ask if there's any chance of getting my job back.

Go to my Doctor's appointment about my ear.

Find a ring?

And meet up with an old friend who'd take a pivotal part in the next phase of my life.

If she agreed to it.

21. ALTAVISTA

LATITUDE: 51° 30' 25" N
LONGITUDE: 0° 8' 28" W

I'd tried to strike up a conversation with a man opposite me on the train. He'd grunted, hidden behind his paper and disembarked at a stop I reckoned was earlier than he'd intended, to escape me.

All I'd done was remark on the weather.

I gripped a hanging strap as the carriage swayed violently left and right into the brightly lit underground station. Colourful advertisements curved down the tube station walls and showed me products I could never need yet felt compelled to buy.

An internet package from a company called Demon.

A mobile phone from a company called The Carphone Warehouse.

And a computer from Tiny PCs Ltd which displayed colour photos on its screen.

Why would anyone want to look at pictures on a computer? What's wrong with a photo album?

I inhaled the musty, stale, subterranean aroma. It didn't matter how many subways, metros or railways I travelled on in the world, London Underground had its own unique smell, which immediately reminded me of shopping, twinkly lights, nightclubs and Fiona.

Fiona.

She loved London.

I smiled, and remembered happy times Christmas shopping, holding hands, walking along Regent Street, marvelling at the Oxford Street decorations, sharing a coffee and a cake in a Piccadilly tea shop.

I wished she were here.

The illuminated, green signs shone 'EXIT'.

"Oi! You're supposed to stand on the right. Move over."

I'd forgotten the etiquette of the London Underground escalators and waved an apology.

The man huffed and pushed past. I heard him mutter, "Bloody tourists."

Everyone moved so fast. People thronged through the ticket gates. A station employee yelled at a young man with a backpack who jumped the barriers and sprinted away.

Chewing gum. Dried chewing gum on all the pavements. Surely there couldn't be so many untidy masticators in the entire city. It spattered everywhere like a masterpiece painted by an energetic chimpanzee.

Buses. I'd forgotten the red, double-decker buses which queued opposite the Ritz hotel. The 'ting-ting' of one of their bells sounded next to me and I watched a middle-aged man in a raincoat run to jump on the rear platform as the bus pulled out.

I heard the rattly diesel engines of black taxis queuing in unbroken, homogeneous lines, with their 'for hire' lights switched off.

How can so many people afford to take a taxi? They're so expensive.

Every shop display showed goods which nobody could ever need, and people queued to buy them.

Fashionable clothes with chunks cut out of them.

Leather handbags. Leather wallets. Leather belts. Leather skirts.

Gold. Sapphires. Rubies. Diamonds.

I jammed my hands in my pockets and avoided people's eyes.

I was a country boy.

A country boy in the big city for the first time.

New Zealand wasn't so obsessed with material possessions, and I wasn't accustomed to this wild spending.

It showed me what a pretentious, materialistic, money-orientated city London was.

I quite liked it.

In fact, I loved it.

I wanted to be part of it again.

I watched people for amusement. Some had mobile phones, which I hadn't seen used in New Zealand or Australia.

My eyebrows rose as a Gordon Gekko-type man dressed in a double-breasted, grey suit, white shirt and yellow tie pulled an aerial out of his device, pushed buttons and raised it to the side of his face. He swivelled to the left and the right, to ensure as many people as possible understood the significance of his call.

"Hello? Yes, I'm calling on my mobile. I'm in Piccadilly. Outside Pret A Manger. I can't be long; these mobile calls are bloody expensive. It's a Nokia sixty-one-fifty; it has a calculator on it. What's yours? I considered one of them; they'll come down in price. I'm on One2one; you're on Orange, aren't you? How's your battery life? Mine's shocking. I must go, got to call my broker. I'll ring you later from the train. Bye."

The entire contents of his call had been about the making of the call. The pretentiousness of this fascinated me.

I inhaled deeply and puffed out my cheeks.

I wanted a mobile phone.

I wanted to stand on a street corner and make calls to inform people of my exact geographical location.

I wanted to be the man in the double-breasted, grey suit.

≈ ≈ ≈

The young, blonde receptionist at my former employer frowned at me as I barged through the entrance door in my jeans and puffa jacket. I didn't recognise her from my time at the company.

"Can I help you? Are you here to collect a parcel?"

My lips formed a straight line. "No. I used to work here. Is Martin in?"

"Sorry, I'm a temp; I'm covering reception this week. Let me look in the directory. She opened a loose-leaf binder and ran her fingers down a list."

"What's his second name?"

"Walker. Martin Walker."

"Nope. No Walkers here. No Martins either, by the looks of it."

"Are you sure?"

"Yep. Nothing listed under W."

I peered over and tried to read her list upside down.

"Does that say Nicholas Hornby?"

She tugged the folder away and held it towards her. "It does."

"Could you call him? Tell him, Simon's here. Simon, who used to work for Martin."

"I'll check if he's available."

She plucked the handset from a switchboard and dialled.

"Mr Hornby? I've a Simon at reception. He says he used to work at this company for someone called Martin. All right, I'll tell him."

She replaced the receiver.

"Take a seat. He won't be long."

Debris from a dead pot plant covered a magazine called 'Print and Packaging Monthly'. I opened it and scanned the pages without reading them. I smelt solvent, glanced up and watched the receptionist brush colour onto her nails.

A door behind her creaked open, and a man wearing a rumpled, untucked shirt limped out. I stood and tugged my jacket down over my belt.

"Hi, Nick. D'you remember me?"

Nick ran his hand through his greasy, lank hair and shrugged. "I'm not sure. Should I?"

"Simon Prior. I worked in Martin's department, in the team with Robin and Helen. We were all made redundant. You must remember me."

He pinched his eyebrows together. "I remember a Simon in sales. About two years ago. Was that you? You look different."

"I've been living overseas. I thought I'd drop in to see Martin, but he's no longer here."

Nick's shoulders slumped, and he stared out of the window behind me.

"Yep, all the old-timers have gone, except me. After the first swathe of redundancies, there was another one. Then another. I reckon your Martin must've been caught up in one of those. The new owners slashed through the workforce. This industry can't keep up with cheap imports from overseas. I'll probably be next."

He exhaled and shook his head.

"I'd better go. They're working us like dogs now. Not like the old days. Take care."

He turned and shuffled into the offices.

150

I stared at the spot where he'd stood, let out a hard sigh and closed my eyes.

Did I want to be part of this life again, in an industry where cost-cutting and job slashing had taken over?

Did I want to spend my days persuading businesses to buy products they didn't want or need?

Did I want to work in sales?

If we return here to live, I need a new career. I don't want to end up like Nick.

I pressed my lips together and departed.

≈ ≈ ≈

The middle-aged medical receptionist clanged open filing cabinet drawers and rammed documents into bulging folders far too full to contain them.

"Can I help you?"

"Good afternoon. I've an appointment with Doctor Atkins."

She shook her head. "No, you haven't. He retired last year."

"Oh. Do I have an appointment with another doctor?"

"Name?"

"Prior. Simon Prior."

She ran her finger down a diary-sized book. "You're seeing Doctor Siva. Take a seat."

I picked up a 1970s copy of *Good Housekeeping* and amused myself studying the out-of-date advertising. I still couldn't believe how popular the Austin Allegro had been. My father had owned three of them, none of which lasted him longer than two years. One was returned to the dealer a day after he'd bought it with the reverse gear jammed and none of the doors locking.

A lady with a small boy entered. His perpetual nose torrent augmented a Danube of snot decorating his sleeve. I squished against the wall and hoped they didn't sit near me.

"Simon?"

A short man entered from a side door, wearing a jumper and casual trousers.

"Good afternoon. I am Doctor Sivasuthan Warnakulasuriya Patabendige."

I briefly wondered how he coped when completing a passport application form which asked for one character per box.

His eyes twinkled above his closely cropped, black beard. "You can call me Doctor Siva. Please, come through."

I sat in his surgery, which used to be Doctor Atkins' surgery. The shelves of old medical journals, the wooden-drawered, antique table and the leather-bound swivel chair had gone, replaced by functional, modern furniture as if I'd accidentally entered the 'office' area of an Ikea showroom during my desperate attempts to locate the exit. A computer terminal stood on the uncluttered, light-brown desk.

"You've come to see me today because for many years, you liked and trusted Doctor Atkins, and you want to investigate whether I am a worthy successor. How can I help you?"

I smiled at his desk-side manner.

"My ear picked up an infection a few days ago whilst in the sea in Australia. I consulted a hospital doctor; she prescribed antibiotics and recommended I see you once it cleared up."

Doctor Siva opened a black, plastic box and extracted his ear-poking tool.

"Which ear is it?"

"This one." I tapped the right side of my skull.

He pulled my lobe and inserted the tool, which felt uncomfortable but not sore.

"A small amount of otitis remaining. You're lucky. You haven't perforated the drum. Have you finished the antibiotics?"

"Nearly. Two days remaining."

"It's healing well. Complete the course and see me if the infection reoccurs."

He paused. "Which hospital did you visit in Australia?"

"One in Brisbane. The Princess Alexandra."

"I think that's where my brother's based. He's a surgeon. Hang on, I'll look him up."

I watched him click his computer's mouse and winced as a screeching noise emanated from behind the screen.

He turned to me and smiled. "It takes a minute to connect."

I pulled my chair closer and gazed at his monitor, which displayed a tiny image of a telephone with a dotted line streaming from it.

The screeching finished.

"Now," said Doctor Siva, "we'll go to altavista.com and type in his name."

He tapped keys and created further screeching.

"Here we go. Yes, he's based at the hospital you visited."

I opened my mouth and shook my head slowly. "How did you find out so quickly?"

"Altavista. It's a search engine. There are others, such as Yahoo and Lycos, but this is the one I use most often."

"Search engine?"

"You connect to the internet, and it helps you search for whatever information you need."

He pointed at the screen and indicated the red, blue and black text.

"This website has a list of post-graduates who studied in Australia, with the hospital trusts they work at."

My eyebrows rose. "Gosh. That's astounding. Like a global phone book."

He rotated the screen back towards him and held up one finger.

"If my prediction is correct, this form of communication will put the encyclopaedia salesmen out of business in less than a decade. Anyway, anything else I can help you with today?"

I shook my head.

"Thanks, Doctor Siva; that's all."

I sprinted down the surgery steps towards the train station. There were still a couple of important tasks to complete.

≈ ≈ ≈

A lady in a smart trouser suit exited the unstaffed reception area of my friend's central London office. She sniffed and inspected me down her nose with the 'are you here to collect a parcel?' look I was rapidly becoming accustomed to.

"May I help you?"

"I'm here to see Sarah."

She rolled her eyes. "Which Sarah? We've three."

"Sarah Wrighton."

"And who shall I say is asking for her?"

"Simon. She's expecting me. I'm an old friend."

"I see. Wait there." She pointed at a chair and swung open a rear door.

I waited. Two men in tight trousers, business shirts and cowboy boots exited the lift and passed through the same door. Their conversation recapped an extravagant dinner where someone else had picked up the bill.

Sarah strode out, grinned, and hugged me. She stood back and held my shoulders.

"It's been so long. How are you?"

I wasn't used to seeing my oldest friend in business clothes. Her cream jacket and matching skirt accompanied light-brown, high-heeled shoes, and she'd tied her long, blonde hair up in a bun.

"I'm well, thanks. Are you okay?"

"I am. Come through to my office. I must finish something which a courier's collecting at 3:30 p.m., then we'll grab a coffee."

She held open the door behind reception, and I stared and gasped.

22. CAPTAIN MAINWARING

LATITUDE: 51° 30' 29" N
LONGITUDE: 0° 7' 53" W

Young men and women sat at desks in rows. Some spoke into headsets, some tapped at computer terminals. A lady guarded a printer as big as a chest freezer and lingered as it clunkety-clunketied reams of paper with a rhythmic, regular motion. Floor to ceiling windows surrounded us, and my pulse quickened as I gaped at the view of Green Park's treetops.

My dream environment. I want to work here.

Sarah pulled out a swivel-chair. "You can sit at Naomi's desk; she's not in today. I'll finish this document." She grinned and pointed at a man opposite her. "Simon, this is Dan. He works in IT."

Dan removed his feet from the desk and swivelled his chair.

"G'day, Simon, is it? How ya going?"

He reached forward to shake my hand. Unlike everyone else in the office, he wore jeans, and a T-shirt which read 'There's no place like 127.0.0.1', a slogan which meant nothing to me.

I grinned. "Are you Australian?"

He smiled and scratched his unshaven chin. "From Melbourne, but I've been here four years."

"I stopped in Australia on the way from New Zealand," I said. "I've been living with my Kiwi girlfriend for the last year."

"Are you back permanently?"

"Nah, flying visit. I head down under again next week. But I think we'll have to return to England. The job situation isn't great."

"Bloody paper clip." Sarah shouted and thumped the desk. She turned to Dan. "How d'you get rid of this stupid cartoon paper clip in Microsoft Word? I'm writing cover letters to accompany this proposal and the bloody thing keeps telling me it looks like I'm trying to write a letter."

155

Dan grinned. "Clippy? He's an icon." He stuck out his bottom lip. "You can't get rid of him."

Sarah bashed her keys. "Right now, I want to throttle him."

Dan sat back in his chair and laughed. "What d'you do in New Zealand?"

"I've played guitar in pubs for pocket money. I worked in print and packaging sales before, in London. But the industry's on its knees. They made me redundant before we left for New Zealand, and it doesn't sound like the situation's improved."

"What's the plan, then?"

I glanced around the office. "We'll have to return to England before we run out of money. I need to decide where life's taking me. I need a new career."

Sarah stood and marched to the printer.

Dan tilted his head back and furrowed his brow. "What about IT? The money's great, there's loads of work and the opportunities are huge. Everyone's moving into it."

I leant forward and blinked. "Really? I used a computer at school, a BBC Micro. But I haven't touched one in the last few years."

"Study Microsoft courses. An MCP, or an MCSE. They don't take long, and the way the industry is, companies are hiring people with barely any experience if they have the certificate. That's what I did, and I've never looked back."

I tore paper from a pad on Sarah's desk, picked up a pen and wrote: Microsoft MCP / MCSE.

"Thanks, Dan. I'll look into it."

"No problem. Here's my card. Email me and let me know how you go. You never know, we might have a job for you here."

Wow.

Sarah returned with her printing. "Ready?"

"Yep." I turned to Dan. "Thanks for the tips. Great to meet you."

"You too." He swivelled his chair, crossed his legs and picked up a magazine.

≈ ≈ ≈

Sarah ordered coffees, and we pulled up chairs at a downstairs café. We'd known each other since our teenage years, and she'd always been a good friend. We'd comforted each other through terrible relationships and break-ups, shopped for Christmas presents for our partners and danced together all night long at London nightclubs. She'd always been the sister I'd never had.

She leant forward and cupped her chin in her palms. "How's New Zealand? How's Fiona? Tell me everything."

"New Zealand's stunning. It's the most beautiful country I've ever seen. Think of snow-capped mountains, ice-blue lakes and pine forests. Have you ever seen a travel programme about Canada? It's similar."

"Sounds perfect. I bet you can't wait to return, away from all this grey sky and traffic." She nodded her head twice sideways towards the window.

I stared out into Piccadilly.

"The problem is, Sarah, you can't eat the scenery. You can't eat the mountains. It's amazing to wake up to beauty every day, but there's no work, there's no money and there's no future. Fiona's earning next to nothing in a hardware store and I'm playing my guitar in pubs for pocket money, but it's not a regular income. I need something more. I'm too ambitious."

A young man marched up and down outside the cafe and shouted into his phone.

I pointed. "I want to be him. I want to talk shit into a mobile all day."

"And you can't in New Zealand?"

"Not where Fiona's from. Not in the South Island. It's too rural."

"What are you going to do?"

"I'm not sure. I need a new career. Your colleague, Dan, suggested some courses I could study to qualify for a job in IT." I grinned. "He said he might even be able to find me a job here, at your work."

Sarah rubbed her chin. "Are you saying you're moving back to London?"

"Probably."

"What about Fiona? Wasn't she kicked out of Britain 'cos her visa ran out?"

"Her visa expired, yes. But, Sarah…" I turned my head away and looked out of the window.

"Yes?"

"I'm going to ask her to marry me. And I wondered if you'd be my best, um, woman?"

Sarah sat on the edge of her chair and held my forearm. "Best woman?"

"You can't be my best man, can you? You're not a man."

Sarah slapped her knee and laughed. She grabbed my hands.

"Of course I will. Wow! Best woman. I can't wait to tell my friends this."

≈ ≈ ≈

Leicester Square in the evening.

Wet.

Crowded.

Exciting.

"Dad, d'you want to see *Cats*?"

I turned around to my father, who'd been momentarily distracted by a purple-haired drag queen strolling past on twelve-inch-high, silver platform soles.

"*Cats*? Andrew Lloyd-Webber? Goodness, I'd love to. Are seats for it really available?"

I glanced at the poster. "This is the half-price ticket booth. They sell off remaining tickets for shows, but you have to go tonight, and you can't choose where you sit."

"It sounds marvellous. I haven't seen it before. It's a shame Fiona isn't here. She would've loved it."

I stared down at my shoes, then up again.

"I know. She loves the nightlife in London. It's not the same in New Zealand."

I completed the transaction with the vendor and showed the tickets to my father.

"Row P," I said. "Not bad. How about a birthday dinner first? Shall we eat at your favourite restaurant in Chinatown?"

≈ ≈ ≈

My father wedged himself in a cramped corner at Mr Wong's and absent-mindedly rearranged utensils. Waiters charged between tables crammed together so tightly that diners touched elbows with people they'd never normally share breathing space with. Puffs of steam emanated from the kitchen, and I inhaled the unique scent of sesame oil. Between the hanging Peking ducks, new customers arrived and shook out umbrellas.

"I enjoy eating at this restaurant," he said. "It always reminds me of when I studied in New York, back in the 1940s. I ate with chopsticks for the first time there. I'm afraid I'm out of practice."

The waiter presented us with entrées of sesame prawn toast and small chicken drumsticks, accompanied by a bowl of prawn crackers.

"Is this what you ate in Hong Kong?" asked Dad, as he picked up his napkin.

My mind recalled the seven-year-old waitress in the dark alleyway, and her grandmother's watery soup. "Not really. This is a westernised version. I think different regions of China have unique cuisines."

My father attempted to spear a piece of sesame prawn toast with the end of a chopstick.

"Dad, it's okay to pick these up."

"What, eat them with my fingers?"

"Of course." I slid my eyes to the left and right. "Save the chopsticks for the main course. Please don't ask for a knife and fork."

My father hesitated before fingering his food and inserting it into his mouth.

We both eyes the last drumstick, and I politely allowed him to claim it as a birthday victory

The waiter collected our plates.

I rubbed the back of my neck and glanced around the restaurant.

Here goes.

Now or never.

"Um, Dad?"

My father peered over his glasses and scrutinised the pictures of radioactive-coloured ice creams on the dessert menu.

"Dad?"

159

He stuffed the pamphlet in the plastic holder. I scraped my hand through my hair.

"I'm going to ask Fiona to marry me."

"Goodness. How wonderful. I can see why. She's a delightful girl. Delightful. It's a big decision, though. Are you sure?"

"I think so. I mean, we've lived together in England and New Zealand for two years now, we enjoy each other's company, we've similar interests. Plus…"

I paused and glanced into my lap. I raised my head again.

"Plus, I can't find a job in New Zealand, so we're probably going to move back to England."

"Really? It'd be wonderful if you came back here. But didn't you apply for a New Zealand permanent visa?"

"Yes, but I need it to return. I'm collecting my visa, flying back to New Zealand and asking her."

"Have you bought a ring?"

I massaged my temples.

"I'd like to buy Fiona a solitaire diamond, but I don't know how I can afford that. The number of jewellery stores I've browsed in the hope something will jump out at me, oh, you'd've laughed. A lady in Australia tried to sell me a ring with a huge, silver penis."

"Goodness. Why on earth would she have thought that'd be suitable for an engagement?"

"I've no idea. And I visited a store in Hong Kong, but I wasn't convinced the diamonds were genuine. I mean, it looked professional, but it'd devastate me if I bought a ring and then found out it was glass."

"What about Ratners?"

"They don't exist anymore. Remember their chairman gave a speech where he said their products were so crap, they wouldn't last as long as a Marks and Spencer prawn sandwich?"

"Oh, yes. Not them, then. You could visit Hatton Garden? That's known for being the centre of the English diamond trade. I went with my father in the 1940s. It suffered terribly from incendiary bombs in the war."

I tugged my bottom lip. "Isn't it a place for wholesale diamond dealing? I have this vision of South African prospectors discussing the entire contents of some third-world nation they've dug up."

160

"Maybe. But there are retail stores too. Why not have a look tomorrow?"

The waiter parked pyramids of crispy fried chicken, rice and stir-fried vegetables in front of us.

"Doesn't this look good?" asked Dad. "Fiona would love this food, wouldn't she? I bet you can't wait to see her again."

≈ ≈ ≈

The Northern Line underground train smelt more familiar the next day. I shielded myself behind my Metro newspaper and avoided other travellers' eyes.

Maybe I'm becoming re-accustomed to London life.

I hadn't visited Hatton Garden before. I pressed my palms and nose to the windows of a large jewellery store. Thousands of rings, earrings and necklaces arranged in military rows on cream trays looked back at me. My eyes glazed over, and my knees weakened as I stared. How the hell would I ever choose one?

Durrants of London.

Abrahams' Diamonds.

Carlo Jewellers.

So many windows.

So many cream-coloured trays.

So many diamonds.

No price labels.

A commissionaire swung open the door of Montfort's Fine Jewels, and I stepped inside. He looked at me from under his shiny, peaked cap as if a dog had strolled off the street and shat on his beige, shag-pile carpet.

I was about to be addressed by Captain Mainwaring.

"Are you here to collect a delivery?"

I smoothed down my jacket. "No, I'm looking for an engagement ring."

He angled his stance away from me and stood erect. "Do you have an appointment?"

"No, sorry."

Why am I apologising?

His chin lowered, and he nodded once. "Wait here."

I inspected my shoes and wondered what I was supposed to do next. The commissionaire continued to stare straight ahead.

A tall, thin salesman in a grey jacket and waistcoat exited from a rear room. He escorted a lady draped in an off-white fur coat, with a matching circular hat. They marched past me without acknowledgement. The commissionaire grabbed the brass door handle and swivelled open the glass door.

The salesman bowed slightly and rubbed his hands as if he were washing in an invisible sink. "Thank you for your business today, Mrs DuBery."

Mrs DuBery held out one gloved hand, which drooped slightly from her wrist. I wondered if the fawning salesman would kneel and kiss it.

She inspected him down her nose. "The alterations must be complete by Friday. I'm speaking at the Lord Mayor's Charity Ball, so they can't be late. I'll have Wilson collect them."

The salesman stooped so low I worried he'd never get up again. "It will be Montfort's pleasure to ensure your jewels are ready for such an auspicious occasion. Please tell your man to ask for me and I'll personally hand them to him."

Mrs DuBery plucked a previously unnoticed light-brown Chihuahua from her white handbag and deposited it on the floor at the end of a thin, red lead. "And don't forget Saskia's collar. It must be sparkling."

"Of course, Mrs DuBery." The salesman made to pat the dog, then withdrew his hand as it bared its teeth. "Aren't you a lucky girl, Saskia? A new diamond collar."

Through the glass exit, I observed a grey-suited chauffeur guarding the rear door of a black, old-fashioned saloon.

"Don't forget. Friday," said Mrs DuBery. Saskia tottled in front of her before being scooped up by the driver and lifted into the car. The salesman clasped his hands and watched them depart.

The commissionaire closed the door and gave a small cough and a tiny nod in my direction. "This, er, gentleman has no appointment."

The salesman paused and looked at me. "Yes?"

I blushed. "I'm searching for an engagement ring for my girlfriend. There's a tray in the window which might have something appropriate."

"I see." He looked at his watch. "I've five minutes before my next client's due. Pop outside and point at the tray for me."

I placed one palm on the door handle, and the commissionaire narrowed his eyes and reached over me to rub the brass with his white gloves.

"The middle tray," I shouted from the pavement.

The concierge swung the door open before I could grab the handle. I followed the salesman to a counter.

"Which particular ring did you have in mind?"

My eyes goggled at a jewel in the centre of the tray, and my heart raced as I imagined it on Fiona's finger. "This one."

23. DIAMOND ACCENT

LATITUDE: 51° 31' 12" N
LONGITUDE: 0° 6' 30" W

The salesman left the ring firmly wedged in the display case.

"That is an eighteen-carat gold band, with a one-carat VS1 clarity-grade diamond. I'll have to confirm the exact price, but I estimate it would retail at over fifteen thousand pounds."

My mouth fell open, and I blinked slowly. "That may be a little outside my budget."

"What is your budget?"

I bit my lip. "Maybe two hundred pounds? I could push to two hundred and fifty."

The salesman removed the tray, pushed up his shirt cuff and looked at his watch. "Excuse me, my next appointment's about to arrive." He returned the tray to the window and called over his shoulder. "Maybe you could try Signet Jewellers?"

"Signet Jewellers?"

He sniffed. "They might have something more within your means."

"All right. Thanks, anyway."

I attempted to annoy the commissionaire by opening the door myself, but he was too quick for me. My palm came in useful to protect my bottom in case he booted my backside as I left.

Across the road, I noticed a store selling antique and second-hand jewellery.

Second-hand? Maybe this'll be cheaper?

The offerings in the window would've benefited from dusting, and the rings' mounts had yellowed, but the jewellery impressed me.

A doorbell tinkled as I entered, and a musty smell filled my nostrils. A short, elderly man wearing a black skull cap pushed down on the counter to help himself stand.

"Yes, m'boy?"

"Could you help me find an engagement ring for my girlfriend?" I pointed behind me. "I've come from across the road, and I can't afford a brand-new one, so I wondered if you had anything second-hand within my budget."

"How much d'you want to spend?"

"Maybe a couple of hundred."

"Sorry, m'boy. I've nothing remotely near that price. You could try Signet Jewellers?"

"That's what everyone recommends. Thanks."

The bell tinkled again as I slammed the door behind me.

≈ ≈ ≈

The fluorescent lights of Signet Jewellers shone down on normal-looking customers. Not ladies in fur coats with tiny dogs squirrelled in their bags. People like me who wore Levi's jeans and puffa jackets.

I crossed the maroon carpet and greeted a salesgirl. Her gold badge announced her name as Natalie.

"Hi. I'm looking for an engagement ring for my girlfriend."

"No problem. What did you have in mind?"

"Maybe a gold band, with a single, solitaire stone? But I can only afford two hundred pounds. Some of the other shops I've visited had nothing for that price."

Natalie smiled. "I'm sure we can find you something. Have a seat and I'll bring out a tray."

I grinned and nodded. She walked to the shop window while I inspected a stand on the glass counter which displayed a selection of earrings under a sign saying £4.99.

Natalie returned and dumped a white plastic tray of assorted rings on the counter. "Here's some to choose from. Anything grab you?"

My eyes widened, and a warm feeling rose from my stomach as one jewel shone and sparkled.

Right in the centre of her tray.

A gold ring, with a single, massive diamond.

I blinked at the ring and hesitated.

This is bound to cost thousands.

I looked up at Natalie and pointed.

"The ring in the middle. How much is it?"

Natalie plucked the ring from the tray with more force and less care than I thought it deserved. She gripped the band and held it up. The ceiling light reflected rainbows through the stone like mist from a fountain on an English spring morning.

"D'you like it? This one's eighty-nine pounds."

"Are you sure? Not eight thousand, nine hundred pounds or anything?"

Natalie checked the label. "It's definitely eighty-nine pounds. Have a look." She showed me the numbers. I wiped the mark between the 89 and the 00 to check it wasn't a dot of fly dirt.

"Wow." I took the ring from her and held it up to scrutinise it. I wondered why no security guard or commissionaire stood nearby to prevent me from absconding with the valuables.

"Yes, sir. That one's popular. A nine-carat gold band with a two-carat cubic zirconia stone fixed in a nine-carat gold setting."

"Cubic what?"

"Cubic zirconia."

"It's not a diamond?"

"Cubic zirconia's a gemstone, and it resembles a diamond, wouldn't you agree? Most people can't tell the difference."

I shook my head and lowered my chin.

"My girlfriend will be able to. What can I buy for two hundred pounds with genuine diamonds? Not cubic whatsernames. D'you have anything, or am I dreaming?"

The salesgirl replaced the ring in its slot and tugged out a neighbouring stone. "This one has genuine diamonds."

"It has? But it's blue."

"Yes, sir. A nine-carat gold band with a topaz stone in a nine-carat gold setting surrounded by twenty-seven diamond accents. One hundred and eighty-nine pounds."

"Diamond accents?"

"Tiny diamonds. Look, hold it up and turn it around. You can see the diamonds."

I twisted it in the light and watched a constellation of microscopic sparkles glisten like bulbs on a Harrods' Christmas tree.

"And these are genuine diamonds?"

"They are. That's the best option within your budget."

I looked at my watch. 2:00 p.m. My task list still comprised a visit to New Zealand house to collect my passport, then return to Dad's to pack, ready for tomorrow's flight.

I set my jaw, looked Natalie in the eyes and nodded.

"I'll take it."

"Great choice, sir. I'll wrap it for you."

She boxed the ring and plopped it in a maroon bag with the Signet Jewellers logo.

≈ ≈ ≈

The New Zealand immigration lady slid my passport over the counter.

"Thanks for your patience. Here's your permanent residency visa for New Zealand. It entitles you to live in New Zealand forever and eventually to apply for citizenship, should you wish. Congratulations. How does it feel?"

I smiled thinly and hesitated.

"Great, I suppose."

I wondered if she expected me to whoop, holler and dance around the room like a winner of Family Feud.

After all Fiona and I had been through, the immigration interviews, the sworn affidavits from notable members of the gentry, trying to remember the colours of each other's toothbrushes, I should've been ecstatic.

Finally, we could live in the same country forever.

Finally, no more separate channels at border control.

Finally, no more fear of being separated by immigration regulations, which had happened to us twice.

The problem was, I didn't think I wanted to live in New Zealand now, and unless I had badly misjudged her, nor did Fiona.

She wanted to live here.

I took the passport, mumbled "thanks," and departed.

My nose was forced into a stranger's armpit on the train back to Dad's and someone else elbowed me in my back. As passengers alighted in the suburbs, and I secured a seat, I reached into my bag and pulled out the passport. I flicked to the page with my brand-new, shiny, blue New Zealand visa in it, studied the writing and replaced it in my bag.

I tugged the ring box out of the Signet Jewellers bag and glanced around the carriage to ensure no-one looked my way. The commuters hid behind their newspapers, oblivious to my actions.

I unclicked the box. The blue topaz offered a dull reflection, and I twisted and turned the ring to make the minuscule diamonds glimmer in the harsh train lights.

It didn't feel right.

It didn't look right.

It wasn't right.

I pursed my lips.

I knew I'd bought the wrong ring.

The train pulled into my father's stop. I closed the box, poked it into my bag and stepped off.

≈ ≈ ≈

Sunday lunch smelt out of place on a Friday evening. Dad stood at the door wearing a white apron and hat that made him resemble the *Little Chef* logo.

"I've cooked roast chicken. Your favourite."

"Yum. I picked up a bottle of wine on the way home. A New Zealand Sauvignon Blanc." I trailed my finger down the bottle and stared into space. "Fiona and I often shared a bottle from this vineyard."

My father sliced the chicken, and I helped myself to vegetables. The gravy dripped from the bowl's lip and spilt on the tablecloth. I remembered it'd done the same every childhood Sunday.

He sipped his wine. "How d'you finish up today? Did you collect your passport?"

"Yep, and it has my New Zealand visa in it, so everything's sorted for boarding the plane tomorrow."

"And what about Hatton Garden? Did you find a ring?"

"I couldn't afford Hatton Garden. The prices were about a million times too much. Two places recommended I visit a shop called Signet Jewellers, so I did, and it was more in my budget."

"Signet Jewellers?" asked Dad. "That rings a bell."

He rubbed his thumb and forefinger on his forehead and gazed into his lap.

"Signet Jewellers. Signet. Signet." He nodded. "I remember. That's what Ratners changed their name to, after their chairman's Marks and Spencer prawn sandwich speech."

I sagged back in my seat and shook my head.

"Are you serious? I've bought Fiona an engagement ring at Ratners?"

I slipped the ring box out of my bag and placed it next to his plate.

"Here. This is what I've ended up with. I'm not sure it's right, though."

My father snapped open the ring box and inspected the contents. He pulled his glasses down his nose and peered more closely.

He turned the box towards me.

"I think something's happened to your ring."

"What d'you mean, something's happened to the ring?" I snatched the box from him and peeked inside.

The ring remained wedged into the slit, but the Topaz stone had dropped out of the mount and rattled around the edge.

"That does it," I said. "This definitely isn't the right ring. How can they sell an engagement ring which barely arrives home without falling apart? Imagine if this happened when I gave it to Fiona?"

"You don't have time to take it back, do you? Would you like me to return it? I'll be in Central London next week."

"Thanks, Dad. I'll have to find a ring in Los Angeles, now." I glanced at the kitchen clock. "Could I make a phone call? I need to tell my host in LA the flight arrival time."

≈ ≈ ≈

1:00 a.m.

I couldn't sleep.

I lay on my right side. The light on the alarm clock glowed at me.

I buried my face in the pillow.

How will I ever afford the right ring for Fiona? One with a diamond which isn't invisible. And which doesn't come to pieces in the box.

I dozed.

2:00 a.m.

I lay on my left side. Streetlights glowed through the thin curtains.

I covered my face with my hands.

I should've bought a ring in Hong Kong. Maybe the diamonds were genuine, after all.

3:00 a.m.

I lay on my back and stared in the direction of the ceiling. A cat sang the final soprano stanza of *Toreador* repeatedly in a nearby garden.

How the hell will I ever find a ring in Los Angeles? I'm only there for two days. Will Richard know where to buy one?

I swung my legs over the side of the bed, opened the door and headed for the bathroom.

≈ ≈ ≈

My father wiped the breakfast dishes.

"Morning. You slept in. Would you like toast? I had mine; I didn't want to wake you."

I rubbed my eyes and glanced at the kitchen clock.

"Sorry; I was awake in the middle of the night."

"Something on your mind?"

"This ring problem. I don't know what to do."

"Maybe you're worrying too much? Fiona's a down-to-earth girl. I'm sure she'll appreciate whatever you buy."

My elbows rested on the table, and I formed a steeple with my fingers

"I'm doing this once and it has to be right. Los Angeles will have rings. The shopping malls are huge."

"What time d'you want to leave for the airport?"

170

"Check-in's at 1:30. Maybe noon?"

≈ ≈ ≈

My father swung the wheel and deposited me outside Heathrow terminal three.

"Bye, Simon. It's been lovely to see you. Call me once you arrive in New Zealand. And good luck with your proposal. Let me know how it goes."

"Thanks, Dad. I'll see you again soon. You could come to New Zealand for the wedding?"

"Of course I will. Let me know as soon as you have a date. Bye."

I slammed the car door and watched him drive away.

A lump formed in my throat.

It didn't seem right, Fiona being so far away.

She belonged here. We both did. Although I'd felt like a stranger in my own country, London was where our immediate future lay.

I tightened my fists, thrust my chest out and shouldered my backpack.

It was time.

It was time for me to fetch her.

It was time for me to board another plane.

≈ ≈ ≈

The first time I'd visited Los Angeles, I'd been an impressionable teenager who'd lived a sheltered life shuttled between a family home and a boys' boarding school.

I'd never seen a Mexican before.

I'd certainly never seen a row of five Mexicans lying prone on a pavement with three policemen pointing guns at them like a scene from *Ricochet*.

The second time I'd visited Los Angeles, Fiona and I had lined up for hours at Disneyland, toured Hollywood and fondled every item of clothing in a gigantic shopping mall.

All tourist activities.

Now I was in the city for the third time, and I was determined to leave my previous impressions of crime, fashion and people dressed as cartoon characters behind.

This time, I anticipated the real LA.

This time, I'd be staying with a local resident.

Unfortunately, I'd forgotten what he looked like.

24. FAJITAS

LATITUDE: 33° 56' 39" N
LONGITUDE: 118° 24' 31" W

I needn't have worried. Richard towered above the other airport visitors, and he'd also helpfully handwritten a sign which said, 'Simon from Byron Bay'.

"Hi. Richard?"

He held out a hand the size of a boxing glove.

"Sure is. Good to see ya. Welcome to Los Angeles."

A leather waistcoat flaunting an eagle emblem covered his white T-shirt, and I spotted his black belt bag around his waist.

I smiled. "Thank you for having me to stay. I'll try not to be any trouble."

"Nonsense. You're no trouble. I've a whole programme of suggestions to do while you're here. We'll discuss them over dinner. Carmen's cooking. D'you like Mexican?"

"Of course. Fiona and I eat it frequently."

Richard slapped my back and almost knocked me flat.

"Not like Carmen's ya don't. Hers is the real deal. Let me take your bag."

He lifted my backpack and marched through the terminal. I hurried after him.

Richard's large, black SUV occupied a space directly outside the terminal doors under a sign that said, 'Official Vehicles Only'. I couldn't see inside the tinted glass, and there seemed to be an unnecessary number of aerials attached to the roof, bonnet and bumper.

He clicked a button, and the doors unlocked. "Hop into the passenger seat. I'll throw your bag in the trunk."

Passenger seat? Hang on, Simon. Remember, the cars are the other way around here.

I stopped myself from opening the driver's door and climbed in on the right-hand side.

Richard started his engine.

"D'you work at the airport?" I asked.

He tilted his head from side to side. "Sometimes. I was tasked to an incident here last Friday."

I pushed out my bottom lip. "Sorry—tasked to an incident?"

Richard cleared his throat. "First time in LA?"

"No, I've visited twice before. I passed through on the way to my uncle's house in San Diego years ago, aged fifteen. Then in 1996, I brought my girlfriend, Fiona, when we emigrated from England to New Zealand. But we only stayed two nights."

Richard joined the freeway traffic. I pushed against the seat back and stamped on an invisible passenger-side brake pedal as he swerved across four lanes.

He tapped his fingers on the dashboard and overtook a truck outlined in bright-red lights, as if Selfridge's Christmas display was travelling along the inside lane. "You seen Hollywood?"

"We visited the part with the celebrity stars on the footpath and the Chinese theatre. If you ask me, it's a dump."

Richard flapped one hand. "Pppfff."

Oh, no. Have I insulted him?

He slapped the steering wheel. "It's a dump all right. I ran a big operation there last month."

My eyebrows furrowed, and I turned towards him.

"Big operation?"

He cleared his throat. "When you were here with your girlfriend, did you see the immense hillside homes of the movie actors and directors?"

"Nope. I'd love to do that. She would've loved that too."

"Great. We'll go tomorrow. You can take photos to show her. And you fly out the following afternoon? That's a quick visit."

"I know. I'd also like to buy some clothes for Fiona. She loves the US malls. I think her favourite was called Fashion Valley. And most importantly"—I grabbed a handle as Richard accelerated onto the 405 freeway—"I need to find a jewellery store."

"I ain't heard of no Fashion Valley," said Richard, "but there's a mall near my neighbourhood. It'll have plenty of clothes and jewellery shops. You can purchase whatever you need."

A phone rang; a sound I wasn't accustomed to in a car. Richard unclipped a handset from beside his right knee and held the receiver on the end of a black, coiled cord. The ensuing conversation seemed to refer to Richard meeting with several people at an undisclosed location.

He replaced the phone.

I raised my eyebrows. "Are you with the police?"

"We sometimes handle joint engagements. Anyway, the shopping mall. We'll head there before you leave."

≈ ≈ ≈

Green, overhead road signs advertised unfamiliar destinations, and we merged onto the 5 freeway. Richard overtook pickup trucks that would've impressed Tommo, sedans and trucks towing trailers, and his headlights offered a view of the concrete road surface. My brain didn't enjoy being on the driver's side of the car bereft of a steering wheel or pedals, and I braced myself constantly.

Richard clicked the indicator, and we exited into the quiet, dark streets of a residential neighbourhood. Dim lights shone from porches. I watched a man push a garbage bin down his driveway.

Richard swung the wheel and reversed into the driveway of a single-storey, detached brick home. I stepped out and tried to open the boot, but it wouldn't unlatch.

He slammed the driver's door. "It's okay; I'll grab your bag. Go ahead inside."

The front door opened to reveal a fit-looking, brown-skinned lady with her arms open wide as if she were about to preach a particularly evangelistic sermon.

"Buenas noches, Simon. I am Carmen, Richard's wife. Welcome, welcome."

She flicked back her bleached-blonde hair and reached up to kiss me, an action I hadn't prepared for. I caught a whiff of perfume, which time-travelled me back to the memorable occasion I'd brushed past Joanna Lumley in Harrods.

"Are you exhausted after your long journey? Richard'll put your bag in the spare room. D'you like fajitas? I made lots; you must be hungry."

She glanced over my shoulder at Richard and threw her arms in the air.

"Don't just stand there." She jabbed her finger. "Put our guest's bag in his room. Then lay plates and cutlery on the table. And the hot sauce. Don't forget the hot sauce. Can't you see the poor boy's tired and hungry?"

Richard swallowed and lowered his gaze. "Right away, my little enchilada."

He marched down a corridor with my bag.

Carmen threw her arm around my waist and steered me inside. "Come. Take off your coat. Sit down."

I followed her into a kitchen and perched on a bar stool.

A large wok sizzled on a stove, alongside a bubbling frying pan. The wonderful smells of Mexican spices immediately reminded me of preparing an Old El Paso kit for Fiona in our little New Zealand home. Carmen grabbed the wok's handle with one perfectly manicured hand and tossed the food. Behind a steamed-up glass oven door, a colourful dish displayed more hot goodies.

"You want a drink?" She opened a double-doored fridge the size of a Swiss bank vault. "Here, I've cola, lemonade, orange, anything you like."

"Lemonade, please. Thank you."

She extracted a can, pffd the ring-pull and slid it towards me with a tumbler. Billows of steam rose from the stove and floated horizontally along the underside of the ceiling.

Richard sat alongside me, undid his black belt bag and clunked it on the counter.

Carmen narrowed her eyes and waved one pointed finger at him. "Don't you sit down. Is the cutlery on the table? Did you put away the laundry yet?"

Richard shuffled off the stool. "Sorry, my little tortilla. I'll do it right away."

He vanished again. I watched Carmen add various spices to the frying pans and remove a jar from the cupboard the size of an old-fashioned milk churn.

She twisted the top, then winced and waggled her wrist.

"Richard, Richard!" she yelled at the open door behind me.

Richard appeared with a sock in each hand. "Yes, my little tomatillo?"

She brandished the jar across the counter.

"Open these jalapeños. You know I can never undo brand-new jars." I briefly considered offering to open it for her, but I didn't feel I should risk the crossfire of their marital salvoes.

Richard's biceps Popeyed as he pinged the lid.

Carmen snatched it from him. "You finished with the laundry yet?"

Richard stood with rounded shoulders and unstuffed the socks from his top pocket, where he'd put them for safekeeping. "Nearly finished, my little quesadilla."

"You still haven't put the plates on the table. And don't forget the sauce."

She turned to me. "You like spicy food?"

I nodded and wondered what she'd have done if I'd said 'no'.

≈ ≈ ≈

Carmen dumped a steaming bowl on the table which could've comfortably fed most of the Yucatán Peninsula, next to a tall pile of tortillas. I wafted the spicy fragrance with one hand and smiled slowly at the familiar sour cream, guacamole and shredded cheese accompaniments. I concluded I'd never eaten this cuisine prepared by a native Mexican before.

My hand covered a yawn, as I realised that, for my body clock, it was 3:00 in the morning.

She picked up a serving spoon and passed it to me. "Are you tired, Simon? You've had a long journey. Richard tells me you flew all the way here from Australia via Hong Kong and London. When we travelled home from Sydney last month that was bad enough, and we only took the one flight."

I nodded. "Yep, my adventure's taken me around the entire world anticlockwise, and right now it's the middle of the night for me."

"Anticlockwise?" said Richard. "What the hell's anticlockwise?"

"Um, the opposite of clockwise?"

"You mean counterclockwise?"

"I suppose so. We say anticlockwise in England." I spooned some salsa.

"What've you boys planned for tomorrow?" asked Carmen.

Richard unscrewed a bottle cap. "Simon's seen Hollywood and Disneyland before, so I thought I'd drive him around Bel Air and Beverly Hills to gape at the homes of the rich and famous. I've seen London on the TV and I know they ain't got places like that. Then the following day, Simon needs to do some shopping. I'll take him to the local mall."

"Pah!" said Carmen. "Not that dump. You've no idea where the right stores are. We'll go to Glendale Galleria. I know it like the back of my hand."

"Yes, my little quesadilla. So the credit card bill tells me."

He turned to me, grinned and held the back of his hand to the side of his mouth. "We've got an agreement. I make the money, she spends it."

WHACK

Richard clutched one hand with the other. "Ow. That hurt."

Carmen replaced the spoon. "I spend money on nice clothes and jewellery to look young and beautiful. It's for you, not me."

Richard swallowed and rubbed the back of his hand. "Yes, my little chimichanga."

I lay my knife and fork on my plate.

"That was delicious. I think I'll head for bed; jetlag's catching up. D'you need a hand clearing away?"

Carmen smiled at me and flicked her hair back. "Of course not. Richard can do that. We'll see you in the morning. Breakfast's *huevos rancheros*. Sleep well."

"Your bedroom's second on the left," said Richard. "Shout out if you need anything."

"Thanks for having me to stay."

What's huevos rancheros?

≈ ≈ ≈

178

A bedside lamp illuminated a large double bed buried under a black duvet, and the opposite wall accommodated a wooden dresser with a television. Richard had propped my backpack against a chair, and I grinned to myself as I discovered a door in the rear wall which opened to a tiny bathroom, with a toilet, sink and shower.

I splashed water on my face, brushed my teeth, pulled off my clothes, tugged back the duvet and plopped on the edge of the bed.

Big mistake.

25. WIN THE WORLD

LATITUDE: 34° 17' 59" N,
LONGITUDE: 118° 27' 34" W

BLUP

The mattress formed a deep, U-shaped valley, and I toppled backwards.

BLUP

I tried to regain a sitting position.

BLUP BLUP BLUP

I flipped onto my stomach, clawed my way to the edge of the bed and fell on the floor, in a movement punctuated by diminishing gurgles.

BLUP BLUP Blup blup blup

Bed: 1; Simon: 0.
I stood, rubbed my chin, then pushed my fist down hard into the mattress.

BLUP

The mattress regained its shape as I removed my fist.

BLUP

I scratched my head and experimented with pushing both fists into the mattress, one after the other.

blooOOOoop blooOOOoop blooOOOoop

I had a vague boyhood memory, when I'd slept over at a school friend's house and spent the entire night needing the toilet.

What's the trick to sleeping on a waterbed?

I sat on the edge and gingerly lay in a sleeping position.

DOOMPH bloop bloop bloop bloop bloop

Not like that.

I lay further away from the edge.

BloOOoop blup blup blup.

Okay, we've successfully lain on the bed. I'll reach over and turn off the bedside lamp.

DOOMPH bloop bloop bloop bloop bloop

Bloody hell. That hurt. Turn off the light first.

I clicked off the bedside lamp, took a brief run up and launched myself face first into the centre of the bed.

BLOOOOOOP

That showed you. I'm not falling out this time.

I tugged the duvet up cautiously, sunk my head into the pillow and switched off my brain.

≈ ≈ ≈

That half-asleep, half-awake period occurred during the night.

Where you think it might be time to wake, but equally it might be a few minutes after midnight.

I turned over to search for a clock.

GLUP Glup glup.

I swore the bed had lost some liquid during the night and wondered if it had saturated the carpet.

Streetlights shining through the blinds assisted me to find the bedside cabinet. I fumbled and heard the crash of the clock.

Damn.

I leant over the edge of the bed and toppled to the floor.

CRASH BLUP Blup blup

Bed: 4; Simon: 1.

I surrender. It doesn't matter what the time is, I'm getting up.

The clock face glowed at me.

4.30 a.m.

Hours until the rest of the household woke. There was no way I'd risk being swallowed by the bed again, so I knelt on the floor and flicked through TV channels.

An old black-and-white cowboy movie, which I watched until all the important characters had tumbled from their horses.

A cooking program in Spanish, which I didn't understand, but the dishes looked yummy.

A repeat of *The Young and the Restless*, which I'd seen in New Zealand.

I finally settled on a quiz show called *Win the World*, which involved teams of contestants answering geography questions to secure an exciting foreign vacation. Some questions seemed remarkably simple. I couldn't believe the teams didn't know Romania was in Europe, or the longest river in Egypt was the Nile.

I tried not to shout at the television, then tripped up on a question about the largest city in the US, and failed to identify the state nickname of South Dakota, but I had an inkling about the capital of Australia.

"It's Canberra," I said in a loud whisper. "Canberra." I threw my hands in the air. "No, don't press 'A'. It's not Sydney. Bloody hell."

The contestant pressed 'A', and a big red 'X' flashed beside them.

I groaned. "Now you need another correct answer to win. Okay. Next question."

The quiz master held up a card.

"What's the name of the island on which Honolulu stands?"

The camera focussed on the other team. Not the one who'd identified Sydney as the capital of Australia. I listened to them mutter amongst themselves.

"It's not Hawaii, is it?" said an immaculately made-up lady to a fat man I presumed was her husband. "I know there's one called Maui, but I think the main one's called Hawaii, same as the state."

"It's Oahu," I informed the contestant, who was not only separated from me by hundreds of kilometres, but, given the 1980s hairstyles they all exhibited, potentially by almost two decades in time. "Oahu. Say Oahu."

Her husband turned to the quiz master. "We'll go with Hawaii."

I thumped my fist on the floor.

"How can you not know that? You're American, for goodness' sake. I know the bloody answer, and I'm English."

"I'm sorry," said the quiz master. "The answer is Oahu."

I shook my hands on either side of my head as the gigantic red 'X' of failure lit up beside the contestants.

The quiz master spoke dramatically. "Teams, it all hangs on this last question. Team Goldstein, if you answer this question correctly, you'll return for our grand final next week, and the chance to compete for two weeks' vacation on the fabulous island of Barbados, in the Caribbean."

The camera panned across a packed auditorium whooping, hollering and clapping.

I couldn't support Team Goldstein. They hadn't listened to my advice that Canberra was the capital of Australia, so they didn't deserve to win. Neither team deserved to win.

"The final question is:"

Dramatic pause.

Occasional yells from the fired-up audience.

"Quiet, please. The final question is: In which European capital city would you find St Paul's Cathedral?"

I held my head in my hands.

Couldn't they have found a harder one? Team Goldstein's bound to win now.

The camera concentrated on their discussion.

"I'm sure it's London," said a short, blonde lady. "I think that's where Prince Charles married Lady Diana."

"Yes!" I shouted. "It's London. Obviously. Say London."

"No way," said a man beside her. "St Paul's is in Rome. It's where the Pope does his speeches."

I threw my hands in the air. "That's St Peter's. Not St Paul's. Don't listen to him."

The team leader turned to the quizmaster.

"We'll say Rome."

"You idiot!" I stood up and gesticulated at the television. "For goodness' sake. I give up. You deserve to lose."

The door opened and Richard's head appeared.

"Are you okay? I heard shouting."

I froze and turned around slowly.

"Sorry, I hope I didn't wake you. This TV quiz show frustrated me."

"D'you want some coffee? I'm fixing some."

"Yes, please. I'll be there right away."

≈ ≈ ≈

Snow-capped mountains surrounded Richard's neighbourhood, a topology which hadn't been evident to me when we'd arrived the previous night.

I sat at the kitchen table and stared out of the window.

"Wow. When us Brits think of Los Angeles, the first thought isn't snow-capped mountains. It's beaches with bikini girls and hunky guys, like *Baywatch*."

Richard nodded. "Yep, that's my winter playground. My buddies and I ski up there."

He pointed at the passageway with his thumb. "Carmen won't accompany me. She don't like the cold. She prefers the beach."

I heard a door close.

"Here she comes. Damn, I haven't fixed her drink." Richard pulled mugs out of the cupboard and rattled teaspoons. The rich smell of percolating coffee filled the air as steam rose from a machine on the counter.

Carmen swept in, dressed in a luxurious kimono with a gold swirly pattern on the cream fabric. Her hair and makeup were as immaculate as the previous night.

"Good morning." She kissed my cheek. "Did you sleep okay?"

I decided not to mention the wrestling match which the water bed had won by knockout in round four.

"Fine, thanks. Although, the time zone difference had me up early, so I watched some TV."

"Are you ready for breakfast? Has Richard fixed your coffee yet?" She glanced at the clock and turned to her husband. "Richard, what have you been doing? Simon's dying of thirst, and you haven't frothed the milk."

Richard rearranged cups as if he were David Copperfield about to perform a complicated magic trick.

"Getting to it right away, my little enchilada."

She huffed. "I'll do it myself. The poor boy's dehydrated."

She opened the fridge and jammed her fists on her hips.

"Richard, I told you to pick up milk yesterday."

Richard slapped his forehead and grimaced.

"The store was out. Right out. Not a single bottle. The delivery truck musta broken down or something. I'll head out and fetch some right away."

Carmen narrowed her eyes and shot him a sidewards glance.

Richard grabbed some car keys from a hook. "Simon, you wanna come for the ride?"

"Sure. I'll put my shoes on."

≈ ≈ ≈

The black SUV swerved out of his driveway. "She's a tough fiery *habanero* sometimes," said Richard, "but she's a good woman. I'm glad you enjoy her cooking."

"Where did you two meet?"

"On the job. She used to be with the LAPD. She ain't no more. Too many tough guys, too many scares, too many colleagues killed or injured. These days she keeps house and spends my money."

He threw his head back and laughed. I tried to imagine the petite, attractive Carmen wielding a weapon during a drugs bust.

"Are you with the LAPD?"

"Nah. But I work alongside them sometimes. D'ya wanna wait here? I won't be long."

He parked the black SUV, hopped out and slammed the door.

I twiddled my thumbs and gazed around the car. Besides Richard's phone mounted by his leg, two radios with black knobs protruded from the dashboard. Rocker switches under the steering wheel displayed symbols which I'd never seen in a car before. One resembled an exploding bomb and another a speaker with lines splaying from it.

Richard had abandoned his unzipped, eagle-insignia belt bag in the driver's footwell.

I stretched my neck and peeked inside.

At the brown, textured grip of a pistol.

26. FANNY PACK

LATITUDE: 34° 7' 54" N
LONGITUDE: 118° 25' 59" W

I glanced around, flinched back from the belt bag and sat bolt upright. I hoped there weren't cameras in this hi-tech vehicle which would betray my inquisitiveness.

Richard opened the door and passed me a rectangular, white bottle, which could've easily been the contents of an entire cow.

He strapped his belt bag around his waist, so it rested in his lap and started the engine.

I rubbed my palm against my lips. "Your belt bag? Does it come with your job? It looks handy for carrying, um, things in."

"What the hell's a belt bag?" asked Richard.

I pointed. "The black bag, around your waist."

"My fanny pack?"

"Fanny pack." I laughed. "Where I come from, fanny means something else. My girlfriend would find your name for it hilarious."

"I sure as hell ain't never heard it called a belt bag. It's standard issue. I always wear it whether or not I'm on duty. Anyway, after one of Carmen's amazing breakfasts, I figured we'd head into the hills. You brought a camera?"

"Yep. And spare film."

"Great. We'll grab some lunch then, this afternoon, I'm gonna show you something different. I reckon it might interest you."

"Sounds intriguing."

"Then we'll head home, have dinner and I'll play the video I took when we dived in Australia. My colleague edited it at work, and it looks great."

"I'd forgotten you had the video camera on our dive; I can't wait."

≈ ≈ ≈

As soon as I stepped in the door, my nostrils filled with exotic, Mexican smells. This was nothing like my father's cornflakes and toast.

Carmen's voice echoed from the kitchen, accompanied by clanging pans.

"Richard. Richard! Knives and forks on the table. Coffee. Come on, where've you been?"

Richard demonstrated the bottle of milk to her. "Yes, my little enchilada. Right away."

Carmen placed down plates. "Huevos rancheros. Eat up."

I gazed at a platter of food which could've comfortably fed the Dodgers baseball team and realised this would be the biggest breakfast I'd ever battled in my life.

≈ ≈ ≈

Richard clicked the house door closed. "If we sneak out without her noticing, she won't assign me any more tasks."

The big SUV pulled out of his drive, and I snapped a picture of the mountaintop snow reflecting in the morning light like a Himalayan postcard. We merged onto the freeway amongst the endless pickup trucks thundering along the sun-warmed concrete.

Richard pushed the indicator stalk down. "We'll turn right on Sepulveda and head up Mulholland."

"Mulholland? I recognise that word from a Tom Petty song."

Richard chuckled. "Excellent memory. 'Freefallin'.'" He sang the third verse badly out of tune. I winced and stared from the passenger window as the road wound past vast mansions with expansive views over the city.

He slowed the car. "Hop out and take some photos. I'll pull over onto this vacant lot."

He parked on a strip of grass next to a real estate agent's sign speared into the ground. I opened the passenger door and nipped around the bonnet.

The vista stretched in front of me; rocky canyons with sporadic clumps of trees poking from crevices, and beyond them, ten concrete lanes of another freeway which bisected tall, commercial buildings. In the background, the skyscrapers of central Los Angeles blurred through the murk.

Los Angeles.

The city of angels.

Why did angels have to live in a yellowy-brown layer of shimmering smog?

I snapped a panorama of photos, then studied the real estate sign.

"Richard, what's actually being sold here?"

I rubbed my chin and paced the tiny patch of grass where Richard had stopped.

Richard leant out of the car window and read the sign, which spiked through the verge halfway between the edge of the road and a precipitous drop into a canyon a few metres away.

"Building land, I guess. Vacant block."

I took a step back and frowned. "Really? This strip doesn't seem wide enough to build anything on."

"Land values are so high here," he explained, "that they fix vast poles into the canyon below and extend the land out. The only part of whatever house they're building that'll be on solid ground'll be the driveway. The rest'll be on poles."

I peered over the edge into the canyon. Scrub grew up the side embedded in the dry, browny-red rock. I coughed, as a breeze whirlwinded dust and puffed it up the cliff.

"I'll show you some finished houses on poles like that," said Richard. "But I'll tell you what, even if I was a multi-millionaire, I'd never buy one of them."

"Are you kidding? The views are to die for."

"Yes, and you might end up dying for them. Would you want to be up on sticks when the ground starts shaking?"

≈ ≈ ≈

We wiggled through neighbourhoods of oversized homes hidden behind high gates. Uniform lawns, unnaturally spinach-coloured for the climate, rolled down to the kerb. I observed gardeners tending herbaceous borders, inhaled the deep perfumes of luxurious foliage and wondered if mere mortals were permitted to drive through these suburbs. Wilshire, Bel Air, Beverly Hills. Richard's tour took me through an entire series of Jackie Collins novels.

He braked outside a huge, monolithic building, which looked like someone had lifted a Château out of the French countryside, flown it across the Atlantic and dropped it in California.

I frowned and pushed my head back.

"Is that a house? It looks a recreation of the Palace of Versailles."

"Yep, it's a house," said Richard. "I reckon it's the biggest in the state."

I stared at the visible parts of the white building and raised my camera. "That's incredible. The size of it. And it looks brand-new."

"It's a few years old. Owned by a TV producer called Aaron Spelling. Everyone hates it. It takes up the space of ten houses, that's to say, ten houses of the size you find up here, which are already ten times the size of a normal house. It has its own barber's, bowling alley, nightclub and space for one hundred cars. Apparently, an entire wing is a wardrobe for his wife's clothes. But because you have money, doesn't mean you have taste, right?"

"Incredible. Thank you for showing me this. It's a different view of Los Angeles from when Fiona and I visited a couple of years ago. I must bring her back and show her."

"We'll grab some lunch at a sushi joint I know, then this afternoon I want to show you something infamous."

"Infamous?"

"Yep. Somewhere a very famous person had a major fall from grace."

As Richard pulled into the traffic, I turned over in my mind who it might be.

≈ ≈ ≈

Richard chauffeured me to a set of high, green, wrought-iron gates, outside a large, mock Tudor-style house. Weeds sprouted through the brown, cobbled driveway, and large plants crawled across the windows.

He wiggled his eyebrows at me.

I pursed my lips. "What are we doing here?"

"Ya know where we are?"

"Is this the house of someone famous?" I paused. "I know, it's someone who used to be famous, but they've fallen on hard times and can't afford a gardener?"

"Close. This is 360 North Rockingham Avenue."

I scratched my head. "Should I know that address?"

"O. J. Simpson. Remember him?"

"O. J. Simpson." I rubbed the back of my neck. "He was in the *Naked Gun* movies with Leslie Nielsen. And before that, he was a sports star."

"Yes, but it's what he did after *Naked Gun* he's remembered for."

I had a vague flashback to a news item which I hadn't cared about.

"Was he the guy who fell from grace?"

Richard puffed and grinned. "I'll say he did. Pretty hard. They arrested him for the murders of his ex-wife and a male friend of hers."

"That's right, I remember. The trial was televised. But wasn't he found innocent? There was a mistrial or something?"

Richard leant towards me and rubbed his hands so hard I expected smoke to rise. "The date's 12th June 1994; nearly four years ago. O. J. Simpson's ex-wife Nicole Brown Simpson and her friend Ronald Goldman are found stabbed to death outside her condominium by"—Richard formed air quotes with his fingers—"persons unknown. Five days later, sports hero, actor and Nicole's ex-husband O. J. Simpson is formally charged with the murders.

He denies the allegations and, like some kinda scene out of *The Blues Brothers,* takes off on a wild-goose chase in a friend's car, pursued by news helicopters, dozens of police vehicles and a heap of private motorists."

I watched Richard recount the details and wondered whether he'd taken part in the pursuit.

"Anyway," he continued, "here's what the prosecution says happened. On the night of the murders, our friend O. J. attends his daughter's dancing function with Nicole, the kid's mother. O. J. also has another girlfriend, but later that same evening, she discovers O. J.'s been out with his ex-wife, so she breaks off their relationship. We can conclude O. J. wouldn't have been in the best frame of mind towards Nicole, right?"

I rubbed my chin and nodded. "Right."

"After his new lady dumps him, the prosecution theorises O. J. heads back to Nicole's house to reconcile with her. Nicole ain't having a bar of it, no way she's getting back with O. J. owing to his history of domestic abuse and, when she refuses, the prosecution alleges O. J. kills her."

He held one finger in the air. "Murder number one."

I nodded.

This would fascinate Fiona. She loves celebrity gossip.

Richard continued. "At that exact point, Nicole's friend Ronald Goldman rocks up and chances upon O. J. standing next to Nicole's dead body, so the prosecution states O. J. kills him as well, to avoid being identified. Murder number two."

My mouth fell open. "Wow. Then what did he do?"

"What the prosecution alleges he did, is jump in his car, return here, to 360 North Rockingham Avenue, take a chauffeur-driven limo to the airport and board a flight."

I tilted my head to the left and right. "What made them so sure it was him? I mean, it could've been a random street robbery which escalated."

Richard shifted in his seat and adjusted his belt bag. "The prosecution argued Nicole had always feared her husband, who had a history of domestic violence. They offered DNA evidence to show blood found near the murder scene belonged to O. J. Then they found Goldman's DNA on a glove discovered at this house right here"—Richard pointed—"360, North Rockingham Avenue, where Goldman had never been in his life; hell, he mighta never met O. J., so there was no rational reason for his DNA to be here at all. Plus, get this, they found the pair to the glove at the crime scene."

"It sounds like an open-and-shut case."

"Everybody reckoned so. They all thought our former idol was headed to jail. It riveted everyone to the TV like when someone shot J. R. Ewing in *Dallas*."

I raised my eyebrows and nodded, then turned to stare at O. J.'s house again. "What happened next?"

"Once the prosecution rested, the lawyers acting for O. J. responded with four points in his defence."

Richard ticked them off on his fingers.

"First, the DNA. The State of California's only proper case was based on DNA from blood drops and stains, such as the glove. The defence argued the DNA had been contaminated and as a result, the actual killer's DNA had degraded. This was a pretty weak argument, to be honest, as they found O. J.'s blood at the crime scene."

Richard paused and held up two fingers.

"Second, the defence argued the entire case was some kinda plot by the authorities to frame O. J. I can tell you for a fact it wasn't; this was puffed up theorisation."

I wondered how Richard knew this, but I let him continue.

"I guess this is the third part of their defence"—he held up another finger—"O. J.'s lawyers went as far as to say the police had planted the evidence. Clearly, the defence was becoming increasingly desperate to assert O. J.'s innocence. Which brings me on to the final point."

He paused and turned to me.

"Can you guess what it was?"

"Nope."

Richard tapped his car's clock. "What's the time, Simon?"

I leant forward and read the glowing display.

"It's 2:37."

"Right. Keep that time in your head."

Without warning, Richard gunned the engine and screeched away from the kerb.

27. LISA KUDROW

LATITUDE: 34° 3' 43" N,
LONGITUDE: 118° 29' 23" W

The black SUV sped past large mansions similar to those on Mulholland Drive, but the next level down on the ostentation scale. People who couldn't afford Mulholland lived here. I gripped the handle above the passenger window as Richard swerved to the right, then swung left onto a road called Sunset Boulevard. He hadn't spoken since we'd left O. J. Simpson's house.

I held on tight as Richard dodged parked cars, and I wondered where we were heading.

"What was the last item in the defence's arsenal?"

Richard smirked as he drove right-handed, his left arm dangling from the window. "I thought you'd never ask. The defence argued O. J. didn't have enough time to return home after the dance function, take the call from his lady ending their relationship, head back over to Nicole's house, murder her and Mr Goldman, retrace his steps to 360 North Rockingham, clean up the evidence of the killings and depart in the limo for the airport. They used the evidence from phone company records of the call with his lady, and the testimony of the limo driver as the start and end brackets of the time period."

Richard paused at an intersection, then screeched the tyres to the right.

"Between those two was a period of around an hour when O. J. couldn't account for his movements. The defence stated this wasn't sufficient time for the murders to have occurred. I'm gonna show you how wrong their theory was."

We lurched around a left turn, then an immediate right.

Richard pointed. "Keep watching the clock. What time is it?"

"2.40. Nope, it changed. 2.41."

"Right. How long have we been driving?"

"Four minutes."

Richard zipped past more mansions, then slammed on the brakes outside a Californian-scale version of a Spanish farmhouse. Huge gables under a terracotta-tiled roof framed half-moon windows and small, intimate balconies. A new, black Mercedes stood on the red brick driveway alongside lawns so green they didn't belong with the arid, Mediterranean landscaping. Mist from a watering system drifted across the pavement and settled on our windscreen.

Richard slapped the dashboard twice. "Here we are." He pointed. "The murder house. This is where it happened. This is where he killed 'em. 875 South Bundy Drive. The current owners changed the street number, for obvious reasons. How long did the journey take?"

I glanced at the clock again.

"It's 2.42. Five minutes."

"All right, you're O. J. Simpson. You took five minutes to drive from your house. You ring the bell, or knock, or whatever, your ex-wife comes out and you stab her to death. Her friend then rocks up, so you stab him too. How long does that take you?"

I gave a nervous laugh. "I'm not familiar with stabbing people, not having done it before. Ten minutes, fifteen minutes?"

"Okay. You take five minutes to drive here, then fifteen minutes to stab your two victims. Therefore, so far, you've been away from home for twenty minutes. O. J. didn't make much effort to clean up the crime scene. So, we add another five minutes. And then, he drives back home."

Richard pulled away from the pavement and executed the entire ride again in the opposite direction. I crossed and uncrossed my legs and watched the everyday lives of wealthy Californians speed past. Richard seemed to be taking this demonstration to extremes in order to prove his point, but I decided to humour him.

We arrived back at 360 North Rockingham Avenue.

Richard exhaled and flopped back in the driver's seat.

"Okay. How long's elapsed in total since we left here?"

"Thirty minutes? Maximum."

"Right. And now O. J. cleans up. He strips off his blood-stained clothes, disposes of any evidence to link himself to the crime, dresses and leaves for the airport. If you were O. J. Simpson, how long would it take you?"

I frowned and shrugged. "I've honestly no idea. Fifteen, twenty minutes?"

"Right. Fifty minutes all up to perform the murders, come home and dispose of the evidence. O. J. couldn't explain his movements for over an hour, but the last element of his defence argued he couldn't have been the murderer, because he didn't have time to do it."

Richard smacked the steering wheel. "Simon, you have just seen a first-hand demonstration of how fabricated that evidence was. Whaddya reckon? D'you agree with me? He had time to drive from his house, kill Nicole and her friend, zoom back and clean up?"

"Definitely."

"D'you reckon he was guilty of the murders?"

I nodded. "Yep."

"Me, too," said Richard. "Me, too."

He indicated and pulled away from the kerb.

I turned the case over in my mind as we rejoined the freeway, and Richard changed lanes between large trucks. I wondered if Fiona had watched the trial.

"How'd he get away with it?"

Richard gripped the wheel. "The politicians were terrified there'd be race riots if they found him guilty. There was a theory some back-room deal was done to ensure O. J. was found not guilty and avoid public disorder. I know that never occurred. But for whatever reason, on October 3rd, the court acquitted O. J. Simpson on both counts, and he walked free."

Richard paused.

"Tellingly, the LAPD chief, who's a personal friend of mine, made the remark that just because the court found O. J. not guilty, doesn't mean there was another murderer. That's a helluva statement, right? And then later on, the families of the victims brought a civil case, in which the court found O. J. guilty and ordered him to pay millions in damages. There ya go. A first-hand insight into the most famous celebrity murder case in recent times."

"Wow. Thank you. That's been much more interesting than Disneyland or Hollywood."

I shifted in my seat and tapped my fingers on the armrest. "You know a lot of detail about the case. Were you involved?"

Richard cleared his throat and pointed at a palace-sized edifice on a hill above the freeway. "Hey, d'ya see that building? That's the new Getty Museum. It's not open yet, but it's going to be massive, isn't it?"

≈ ≈ ≈

I woke when Richard switched off the engine.

"Home again. Jetlag catching up with ya?"

I wiped dribble from my mouth. "Wow, sorry. Thanks for a great day. You've been a fantastic tour guide. I'd never have seen Mulholland or all those big houses by myself."

Richard unlocked the front door. "We're home."

Carmen appeared wearing a dress which made her look like Jennifer Lopez about to pose on the red carpet. She air-kissed me twice, then stood back and rubbed my upper arm. "Have you had a good day? You look tired."

She turned to Richard and planted her hands on her hips. "What are you doing, wearing out our guest? He's exhausted, the poor boy."

She stroked my shoulder. "Simon, stretch out on the recliner. Pick a TV channel and put your feet up."

Her finger wagged at her husband. "Richard, don't stand there; fetch Simon a drink. I'll have a soda while you're at the fridge. And set the table for dinner."

Richard rubbed the back of his neck. "Yes, my little quesadilla. Right away."

He demonstrated how the living room armchair reclined by pushing a small button on the side. I'd never seen this feature before, and once he'd left the room I devoted a suitable amount of time to ensuring it functioned to my satisfaction.

I switched on the TV and flicked through the channels.

Beverly Hills 90210. I briefly watched to see whether the filming locations had featured in the afternoon's itinerary.

Frasier. Nope. I'd enjoyed *Cheers*, but I'd never appreciated the spin-off.

Friends. I'd seen this episode before, but my secret Lisa Kudrow crush ensured the repeat held my attention.

Richard *pffd* a can of Dr Pepper and unclipped his belt bag. "D'you wanna watch the dive video of Australia?"

"I'd love to."

Richard untangled cables and plugged in a video cassette recorder. "Pass me the remote."

I blew Lisa Kudrow a secret goodbye kiss and dreamt she'd returned the gesture.

A menu flashed on the screen.

Richard pressed play, and I leant forwards on my elbows as the scene immediately drew me back three weeks. Tommo and I chatted in the video as we kitted up on the boat, although the words weren't distinct.

I turned to Richard and grinned. "Wow. I never knew you were filming at that point."

"I tested the camera controls before I jumped in the water. Okay, here we go; we're diving."

The scene changed to a view of Richard's legs; then the camera panned around suddenly, and I heard bubbles in the background.

I grinned and nodded. "That's fantastic. I didn't know it recorded sound."

"All you can hear underwater is bloop-bloop-bloop. It adds to the experience, though."

The ocean exploded in front of the camera as Tommo and I fell backward into the water. I watched us make the okay sign to each other, then the video showed Tommo and me swimming into the trench.

"This part's dark," said Richard. "There's not much daylight at that depth."

I noticed the brown, flat-headed shark flip into a crevice.

"There's the little wobbegong," said Richard. "Better tell your friends the sharks are scared of you, tough guy."

We both laughed. Richard pointed. "See the turtle swimming ahead? That's the same one I videoed later."

"I remember this part," I said. "My previous night's hangover and the motion of the waves against the sea floor made me nauseous." I pointed at myself in the video. "Right now, I'm trying not to vomit underwater."

"I thought you looked off-colour, but I figured it was your normal appearance."

I observed myself stroking the big grouper fish and Tommo patting it. The turtle we'd seen earlier reappeared.

"Now," said Richard. "This is the good bit. Watch closely."

I perched on the edge of my seat, as the screen showed me pretending to be James Bond, and Tommo the baddie wrestling with me underwater. Richard paused the video.

"There, in the background. Hang on, I'll rewind it. Look. I did see the manta rays; I just didn't realise it." He raised his clenched fists in a triumphant gesture. "I showed my buddies and they're suitably jealous."

I gave him two thumbs-up. "That's fantastic, Richard. I'm so pleased they're visible on the video."

"Richard," called Carmen, "what are you doing? I asked you to fetch me a drink and set the table."

His face paled, and he swallowed.

"Coming, my little caracola."

≈ ≈ ≈

"Another Dr Pepper?" asked Richard.

"Sure, thanks."

Carmen dumped a Sierra Nevada of food on the table, piled in a colourful, rectangular dish and covered with cheese, spring onion slices and olives.

I closed my eyes and inhaled deeply through my nose. "Wow, this looks amazing. What are we eating tonight?"

Carmen waved both hands across the food.

"*Enchiladas Coloradas de Carne*. Hot beef enchiladas." She passed me a small bowl. "Here, sour cream to cool it down."

I helped myself to both, cut off a piece of enchilada and placed it on my tongue. The mixture of the hot food and sour cream averaged to a spiciness I could just about withstand.

Carmen blew on her food. "Where did Richard take you today? I hope he showed you everything you wanted to see."

"I had a great day, thanks. Richard's a fantastic tour guide. He really knows Los Angeles."

Carmen laughed once. "Pah. He knows the dodgy areas. Which was your favourite part?"

"The homes of the stars. Some of those places are extraordinary."

I turned to Richard. "Whose house was that on ten blocks? A movie producer?"

"Aaron Spelling. One wing of that house is entirely a wardrobe for his wife's clothes."

Carmen placed a hand on her chest and gazed upwards. "Ah, a woman after my own heart."

Richard rolled his eyes. "Yeah, but Aaron Spelling has a higher credit card limit than me."

Carmen glared at him, then turned to me and smiled.

"And what did you see in the afternoon?"

"Richard took me on this interesting excursion, to show that O. J. Simpson's murder defence wasn't valid."

Carmen clanged her cutlery on the table and turned up her hands towards Richard. "What the hell did you do that for?"

28. DYNASTY

LATITUDE: 34° 8' 47" N
LONGITUDE: 118° 15' 23" W

"Every guest we have," said Carmen. "Every guest. Why d'you take them on that O. J. Simpson drive? I know you're proud of your work, but isn't that getting old?"

Richard's chin dipped. "I thought Simon might be interested."

"I enjoyed it," I said. "I'd never have that experience on an organised tour. Fiona'll be fascinated when I tell her."

"See," said Richard, pointing at me, "our guest enjoyed it. Sometimes I know what I'm doing. OW."

Richard rubbed the back of his hand. Carmen replaced the serving spoon and turned to me.

"Tomorrow we're going shopping, hey? My favourite activity. We'll head to Glendale Galleria. Richard can drop us outside, and I'll take you on my own excursion which'll be much more enjoyable than revisiting murder scenes. I'll show you where the best shops are."

"I know where the best shops are," said Richard. "I just have to study the credit card bill. OW."

I tried to distract Carmen from the corporal punishment which she delighted in dishing out. "You'd have fun with my girlfriend. She loves shopping."

"Next time you come to LA, you must bring her. But tomorrow we'll find her a nice outfit. D'you have a photo of her?"

"Yes, I'll fetch it."

I stood up and nipped to my bedroom.

"Here." I handed Carmen a picture of Fiona and me on the farm in New Zealand. Richard leant over to look, and Carmen brushed him away.

"Pretty girl. You're lucky. And she looks about my size. I can try on some dresses, and we'll see if they fit."

"Yeh," said Richard. "Remember you're shopping for Fiona. Don't try on too many. OW."

I leant forwards. "Is there a jewellery shop in Glendale Galleria?"

Carmen nodded. "Several. Did you want to buy Fiona some earrings, or maybe a necklace?"

I glanced down in my lap, then up again. "Actually, I wanted to find an engagement ring."

Carmen's eyes sparkled, and she fanned herself with one hand.

"Oh, my. How romantic. I have to help you with this. I'll take you to my favourite store; Helzberg Diamonds."

She narrowed her eyes at Richard. "I might choose myself something while we're there."

Richard covered his eyes with his hand. "Helzberg Diamonds. I recognise that name from the bills. OW."

We finished dinner, and I prepared for my evening tournament with the waterbed.

≈ ≈ ≈

I'd no idea how I'd ever consume the Greek urn-sized bucket of soft drink a greeter presented me with upon entering the mall. The cup felt cold in my hands, and I sucked on the straw.

"Wow. They don't give you a free drink when you enter a mall in England. I might have to dump it in a bin, though. I'll never be able to finish 64 ounces of cola."

Carmen tossed her hair back. "Plus, you'll need two hands to carry all our purchases, right?"

The mall clientele primarily comprised families dressed uniformly in oversized T-shirts down to their knees. Some pushed prams, and all consumed food and drink as they strolled, in order not to waste valuable shopping time. I watched one man eat a hot dog in two bites while simultaneously carrying three store bags and pushing a stroller. Tomato ketchup squirted sideways onto the floor of the mall where it remained for a following mobile diner to skid on.

We stopped outside a jewellery store and inspected the various offerings in the window. All had small tickets attached to them, but none of the labels showed pricing.

Here we go again. Another shop I can't afford.

"Helzberg Diamonds," said Carmen. She pointed to the window display, at a pair of long, lozenge-shaped, silvery-white earrings which resembled something Joan Collins might have worn on *Dynasty*. "What d'you think? D'you reckon these'd look good on me?"

"Sure."

An immaculately dressed man with floppy peroxide-blonde hair addressed us as we entered.

"Thank you for visiting our emporium today." He flicked his hair back and gesticulated extravagantly. "My name's David, and I'll be ever so pleased to assist you. Was there anything in particular your heart desired?"

He shook our hands and immediately left me with the subtle scent of expensive aftershave. This would be a different experience to my treatment at the hands of Captain Mainwaring in Hatton Garden.

David slid out two chairs in front of a wooden desk, gave a Shakespearian bow and offered us an immaculate, uniformly shaped display of icicle-coloured teeth I hadn't imagined possible outside the world of Madison Avenue. He pulled out a chair on the other side of the desk, brushed invisible crumbs from the seat and sat.

I angled forward. "I'm searching for an engagement ring. There are some in the window I'd like to look at."

David raised his closed eyes and crossed his palms over his chest theatrically. "Oh, how simply romantic. A joining of souls. May I be the first to congratulate both of you."

Carmen and I leant away from each other.

"Oh, no," I said, "we're not together."

Carmen rested her elbows on the desk, cupped her chin in her hands, leant towards David and smiled. "Thank you, but I'm probably old enough to be his mother. I'm already married to someone else."

David shut his eyes gently and flopped one hand. "My, my. I'm not telling if you don't. Tee-hee-hee."

My cheeks reddened, and I tried to steer the conversation where it was supposed to be going.

"It's for my girlfriend. We live overseas and I'm proposing when I see her again in a couple of days. Could you show me a selection of rings?"

David cleared his throat. "Of course." He stood and walked to the window.

Carmen placed her hand on my knee and grinned. "Fancy that. He thought we were a couple. How flattering." She tossed her hair back. "I know I don't look my age, but I don't think I could pass as a fiancée for a.. how old are you?"

"Twenty-nine."

"Right. Guess how old I am."

I gritted my teeth.

Oh, great. Too old, and I insult her, too young, and she'll know I'm lying.

"I don't know, um, Forty-two?"

Carmen flicked one hand. "You're such a charmer. I'm fifty-one."

Phew.

"Wow," I said. "You don't look it at all."

Carmen smiled and smoothed down her top. "I know. Sometimes people think my daughter and I are sisters."

David returned with a tray of jewellery. My eye immediately drew to a gold ring at the rear with a diamond as big as a decent-sized garden pea. He placed the tray on the counter.

"Anything that attracts you?"

I nodded my head rapidly.

"The one at the back with the diamond."

"An excellent choice. An eighteen-carat gold band, with a quality jewel mounted in it." He slipped on a single white glove like a member of the Michael Jackson fan club, tugged the ring from its slot and handed it to me.

I turned it over in my hand.

I pincered it between my thumb and forefinger.

I held it up to the light.

My mouth hung open, and I imagined myself on one knee, presenting Fiona with it.

Carmen placed her palms together, pointing upwards. "Oh, Simon, it's so beautiful. Fiona'll love that."

I tried it on my finger, but it wouldn't fit.

"The young lady in question could take it to a local jeweller to have the band altered if needed," said David.

I imagined it on Fiona's finger.

But can I afford it?

I turned to David.

"How much is it, please?"

He took the ring and read the secret code of numbers on the label.

The store lights glinted through the diamond, and I blinked.

He lay the ring carefully on a white cloth as if he were a valuer on the *Antiques Roadshow*.

"This particular engagement ring is priced at nine thousand, eight hundred dollars."

I raised my eyebrows, breathed out noisily and stared into my lap.

Carmen pursed her lips.

"It is a significant stone," said David.

"I'm sure it is," I said. "But I paid a third of that for my car. D'you have anything more in my price range?"

"What, exactly, is your price range?"

"A lot less than that. Can I look at this one at the front?" I pointed at a ring with multiple tiny diamonds mounted above a gold band.

David plucked the ring from the tray and lay it in his palm.

"This one would be significantly more affordable. An eighteen-carat gold band again, although you'll notice it's considerably thinner than your previous choice. Fifteen diamonds arranged among the setting, so your young lady will have, um, fifteen times more diamonds."

He handed me the ring. My thumb and forefinger absorbed the gold band. I watched the top of the ring sparkle and smiled as I distinguished individual gems.

"How much is this one?"

David examined the label.

"This one would be one thousand, four hundred dollars."

I winced and clenched my teeth. "We're closer, but still about a thousand dollars too much."

"You know what," said Carmen. "I think we'll try some more stores."

David sniffed and delicately replaced the ring. "Do remember, you get what you pay for."

≈ ≈ ≈

Carmen marched away from the shop. "I'm so sorry. Helzberg Diamonds is far too expensive. What was I thinking, taking you in there? Other stores in the mall might be more in your price range."

The escalator creaked as we ascended to the first floor and passed rows of shops containing garment-embellished mannequins contorted in assorted catwalk poses. I dodged approaching people as if I were Terrell Davis about to score a touchdown, then we paused outside a shop called Zales.

My shoulders slumped as the memory returned of Ratners or whatever they called themselves today.

Fifty customers jostled inside the store. Many had dressed for a day at the beach and all of them displayed tattoos.

I contemplated one couple as they slipped car engine-themed rings on each other's fingers.

Carmen folded her arms. "D'you want to go in? It seems crowded."

"It also seems more in my budget, judging by the clientele."

Carmen cocked her head to one side. "Yep, I think I recognise some of them from my LAPD career."

We navigated to a glass display cabinet with trays of rings on top of it.

"Wow," I said. "These rings are so cheap; they don't lock them away." I picked up a silver-coloured, shiny, chrome ring attached to a piece of card. "This one's less than twenty dollars. I could afford something here."

Carmen pursed her lips and glanced behind her. "I know. But you wanted genuine diamonds."

I waved at an assistant. "Hello, excuse me?"

She dinged the till, passed a customer their purchase and nipped in front of me.

I pointed. "Could I please look at this tray of rings?"

"Yep." She slid open the display case door, dumped the tray in front of me and dealt with another client.

Carmen sniffed. "No white gloves here."

I gestured at the tray. "They're like the rings at the last shop; but this store's so cheap. I wonder what's different about it?"

Carmen peered at the jewellery and furrowed her brow. "What is it they say? All that glitters is not gold?"

"It looks like gold." I lifted a ring and twisted it in the light. I couldn't believe, in this shop packed full of people, I could hold what might have been a one-thousand-dollar ring unsupervised.

The assistant returned. "Anything you like?"

I held up a ring containing a ball bearing-sized diamond. "How much is this, please?"

"The price is on it. One hundred and seventy-nine dollars."

I glanced up, then back at the ring. "It seems incredibly cheap. Is it a real diamond? It's not glass, or cubic zirconia, or whatever fake diamonds are called?"

"Nope, that's a genuine diamond. We have a sale on, so the price on all engagement rings is thirty percent off until next weekend."

I tapped the counter twice. "Carmen, I'm going to buy this. Less than two hundred US dollars, for a gold ring with a diamond on it. It's perfect."

I tugged my wallet from my pocket and ruffled through identically sized notes to find two one-hundreds.

Carmen reached across me, plucked the ring from my hand and held it up. "Hang on, Simon. Before you hand over your cash, let me inspect it."

"But this is the first genuine diamond ring I've seen anywhere that I can afford."

Carmen rotated the ring, so the gold band lay on top and brandished it at the assistant. "What's the band actually made from?"

"It's sterling silver with fourteen carat gold plate."

Carmen showed it to me and shook her head. "See, it's not solid gold. In a few months on Fiona's finger, the gold colour will rub off, and the silver'll show through."

She flashed a cold smile at the assistant. "And the diamonds. Are they real?"

"Sure are. We wouldn't be allowed to call them diamonds if they weren't."

Carmen frowned and twisted the ring in her hand. She peered closely, then replaced it and extracted a second one from the tray. This boasted a price tag of $399 and comprised a gold-coloured ring with a larger diamond mounted in the top.

"That one looks the same as the ten-thousand-dollar diamond in the other shop," I said. "You're paying a lot for shop fittings and plush seats, aren't you? I might stretch my budget to afford that."

Carmen shook her head. "These can't be real diamonds. A genuine diamond this size would be thousands."

"They're synthetic diamonds," said the assistant. "They're real diamonds, but they're not mined; they're manufactured in a laboratory."

"Synthetic?" I blinked rapidly as my vision of kneeling in front of Fiona evaporated. "They're fake?"

The assistant folded her arms. "They're not fake. The difference between mined diamonds and synthetic diamonds is they're made in a lab. Everything else is the same."

"Pah!" said Carmen. "They're fake. Artificial. That's why they're so cheap."

The assistant bit down on her lip. "Most people can't distinguish them from mined diamonds."

I replaced my wallet in my pocket. "I'm sure Fiona'll be able to. Thank you, Carmen."

Carmen linked arms with me. "Let's find another shop." She hissed at the assistant. "One which doesn't sell fakes."

≈ ≈ ≈

We shopped all afternoon.

I bought a jacket for Fiona.

Carmen bought several jackets for herself.

I bought a top for Fiona.

Carmen bought several tops for herself.

We completely and totally failed to buy a ring.

Every genuine diamond was too expensive.

Everything affordable was fake.

I rubbed my temples and slouched as Richard pulled up outside the mall. His eyes bulged at the bags in Carmen's arms. "I thought you two were shopping for Simon today?"

"We were, but I found so many bargains in the spring sales, I had to save some money."

Richard did a double take. "Whaddya mean you had to save some money?" He loaded the bags into the trunk.

Carmen tossed her hair and opened the passenger door. "Yep, I had to save some money. I didn't pay full price for anything."

I slid into the back seat, and Richard swung out of the car park.

"Did you find a ring for Fiona?"

I looked down at the footwell.

"No. I want to propose with a genuine diamond. I mean, she has to wear it for the rest of her life. But everything that's in my price range is fake, or the diamonds are so titchy you need the Hubble space telescope to see them."

Richard drummed his fingers on the steering wheel. "Can you describe what you're looking for?"

"I'm searching for a gold band with a simple, single diamond. Not cubic whatever-it's-called, not a synthetic, factory-made fake. A real, one hundred percent genuine diamond. But they all cost thousands. My budget's about $400, and that's stretching it."

I held my face in my palms. "I don't know what to do now."

Richard rubbed his hand across his chin, then swung the wheel and pulled off the freeway.

"Hey, where are we going?" asked Carmen. "This isn't the way home."

"I just remembered," said Richard. "I need to collect something important from my office."

29. REAL DIAMONDS

LATITUDE: 34° 2' 34" N,
LONGITUDE: 118° 14' 46" W

Richard pulled up outside a brown, rectangular building and parked in a space with an 'Agency Vehicles Only' sign.

Traffic cruised past in both directions and distant police sirens formed an atmospheric backdrop to the wind-blown commercial street.

He turned to me. "I won't be long."

"Too right, you won't," said Carmen. She clicked her fingernails against the dashboard. "I need to hurry home to try on my new clothes."

Richard slammed the car door and bounded up steps into the building.

Carmen spoke over her shoulder. "I'm so sorry we didn't purchase a ring. D'you think you'll find one in New Zealand?"

"I guess so. But I wanted it to be a big surprise." I scratched my cheek. "I thought I'd kneel in front of her at the airport."

Carmen reached around and patted my arm. "You're such a romantic. When Richard proposed, he handed the ring across the table at Denny's."

Denny's.

My mind drifted back to tropical Hawaiian breezes, sitting opposite Fiona in the outdoor restaurant, on our journey to Tonga.

Was that really over a year ago?

Richard strode back to the car, swung the door open and leapt in. He grinned and gave me two thumbs-up.

"What are you looking so pleased about?" asked Carmen, crossing her arms. "Take me home, now."

"Hang on," said Richard. He reached into his belt bag and extracted a small, cubic, burgundy-coloured container. "Would this do?"

211

He passed me the box.

I peeked inside, and my eyes bulged.

"Are those real diamonds?"

"They are," said Richard. "One hundred percent genuine."

I rubbed my eyes and inspected the box again.

I stared at the gold band clasped in the slit. The light reflected from a flower arrangement of nine translucent, shiny diamonds mounted on a dull, gold band. The box didn't click closed properly as it would have when it was brand new, and I didn't dare slip the ring out in case I dropped it in Richard's car.

My head shook slightly. "I don't understand. Where did this come from?" I glanced at the brown building. "What is this place?"

Richard pulled away from the kerb.

"It's my office. We have occasional auctions where we sell off valuables which come into our possession."

I frowned and pointed at the ring. "Is this stolen goods?"

"Yes, but it's legitimate. We sell these after we've exhausted all efforts trying to find the owners. The next auction's on Monday. I made an early bid. If I hadn't bought it, someone else would've. I rummaged through the collection, but I couldn't find a solitaire. That's the closest we had."

I stared into the box. The band might've been thinner than the ones I'd seen in Hatton Garden and Helzberg Diamonds, and the stones might've been smaller, but here it was, a genuine, diamond ring.

I imagined myself kneeling in front of Fiona, opening this small, burgundy-coloured box and seeing her expression.

"Thank you so much, Richard. Um, how much did you bid?"

"Three hundred and fifty dollars. You can pay me when we reach home."

≈ ≈ ≈

The waterbed glooped from side to side as I piled my possessions like an East End market trader, stood back and held my forehead.

I'd no idea how I'd cram everything from my travels into the backpack.

212

The dolphin dress from Australia.

The sunset painting of the junks from Hong Kong.

The jacket and top from Los Angeles.

And most importantly, the ring.

The ring displayed in its burgundy, cubic box on the bedside table. Fiona would love it.

I bounced on my toes.

She'll have to say yes with a ring like this one.

Carmen had polished it, and the gold band reflected light as I picked it up and twisted it around and around.

I took a deep breath, closed my eyes and wondered who'd owned this ring before. Maybe it was the lady whose clothes collection occupied an entire house wing. I wished it was her, as she probably owned hundreds of rings and wouldn't miss one.

I hoped it hadn't been stolen from someone like me, who could never have afforded to lose it. But, as Richard said, they couldn't reunite it with its former owner, and if I hadn't bought it, someone else would've.

I held it up to the light again and replaced it in its box.

Richard entered. "How's the packing going?" He laughed as he saw me surrounded by Everests of luggage. "Oh. Not too good. D'you have enough space in your bag for all that?"

"I have my carry-on too. I reckon I'll squeeze it in."

Richard grinned. "Good luck. Dinner'll be about fifteen minutes."

I heard Carmen's voice. "Richard. Richard! Empty the trash, and then put some cutlery on the table. And wash your hands in between."

"Yes, my little quesadilla. Coming right away."

He closed the bedroom door behind him, and I contemplated my million kilos of garments.

≈ ≈ ≈

Carmen lay another gargantuan plate of food in front of me, and I breathed in the prevailing steam of Mexican spices. "What have we tonight, Carmen?"

"Flautas. Little flutes. Rolled tacos with meat in hot sauce, salsa, guacamole and cheese. Enjoy."

It tasted similar to every dish she'd produced, and I concluded tacos, enchiladas, huevos racheros and now flautas were all the same ingredients arranged in a slightly different order. Not that I was complaining, but I didn't want to eat any more Mexican food, and I looked forward to one of Fiona's mother's juicy steaks, or spaghetti Bolognese.

"Did you fit it all in?" asked Richard.

I cracked my knuckles. "Yes, but I'm sure my backpack's way overweight and I don't know how I'll lift my cabin bag into the overhead locker. And it might not fit under the seat in front of me."

"Let me help you," said Richard. He stood, reached up to a shelf and produced a black, wrinkled piece of canvas. "Here. Open it."

I turned the object over, tugged a strap and it unfolded into a belt bag the same as his.

"I noticed you admiring my fanny pack," he said, "so I picked one up for you. We've got loads of uniform kicking around at work, handed back by ex-employees, or people who've updated their kit. It'll come in handy on the plane."

"Wow. Thank you." I looked up at Richard and Carmen. "You guys have been so good to me. I hope I can repay the hospitality one day."

"Our pleasure," said Carmen. "You must come again and bring Fiona, so I can take her shopping. It's been lovely having an English gentleman stay with us. Hasn't it, Richard?"

"Yep. And thanks again for being my dive buddy in Australia. I had fun."

I flipped the bag over and exposed an American eagle logo.

"That's an old design," said Richard. "I tried to find a plain one, but they all have something on them." He held out his hand. "Pass it back to me a second."

He unzipped it and showed me the interior. "If you fold this part, it should have a secret pocket. Yep, here it is, see? You zip it up, and cover it with the flap, and now, anyone who looks in it can't see the secret section. You could store your passport and money in it."

I peeked inside and realised this was where I'd glimpsed Richard's gun.

"Wow. I know exactly what I'm going to hide in there." I jumped up, strode to my bedroom, returned with the ring and carefully concealed the box in the secret pocket.

"Thanks so much, Richard. I was worried about leaving the ring unattended in the overhead locker. Now I won't have to."

Carmen glanced at the clock. "Eat up. You need to depart for your flight."

If I'd known what was going to occur when I arrived in New Zealand, I'd never have accepted his gift.

≈ ≈ ≈

"Have your bags ready to go through the scanner, please. All bags to be scanned."

I shuffled through the LAX security check with my hand luggage. The plump, female officer in charge of the queue looked increasingly annoyed at the line of ignorant passengers who couldn't follow her basic commands.

"Yes, ma'am. Your handbag. I don't care if it's Gucci, it still has to go through the scanner. No, ma'am, I don't know who you are, but if you wanna fly anywhere today, we're gonna have to scan your bag, same as everyone else."

She addressed the queue in front of me. "Keep moving, keep moving. Have your bags ready. All bags, all bags." She gazed down at a small child. "Sweetie, I'll have to scan teddy. Pass him up to me."

I heaved my cabin bag onto the conveyor belt and tried to make it appear easy to carry. It must've weighed triple what it was supposed to, and I'd had to fight to zip it up. The officer pointed. "You sure you don't wanna check that in?"

I pressed my lips together and shook my head. "I'll take the risk, thanks."

She peered over at my waist. "You got a fanny pack? That'll have to go through as well."

"Really? I don't want to let go of it."

"Yes, sir. Pass it to me."

I unclipped the black belt bag and handed it over, then paused until I'd watched it enter the machine.

I stepped through the body scanner in front of me and heard BEEEEEP.

The body-scanning agent held up one flat palm towards me.

"D'you have anything metal in your pockets, sir?"

I pushed my hands into my trousers. "No."

"Are you wearing a belt with a large buckle?"

"No."

I glanced to the right. Passengers who'd successfully negotiated the security check collected their bags. My cabin luggage lay unattended. I couldn't see the belt bag.

Shit. Has someone picked it up?

I clenched and unclenched my fists and hyperventilated.

"Sir, my colleague's going to pat you down. Could you please stand with your arms outstretched?"

I lifted my limbs as if I were a small child pretending to be an aeroplane. The agent slowly gripped my upper left arm and ran his hands along my sleeve to my wrist. I gazed behind him. My cabin baggage continued its solitary vigil at the end of the conveyor belt. No belt bag.

Come on, come on. Hurry.

The agent started on my right arm.

I twisted towards the scanning machine.

"Stand still, sir."

He rubbed down one trouser leg, then the other.

Faster, faster. Please let the bag be there.

"All right, sir. You're free to go."

I took rapid, shallow breaths and darted glances everywhere.

"Excuse me?" I waved at an officer. "Have you seen a fanny pack?"

216

30. SPELLING BEE

LATITUDE: 7° 0' 45" N,
LONGITUDE: 149° 59' 54" W

I wiped sweat from my forehead.

Please let it be here. Please don't let anyone have taken it.

The officer rummaged through articles on a table behind her and held up a black item. "Is this it?"

"Yes. Could I have it?"

She conferred with a colleague, who watched a screen showing an x-ray view of bags as they passed through the scanner.

I bit my nails.

"Here you are, sir. Something showed up in the scanner, so we had to search it by hand."

The cubic ring box responded to my fingers as I grabbed the bag from her.

I pressed a palm to my heart, stared up at the ceiling and muttered, "Thank you."

≈ ≈ ≈

"Good evening, sir. 37G? Head down the aisle behind me, and it's on your right."

The bright, friendly smile of the Air New Zealand steward contrasted with the officialdom of border security, and I grinned, pushed my shoulders back and tried to make my cabin baggage appear as light as possible. As I squeezed through the galley area, a crew member removed steaming, white towels from a heater. I swapped the bag to my right arm and continued.

Seat 37G was on the end of the central row of four in the jumbo jet.

I heaved my cabin baggage above my head, stuffed the belt bag under the seat in front of me, sat down and fastened my seatbelt.

No-one sat in the other three seats.

Yet.

Would this be like the flight from Hong Kong to London?

Would I have four seats to myself?

Would I be able to stretch out and sleep for the entire twelve-hour journey to New Zealand?

New Zealand. I'll pick a perfect location, kneel and propose, and she'll say yes.

The queue of passengers boarded the plane.

A tall man who needed to fold up like a Swiss army knife to fit into an economy class seat approached. He glanced left and right at the seat numbers.

Please keep walking. This isn't your row.

He passed by, and I breathed out.

A couple with a tiny baby, currently fast asleep, but with the potential energy to compete with a World War II air-raid siren lugged bags towards me.

Oh, no. Are these your seats?

They stopped a few rows ahead of me and arranged their belongings.

Phew.

A bearded, scruffy man who looked like he'd need to occupy more than one seat squished along the aisle.

Please pass me. Please pass me. Please pass me. Yes!

The line of passengers trickled to a halt, and the cabin crew clicked closed the overhead lockers.

I leant against the headrest and smiled.

Four seats to myself on a full plane. Score one.

"Good evening, ladies and gentlemen. My name's Colin, and I'll be your chief steward tonight. Joining me in the forward cabin are Sharon, Michael and Kate. Anthony, Cherie, Leigh, Carrie, Jackie and Scott will look after you lucky people in economy class. Thank you for making your way quickly to your seats to enable us to depart on time. We're just boarding the final passengers, and we'll be on our way, so sit back, relax and enjoy the Air New Zealand experience."

Final passengers?

I couldn't see anyone standing except the cabin crew.

I sat up and peered over heads.

My fingers drummed on the armrest.

"Cabin crew, prepare the cabin for departure."

I glanced up, as a harassed lady shepherded two children towards me.

"Josh, stop. In here. These are our seats."

Josh mountaineered over the dividing arms and plopped into the seat next to me.

"Hi," he said in a Californian accent. "I'm Josh. Are you going to New Zealand too?"

His short, blonde hair spiked in every direction, and I noticed a spattering of freckles traversing his nose. His mother followed him, and her teenage daughter sat on her other side.

I smiled at him. "I think we all are. At least, I hope we are."

Josh grinned. "You're funny. D'you want to help me with my spelling? My Mom says I have to finish it while I'm on the plane so I can enjoy my holiday."

His mother tapped his arm. "I'm sure the gentleman has something else he'd prefer doing."

Her soft, New Zealand accent surprised me and immediately reminded me of Fiona.

"I don't mind helping," I said, "although it's been years since I attended school."

Josh turned to his mother and gave her a triumphant grin. "Yes!" He danced in his seat and fist-pumped the air with both arms as if he'd achieved a new high score in *Super Mario*.

"Josh," said his mother, "the nice man's agreed to help you. Not to do it for you."

"I know, I know," said Josh.

His mother spoke to me. "We're returning to New Zealand to visit my parents. My husband's American, and we live in San Diego. We haven't been back to Auckland for three years; their grandparents normally come to California. But my mother had a fall, and she's nervous about flying now, so it's time for us to head back."

"Yep," said Josh, "and Grandpaw's going to let me sit beside him on his ride-on lawn mower. He might let me drive it."

He gave me another huge grin, and I briefly wondered how he managed to eat with two missing front teeth.

"Wow. That's so cool," I said. I pointed at the aisle. "Shall we look at your homework once they've shown the safety demonstration?"

≈ ≈ ≈

"Ladies and gentlemen, this is First Officer Clive Fowles from the flight deck. We've reached our cruising altitude of 38,000 feet, and the captain's switched off the seatbelt sign, so you're free to move around the cabin. We've a good tail-wind, and we expect to have you on the ground ahead of schedule. I'll be back with a more precise update on our arrival time shortly before we land."

Josh pressed buttons on the seat-back entertainment. "We can watch *Batman*. D'you want to watch it with me? Please, please?"

I glanced at his mother. "Let's do your homework first. Then we'll watch it. I promise."

Josh tugged out an exercise book, a printed sheet of paper and a pencil. "You say the words, and I'll write them down. Then you tell me how many I spelt right." He folded down his tray table and passed me the printed sheet.

I assumed a TV announcer's voice and pretended to speak into a microphone. "We're here at the International Air New Zealand Spelling Bee, and playing for a place in the finals; it's Josh."

Josh giggled. His mother smiled at me and mouthed, "Thank you."

"Josh, are... you... ready?"

Josh smiled and nodded.

I ran my finger down his list. "And your first word, for five points, is... lettuce."

Josh licked the end of his pencil. I peeked over his shoulder and observed him correctly spell the word in neat, slow, cursive writing.

"That's the correct answer. Your second word, for ten points, is... furniture."

Josh wrote carefully. He looked up at me.

"Correct. And your third word, for twenty points, is... antidisestablishmentarianism."

Josh paused, lifted his pencil and stared at the paper wide-eyed, then turned to me. His mother slapped a hand to her mouth, and lines formed in the corners of her eyes.

I couldn't keep a straight face.

He grinned slowly. "That word's not on my list. You made it up."

"Okay. You caught me. But it's an actual word."

We spent the next ten minutes finishing the spelling, then I kept my promise, and we watched *Batman*. The cabin crew served dinner, then, after they'd cleared away, Josh's mom passed him a blanket and a teddy. He stuffed his thumb in his mouth, curled up and slept on my leg.

≈ ≈ ≈

The main cabin lights illuminated suddenly. Josh lay on his mother's lap, and one of his feet stretched across me. A hot food smell drifted from the rear of the plane.

"Ladies and gentlemen, good morning. First Officer Clive Fowles speaking from the flight deck again. We've made good time tonight, and we'll have you on the ground twenty minutes early, at 5:30 in the morning. The weather in Auckland is 27 degrees and humid, with occasional showers. The cabin crew will shortly be serving a light breakfast. We hope you've enjoyed flying with Air New Zealand, and we look forward to seeing you on board again soon."

Josh's mother tapped his arm. "Josh, wake up. We're nearly there."

He sat up instantly and didn't seem entirely sure where he was. I glanced over and observed his sister obscured under an eye-mask and headphones.

He turned to me. "Are we in New Zealand?"

"Soon. It'll be breakfast time in a minute."

I reached down to make sure nobody'd stolen the belt bag during the night. The outline of the ring box responded to my prod.

Josh rubbed his eyes and grinned at me. "When we land in New Zealand, can you come to my grandpaw's house with me? Please, please? Please say you will."

"I'd love to, Josh, but I have to board another aeroplane. I'm flying to Christchurch."

He ruffled his hair. "Christchurch? Is that an actual place, or is it just a church?"

"It's another city in New Zealand. I'm meeting my girlfriend there, and I'm asking her to marry me."

Josh's eyes opened wide. "Woh, that's so cool." He tapped his mother's leg. "Mom, Mom, Simon's getting married, Mom. In Christchurch."

His mother smiled at me. "Congratulations."

"Excuse me, sir?" said a flight attendant at my elbow. "Would you like porridge with fruit, or an omelette?"

I unclipped my tray table. "I'll have an omelette, please."

She tonged a roll, added it to a tray of wrapped-up goodies and clacked it in front of me.

"And what'll your son have, sir?"

I was about to say, "He's not my son", but I hesitated and turned to my left.

"Josh, would you like an omelette, or porridge?"

"Does she have Lucky Charms?"

"She hasn't. She has omelette, or porridge."

Josh poked out his bottom lip. "What are you having?"

"I'm having an omelette."

He nodded violently. "All right. I'll have an omelette too."

The lady passed Josh his tray, and we had lots of fun opening the jam without emptying it all over us, trying to spread cold butter on soft bread and making sure the orange juice didn't slop over the edge of the little plastic cup.

≈ ≈ ≈

Josh gripped my hand as we lugged our carry-ons through Auckland airport. I didn't think I should negotiate passport inspection with his family. There might be an issue with my new visa, and I didn't want to hold them up.

I paused and bent down to him. "Go through border control with your mum and sister. I'll be right behind you."

"Promise?"

"Promise."

I hesitated as I approached the immigration agent.

She took my British passport, flicked to the visa page and thumped her stamp. "Next, please."

I frowned and shook my head. "Is that it?"

No 'welcome to our newest permanent resident?'

No fanfare?

No congratulations?

"Yes, sir. Please continue." She glanced behind me. "Next, please."

I stuffed the passport in the belt bag and caught up with Josh's family.

We stood at the baggage carousel and waited for their hold luggage. Josh gripped me, and I didn't know what I'd do when the family's bags arrived, and they left for Grandpaw's house while I rode the bus to the domestic terminal. We'd both be upset.

He released my hand and pointed. "Mom, look. A dog."

We watched a short, fit, uniformed man lead a black Labrador onto the baggage carousel. The dog scrambled over the bags as they joined the conveyor belt.

Josh watched. "What's it doing? Why's the dog allowed to jump over the bags?"

"It's a specially trained dog," I said. "It's making sure nobody has anything in their luggage they shouldn't have."

The dog leapt off the carousel.

"This way, Lucy," called the handler.

Lucy didn't go that way.

Lucy sat firmly at my feet.

31. KOJAK

LATITUDE: 37° 0' 33" S
LONGITUDE: 174° 47' 11" E

Lucy's handler shoved a rolled-up rag in her mouth and ruffled her fur.

"Good girl, Lucy, what a good girl."

His expression changed more instantly than I'd ever seen anyone's change before.

Lucy was his friend.

I wasn't.

"Sir, the dog has indicated you may be carrying illegal narcotics. I need you to come with me to the secure area."

I froze, and the tops of my cheeks tingled.

"Pardon?" I pointed at my chest. "D'you mean me?"

"Yes, sir. This way, please."

I raised my palms and frowned. "But I've never had anything to do with drugs."

"The dog has indicated you're in possession of controlled substances, so I need you to accompany me."

I smiled and shook my head. "I'll come with you, but it's a waste of time. You won't find anything."

I lifted my cabin bag, swivelled the belt bag around to my back and traipsed after the dog handler.

A small voice behind me said, "Mommy, why is Simon going with the cop? He didn't say goodbye."

A flush crept across my cheeks, and I turned around and gave Josh a tiny wave.

"Are they with you, sir?" asked the officer.

I shook my head. "Just people I talked with on the plane." I swept my spare arm. "Listen, this is a mistake. I've never taken drugs in my life. Something's not right here."

"The dog's indicated you have narcotics with you, sir. We need to check further."

His boots echoed on the concrete floor of a large, clinical white room. Officers searched through other passengers' bags on shiny, metal tables.

The agent pointed to a vacant one.

"Stand here, sir. Give your passport to this officer."

He pointed to a second, shaven-headed man who stood behind the table and reminded me of *Kojak*.

The first officer led the dog away through a rear door.

"Your passport?" demanded Kojak.

I reckoned he would have been very comfortable dishing out orders on a parade ground.

"All right, all right, I'll find it." I unzipped the belt bag and handed the document over.

I planted my feet wide apart and crossed my arms over my chest.

"Listen to me. I don't know why your dog thinks I'm carrying drugs. I've never taken drugs in my life. This is all a mistake."

"Wait here. Don't move."

He confiscated my passport and disappeared through a rear door, which slammed like a cell in *The Green Mile*.

I stood helplessly beside the metal table and bit my nails until my fingers turned red.

Sweat broke out on my forehead.

Maybe someone's planted something on me?

I shoved my hands in my front pockets and tugged out a handkerchief.

I shoved them in my back pockets, which were empty.

I slid a finger into the little pocket in my Levi's which I always used for bus tickets.

Nothing.

I checked through the inner and outer pockets of my jacket. I removed stubs of boarding passes, restaurant receipts and a Snickers wrapper.

Kojak returned. "We can see you on the cameras. We're watching you go through your pockets."

My face and neck flushed, and my muscles tensed. "Of course I'm going through my pockets." I held my arms out wide and leant towards him. "Why the hell wouldn't I be? I know I don't have any drugs, and your dog says I do, so I'm wondering if someone planted something on me."

The officer raised his nose in the air. "Planted something? I've heard that before. You're making yourself look more guilty. If I were you, I'd stand still and keep my hands by my sides."

I didn't think anyone had said those words to me since Mr Giles confiscated my loaded water pistol at primary school.

Kojak disappeared again. The blood drained from my face as I stared at the ground.

This was a mistake, and I knew it.

I didn't have any drugs.

How the hell did I get into this mess?

The two officers reappeared without their dog.

"Here's what's going to happen," said the first one. "I'll repeat, the dog's indicated you may be carrying illicit narcotics."

I pressed my hands hard against my cheeks with my eyes open wide.

"Your dog's got it wrong."

The officer ignored me.

"First, we'll take you into an interview room and ask a few questions. Then we'll look through your bags."

I thumped the metal counter. "How long is this all going to take? I have to catch a flight to Christchurch in ninety minutes."

The first officer pointed at my hand luggage and the belt bag.

"If we find anything we shouldn't, you won't be going anywhere in ninety minutes."

A man wearing a baggage handler's orange vest wheeled a small sack barrow towards us. I blinked as I recognised its contents.

"Why the hell d'you have my backpack? I checked it through to Christchurch."

The officer cleared his throat and continued.

"After we've inspected all your bags"—he pointed again—"including your hold baggage, we'll perform a strip search."

I threw up both arms. "Strip search? Are you bloody serious? This is crazy; I've never taken drugs in my life. Can I sue?"

The officers turned away from me and conferred.

"You're permitted to speak with the duty solicitor by telephone. Would you like me to contact him for you?"

I lifted my chin. "Yeah, I want to, before we go any further." I clenched my teeth. "This is bloody ridiculous."

He sighed. "All right, I'll call him. Wait here."

I stared at his back as he walked away.

This is all so wrong. I've got nothing.

The officer returned. "Come and use this phone. Just to let you know, I'll be listening on the extension."

He led me to a telephone mounted in the corner of the room. I took the handset and turned towards the wall.

"Hello?"

"This is Paramjeet Singh, the duty solicitor. What can I do for you?"

He sighed heavily, but I wasn't about to apologise for the 7:00 a.m. call.

"You have to help me. I've stepped off a flight from Los Angeles. A drug dog's indicated I'm carrying illegal substances." My knuckles whitened as I gripped the receiver. "I've never taken drugs in my life, and they say they're going to strip search me. How can they do this, when I'm innocent? Can't you take out an injunction or something to prevent them? I need help, now."

Another heavy sigh. "Unfortunately, when it comes to border control officers, you have no rights to prevent them performing their duties. You say the dog indicated you're carrying drugs?"

"Yes, but I…"

"And they're going to perform a strip search?"

"That's what they said. How can they…?"

"I can't stop them from performing the strip search. But once they've finished, and they've found whatever it is the dog's indicated you're carrying, ask them to call me back, and I'll help you further with your defence."

I ran a hand through my hair and panted. "Are you kidding? They won't find anything. Unless something's been planted on me, and I've checked all my pockets, and they're empty, although they didn't like me doing that, and they told me to stop, and…"

"Sir, let them find whatever they think they're going to find, and then call me back. There's nothing more I can do for you at this stage."

"But…"

"Sorry, sir. Call me back if you need me. Goodbye."

CLICK

I dangled the phone cord, then replaced the handset.

Kojak tapped my shoulder. "The quicker we start the process, the quicker it's over."

My eyes stared down at my feet, then I looked up. "I'm telling you; I don't have any drugs."

"Then you've nothing to worry about, have you? Bring your bags and follow me."

I opened and closed my mouth, but no words came out.

He motioned me to follow him through the door at the rear of the holding area, into a small room which contained a table and four chairs. The other officer tailed us and closed the door. A square, brown, electronic device rested on the table's corner, and a one-way window looked out into the holding area.

"Sit down here."

I bit my nails and sat.

The bald officer held my passport open at the photo page and pressed a button.

CLICK

"Interview with Simon Prior, 7:04 a.m. 3rd March 1998."

Sweat prickled on my brow.

He looked up at me.

"A few questions, then we'll perform the search. First, we'll confirm some details. Your full name is Simon Michael Prior?"

"Yes."

"Date of birth?"

I tapped the table twice.

"It's in the passport you're holding."

The officer rolled his eyes. "Mr Prior, the more you co-operate with us, the quicker we finish this process. Your date of birth?"

I spelt out the date.

"And your occupation is?"

I sighed. "I'm a musician."

The officers narrowed their eyes at each other, smiled and nodded.

I whacked the table with my hand. "Just because I'm a musician doesn't automatically mean I take drugs. Elton John entered New Zealand a couple of months ago. Did you strip search him?"

I had a brief thought of Elton John naked and dismissed it rapidly.

"We would have done, if the drug dog had showed he was carrying. What's the purpose of your visit to New Zealand today?"

"Visit? I live here." I sat back in the chair and folded my arms. "If you turn to the correct page in my passport, you'll see I have a permanent visa."

The officer flicked through the pages and inspected my new visa affixed in my passport at the New Zealand consulate. He scribbled notes on his pad.

"Where did you fly in from today?"

"Los Angeles. But I originally came from London."

"What were you doing in London?"

"Visiting my father."

"What were you doing in Los Angeles?"

"I stopped for a couple of nights on my way from London."

"Did anyone give you anything in London to carry on the flight for them?"

"No."

"Did anyone give you anything in Los Angeles to carry on the flight for them?"

"No." I shook my head vigorously. "I mean, the man I stayed with gave me a gift, but it was for me to keep. Not to carry for him."

"Can you show me the gift?"

I clasped the belt bag by its strap. "This bag."

The officer took it from me. He unzipped it, peeked inside and furrowed his brow, then dangled it and pointed. "This insignia is a symbol of the US government. Where did you get this?"

"My host in Los Angeles gave it to me. I told you that."

"What was his name?"

"Richard."

"Second name?"

Cold sweat materialised on my forehead. I realised I'd never known Richard's full name.

"Um, I don't know."

The officer glanced sideways at his colleague.

"You stayed with this Richard in Los Angeles, and you don't know his last name?"

"No."

"Where did he live?"

I wiped sweat from my forehead. "Near the mountains."

"The address?"

"Erm, I don't know that, either. He collected me from the airport and dropped me off, so I never discovered his exact address. His suburb was near a shopping centre called Glendale Galleria. I have his phone number, if it helps?"

"Maybe. How d'you know Richard?"

"I met him on holiday in Australia. We scuba dived together, then he invited me to stay."

The agent lifted the bag again, tilted his head and inspected the insignia.

"Why would he possess a bag like this?"

"How would I know?" I shrugged. "He uses one himself to carry a gun."

The officer jotted more notes.

"Why did he give you the bag?"

230

"I told you. A present. He said it was old uniform from his work."

"Who does he work for?"

My face sagged. "Um, I don't know that, either. He was pretty secretive."

Kojak turned the bag over and placed it aside.

The other officer tugged on a translucent glove like a physician about to perform open heart surgery. I froze at the thought he might ask me to bend over.

"We'll perform a thorough search of your luggage," he said. "Before we begin, could you please inform us if you've anything in there which shouldn't be? Like illegal drugs, for instance."

My palms pressed on the table, and I leant forwards.

"I told you; I've never had anything to do with drugs. There's nothing, unless someone planted it."

The officer pulled on the other glove. "And could you tell me if you've anything in your luggage I might hurt myself on, such as a knife or a syringe?"

"No." I stood and balled my fist. "Can you stop addressing me like I'm a criminal? I've done nothing wrong."

"Sit down, Mr Prior," said the shiny headed one. "You've told us a stranger who you stayed with gave you a bag. You've told us you don't know his full name or where he lives. You've told us he carries a gun. Our drug dog's indicated you're carrying illicit substances. It's not looking great for you, is it?"

I folded my hands in my lap as the first officer unzipped my backpack. He lifted out clothes, shoes and books. He rummaged through my possessions and removed Fiona's dresses, tops and skirts.

My face flushed. "They're presents for my girlfriend."

The officer showed no interest.

He felt around the edges of the empty bag, along the seams and around the straps, then repeated the process with my hand luggage. Sweat ran down my face as he unzipped the belt bag and removed my wallet. He felt inside the lining, discovered the outline of the ring box and unzipped the secret compartment. He didn't ask about the ring, and I wasn't volunteering anything. If they were suspicious about Richard giving me a belt bag, what would they say about an ex-stolen diamond ring?

He replaced the wallet and ring box in the belt bag and zipped it up.

I crossed my arms and smiled. "You found nothing."

"Not yet," said the officer. "But if it's here, we will."

He turned to Kojak.

"Shall I bring Lucy in?"

"Yep."

Here we go. My best friend, Lucy.

He returned with the Labrador and ran her over my possessions.

"Come on, Lucy. Good girl, good girl. Find it, Lucy, find it."

Lucy ignored my backpack.

She ignored my carry-on.

Lucy sat and stared at the belt bag.

32. NAKED

LATITUDE: 37° 0' 23" S,
LONGITUDE: 174° 47' 29" E

"Good girl, Lucy, well done." The dog agent gave Lucy her treat and led her away.

"Mr Prior, the dog's indicated this bag," said the bald agent. "We'll swab it and perform chemical tests."

I sat upright and my eyes widened.

"Will I get it back?"

"That depends on what we find."

The dog agent returned with a third officer, who departed with the belt bag.

Kojak planted his hands on his hips. "While the chemicals team test your bag, we'll perform the strip search. Undress to your underpants, please."

My knees shook as I stood. "What, here? Is that window definitely one-way? No-one can see in?"

"Nobody will see you except us. The idea is you spend as little time naked as possible."

I removed my top half and placed my clothes on the chair I'd been sitting on. I took off my shoes, then my trousers.

The officers inspected me from all angles as if I were a second-hand Ford Escort they weren't sure about purchasing.

I twisted away from their gaze and covered my body with my arms.

Kojak frowned, stepped forward and pointed. "What did you drop on the floor?"

The agent reached down and pincered a tiny item between his thumb and forefinger.

I blushed. "Erm, I reckon that's belly button fluff."

He held the offending article up to the light, turned to his colleague and grinned. "We'd be pretty desperate if we were looking for something that small."

They laughed. This was the first laughter I'd heard since they'd begun their process. I smiled thinly and figured they wouldn't permit me to join in.

"Lift your arms, please."

I raised them, and they inspected my armpits.

They stood in front of me.

"Last part. Take off your underwear."

I concluded they enjoyed humiliating innocent travellers. I pulled down my underpants and stood stark naked in front of two fully uniformed, jack-booted strangers.

"Lift yourself up so we can have a look."

My cheeks burnt as I slid my hand between my legs and displayed the underside of my scrotum.

"All right, you're clean. Get dressed."

I tugged my underpants up as quickly as I could, then turned my other clothes the right way around and replaced them. I sat in the chair and pulled on my shoes.

A knock at the door.

The third officer returned with the belt bag. "We've run the tests, and they're negative."

The first officer turned to me. "Looks like you're in the clear. Repack your bags."

I considered this rather rude, as they were the ones who'd unpacked them.

He passed me the belt bag, and I squeezed the comforting shape of the ring box.

I turned to the officers and threw one hand up. "I told you I didn't have any drugs. You might need to buy a new dog, 'cos Lucy doesn't work too well."

The officers folded their arms.

I stuffed clothes into my bags significantly less neatly than before, held up my chin and took a step forward. "Seeing as this whole thing is your mistake, could you drive me to the domestic terminal? I'll miss my connecting flight now."

"Sorry, we can't do that."

I clipped the belt bag around my waist, shouldered my backpack and picked up my luggage.

"Could you at least call the airline to explain what's happened and ask them to hold the plane?"

"No, sorry."

The officer held the door open. "Just head through the green channel."

I shook one fist. "Of course I'm going to head through the bloody green channel. If I had anything to declare, you'd already know about it, wouldn't you?"

I puffed theatrically and marched out. I had ten minutes to reach the domestic terminal, one kilometre distant.

As I strode into the green channel, I heard a voice shout behind me.

"Stop!"

The first border officer marched towards me like the T-1000 in *Terminator 2—Judgment Day*.

I spread my arms wide. "What? What d'you want now? D'you want to bloody x-ray me or something?"

"You forgot this. Here."

He handed me my passport.

I stared at him wide-eyed. "I forgot it? You bloody forgot to give it back to me. This hasn't been your finest day, has it?"

I figured I'd pushed my luck as far as possible with border force, and I scooted through the green channel to freedom.

≈ ≈ ≈

The inter-terminal bus drove away as I sprinted through the terminal exit, and I dashed after it and banged on its window. The doors opened, and I collapsed up the steps in a heap of backpacks and belt bags.

I panted and placed one hand on my chest. "Thank you so much."

The Māori driver grinned. "Chill, bro. You look like you need a break. Not eight in the morning and your face says you've had a bad day already."

I rubbed both hands through my hair. "More than you'd know, my friend, more than you'd know."

The bus lurched around the corners and stopped at the domestic terminal.

"Paging the last remaining passenger for flight NZ53 to Christchurch. Paging the last remaining passenger for flight NZ53. If Mr Simon Prior is in the building, your flight is closing at gate nine. That's Mr Simon Prior. Paging Mr Simon Prior."

Shit, shit, shit. Thank goodness I already have my boarding pass.

The line for scanning zigzagged miles back to the doors. I tore past it, nipped under a temporary barrier and entered a separate queue which said, 'operational staff only'. Two men in pilot's uniforms stepped through the scanner ahead of me.

"This is for crew only," said a brother of the agents who'd stripped me naked.

"Can you let me through, please? They're paging me. My flight's about to close. I don't have time to queue with everyone else."

He folded his arms. "Crew only. You'll have to wait in line."

I placed my palms together in prayer. "Please? I'm late because border security detained me for no reason. Plus, my girlfriend's meeting me off this flight and I'm proposing to her. I have to make this flight. Please?"

Maybe it was my hyperventilation.

Maybe he wanted to make amends for the Auckland strip show.

Maybe it was the mention of my forthcoming proposal.

The agent glanced behind him, sighed and invited me to dump my baggage on the conveyor belt. I strode through the people-scanner.

Nothing beeped, so I grabbed my bags and ran. I heard the agent shout 'good luck' behind me.

Gate nine.

Gate nine.

Where the hell's gate nine?

"Last call for Mr Simon Prior. Your flight has closed at gate nine. If you are in the terminal, please present yourself at gate nine. The flight has closed. That's Mr Simon Prior."

I span on my heels and scanned up and down the concourse.

BEEP BEEP BEEP

An airport employee approached in an electric car.

"Quick, can you take me to gate nine?"

"Gate nine, sir?" He pointed with his entire arm. "It's right down the end."

I employed the prayer gesture again. If it worked with the scanner guy, it might work with the electric car driver.

"Please, can you take me? My flight's closed and they're paging me." I pointed up at the ceiling speaker. "I have to make this flight."

"All right, hop on." He grinned. "Try to look as elderly as possible."

I threw my bags up, jumped next to him and had a brief experience of how the Queen must feel sailing along, while the great unwashed proletariat was forced to stand and wait.

"Gate nine, sir."

"Thank you so much."

I charged towards the airline staff, leant on the counter with one hand and panted.

"I'm... Simon... Prior. You were paging me."

"Goodness, Mr Prior, we almost left without you. D'you have your boarding pass? Thank you."

I pointed at my backpack. "I didn't have time to check in my bag."

"Give it to me. I'll radio the baggage handlers." She scrawled my name and flight number on a temporary tag and twanged it around the handle.

I took a deep breath, released it slowly and strode down the air bridge onto a full plane, where over one hundred people paused mid-conversation and glared. I ducked my head as I hurried down the aisle. The overhead lockers had all been closed, so my hand luggage squished under the seat in front of me, and I sidled in next to a middle-aged man wearing a suit.

He turned to me and jabbed a finger. "They held the plane for you, y'know." He made a show of tapping his watch. "We're late taking off."

I avoided his gaze and unclipped the belt bag.

"I'm really sorry. You're not going to believe what a morning I've had."

≈ ≈ ≈

"Ladies and gentlemen, welcome to Christchurch, where the local time is 9:15 a.m. Please remain seated until the seatbelt sign has been switched off. For those visiting, enjoy your stay, and for those who live here, welcome home. On behalf of Captain Robert Harris, First Officer Tim Collins and the rest of the crew, may we thank you for flying Air New Zealand today, and we look forward to seeing you again soon."

I pushed up my sleeves, picked up the belt bag and squeezed the reassuring outline of the ring box.

Nearly there.

I bit my nails.

Fiona.

Will she have changed?

I rubbed my chin.

Where would I propose?

As soon as I saw her in arrivals? Standing by the Southern Alps panoramic photo where we'd arranged to meet? In front of all the airport visitors?

Maybe not, Fiona would feel embarrassed.

In the car?

Not very romantic.

Maybe stop at the first beauty spot on the road to the mountains?

Yes.

I'll be the best boyfriend ever.

The best fiancé.

I'll be the best fiancé ever.

As soon as the plane stopped, everyone leapt up to retrieve their hand luggage. I tugged mine out from under the seat in front where it had enjoyed an uncomfortable, squashy journey and stood in the queue to depart.

One thousand gigantic, tropical butterflies flapped in my stomach simultaneously.

The lady in front elbowed me, and the lump of the ring box dug into my hip.

I peered around the passengers towards the front of the plane. People began to depart.

I fidgeted and huffed, then politely allowed people in the row in front of me to spend forever gathering their bags.

Come on, come on. Hurry, hurry. This is the most important day of my life.

They departed, and I doink-doink-doinked my hand luggage along the aisle after them.

A flight attendant smiled at me and repeated the phrase she'd said to every departing passenger. "Thank you. Have a great day."

I grinned back at her.

"Oh, I will. This'll be the greatest day ever."

33. THE ANTICLOCKWISE PROPOSAL

LATITUDE: 43° 29' 15" S
LONGITUDE: 172° 32' 15" E

One hundred people stared at the baggage carousel, willing it to move.

The man next to me inspected his watch every ten seconds and huffed dramatically.

I rubbed the ring box through the belt bag and reflected on everything that had brought me to this point.

The moonlight beach in Queensland, where Veronica had made me kneel with the shell and practise my proposal.

Dinner with my father, where he'd approved my choice of fiancée. I heard his words in my head: "*She's a delightful girl. Delightful.*"

Shopping for a ring in Hong Kong, Hatton Garden and then Glendale Galleria with Carmen.

Not finding one I liked and could afford.

My joy at the ring Richard produced.

I spun around on my toes and waved both clenched fists in the air.

Other passengers sidled away from me.

I forgave the fake diamond vendors.

I forgave Captain Mainwaring.

I forgave Lucy the drug dog.

I forgave the Auckland border security agents.

I'd flown around the entire world, anticlockwise.

I'd arrived at conclusions about myself, about my relationship, about my future.

Fiona's future.

Our future.

BEEP BEEP BEEP

The three customary, battered bags circumnavigated the carousel. They whopped through the black, plastic, flappy things, then began a second lap.

After several circulations, my backpack appeared, so I threw it over my shoulder, picked up my hand luggage and marched to meet my future wife.

≈ ≈ ≈

The Southern Alps mural covered one entire wall. I scanned people's heads and hesitated.

Is that her? She looks different.

Fiona glanced up and paused, then ran towards me. I lifted her and swung her around and around. She squeezed me tightly, and the ring box pressed into my hip.

Please don't ask me what that lump is. Not yet.

She released me and stood back. "You smell."

"Thanks. That's a nice way to greet your boyfriend who you haven't seen for a month."

I looked her up and down.

"You've changed. You've had a haircut."

"Yep. I fancied a short bob. D'you like it?"

"It's lovely. It looks like Lisa Kudrow's new style."

She took my hand, and we headed to the car park.

≈ ≈ ≈

Fiona swung the Honda onto the main road west. Autumn had come early to the South Island, and I leant out of the passenger window and inhaled the fresh, cool air of New Zealand.

I jiggled in my seat.

Fiona shivered. "Close the window; it's cold."

"I want to smell the fresh air. I've been cooped up on a plane for the best part of a day."

"Stop biting your nails. What are you nervous about?"

241

"Sorry." I gripped one hand with the other. "It's great to see you."

"Did you have a pleasant flight?"

"Yep. Right until Auckland airport, where some useless drug dog indicated I was carrying illegal substances. Can you believe it? They went through all my belongings and strip-searched me."

Fiona's mouth fell open, and she shook her head.

"What, completely naked?"

"Yes. In a private room. Naturally, they found nothing. I don't know why the dog thought I had drugs. This belt bag interested it."

Fiona glanced in my lap.

"I haven't seen that before. Did you buy it?"

"No. A present from my host in Los Angeles."

"You haven't been staying with druggies, have you?"

"Nothing like that. He was some kind of law enforcement agent, although I never found out exactly what he did."

"There's your answer. Maybe he was with the drug squad and the bag had contained drugs from an arrest. Those dogs' noses are very sensitive."

I sucked in a deep breath. "There's something else inside it which might interest you."

"I didn't want any presents. Unless… is it something from Fashion Valley? It is, isn't it?"

I crossed and uncrossed my legs and ran my hands through my hair.

"It's not really a present."

This is it.

"Um, Fiona?"

"Yes?"

"Could you pull over in the next layby?"

"Why? We need to hurry home. Mum's cooking a big lunch to welcome you back."

I blinked and cleared my throat. "Could we stop for a few minutes?"

"D'you feel sick?"

"No, I just need to stop, okay? Here." I pointed to a small, gravel car park. Fiona swung the wheel, parked and pulled on the handbrake.

I held a huge breath, then released it.

This is it. You have the ring. You can feel it, in the bag.

The passenger door swung open.

"I'll wait in the car," said Fiona.

"I want you to get out too."

"Why? It's cold."

"Please? For a minute. I have to show you something."

"Can't you show me later at home?"

"I need to show you now. Please?"

Fiona unclicked her seatbelt. "Okay, mystery man. Make it quick; I don't have a jacket."

She shot me a sideways glance and opened her door.

I waved the back of my hand at her. "You have to get out first."

Fiona rolled her eyes, stepped out of the car and slammed the door. She hugged herself and rubbed her arms, as the wind blew her hair behind her like one of Christie Turlington's photo shoots.

I unclipped the belt bag, swivelled it around me and unzipped it. The ring box stuck in the secret pocket. I tugged it hard, and it flew out and fell in the footwell.

Fiona opened the driver's door. "What are you doing? Hurry, I'm cold."

"Shut the door. I'm coming now."

I rummaged for the ring box under the seat. My fingers shook as they closed around it. I stepped out of the car, and the belt bag fell off my lap onto the gravel.

I pointed at the ground. "Stand here."

Fiona shrugged. "Why?"

"Oh, for goodness' sake, please stand here." I pointed. "Just there."

The Southern Alps mountains soared behind her. Autumn wasn't sufficiently advanced for snow to have fallen yet, and their green slopes reflected orangey gold in the sunrise. Morning mist steamed on the fields, cows mooed enthusiastically, and birds warbled. I paused and inhaled the wonderful essence of New Zealand.

"Quick, whatever you're doing," said Fiona. "It's freezing. The wind cuts right through me."

This is it.

I knelt down on one knee and secreted the box in my hand.

"Fiona?"

"What?" She hugged herself. "I'm going to climb back in the car. It's so cold."

Here goes.

I opened the box in her direction.

I recited the words Veronica taught me, all those weeks ago on the beach at Mooloolaba.

"Fiona, I have missed you so much. I want to be with you forever. Please, will you marry me?"

She tilted her head and frowned.

That's not the reaction I expected.

I furrowed my brow and lifted the box higher.

"Well? Will you?"

Fiona pointed at the box.

"Is something supposed to be in there?"

34. TIME TO PLAN

LATITUDE: 43° 26' 21" S
LONGITUDE: 172° 9' 20" E

The world stopped turning.

The traffic ceased.

The cows paused mid-moo.

The birds fell silent.

My face tingled. Sweat formed on my brow.

I had the first inkling something had gone terribly, terribly wrong.

I wanted to turn the box around to look at it.

But the last thing I wanted to do was turn the box around to look at it.

I had to.

I had to turn the box around.

I brought it towards me, twisted it and peeked in.

Empty.

≈ ≈ ≈

"I'm getting back in the car," said Fiona. "It's icy out here."

She sat in the driver's seat and slammed the door.

I knelt and stared into the ring box.

I twisted it around in my hand.

I looked underneath it.

I searched at my feet, among the gravel, under the car, looking for anything shiny.

I planted my hand on my forehead and panted.

I tugged everything from the belt bag. My passport, a pen, coins in Australian, Hong Kong, English and American denominations.

A boarding pass stub blew away. My hand grabbed at it, then I watched it fly off towards the mountains.

I pushed my hand into the belt bag.

I poked my fingers into the corners of the secret compartment.

I groped all around the main pocket.

Nothing.

I rubbed my temples. I turned the belt bag upside down and shook it out. A previously unnoticed foreign coin clinked on the gravel.

Where the hell is it?

I stood and pushed my hands into all my pockets, even the back ones. Even the one for holding bus tickets.

Did the scanner agent in Los Angeles take it? Was it kept by Auckland airport's chemicals team? Did someone steal it on the plane? When did I last actually see the ring?

I rummaged through the bag again.

I fell down on my hands and knees and swept over the gravel gently where I'd knelt.

Fiona lowered the passenger window. I heard the whoosh of the hot air blower.

"Simon, get in the car."

How am I going to explain this?

I stood and poked my head through the window.

"Fiona, I need to keep searching. I've lost something."

Fiona furrowed her brow and her lips straightened. "Have you lost whatever was supposed to be in that box?"

Tears ran down my face. "Yes. I spent forever looking for the most beautiful diamond ring. All around the world, in Australia, Hong Kong, London and Los Angeles. I wanted to propose to you and ask you to marry me and it was all going to be perfect and now the ring's disappeared and everything's gone wrong and I'm a stupid, useless boyfriend."

I wiped my face with gravelly, filthy hands, opened the car door and slumped into the passenger seat.

Fiona laughed and covered her mouth.

I thumped the dashboard. "It's not bloody funny."

She giggled. "Sorry, but with that dirt all over your face, you look like something from *Rambo*."

I pulled down the vanity mirror and wiped my face with my hands, which made my black makeup worse.

Fiona leant towards me and pointed.

"Simon, what's that?"

I lifted my shoes.

"Where?"

"Under the floor mat."

I groped around at my feet.

Something hard and ring-shaped responded to my fingers.

My heart thumped as fast as the snare drum at the start of the National Anthem.

I didn't dare look.

I couldn't look.

I looked.

My hands quivered as I gripped it in front of me.

I flopped backwards, and my shoulders slumped.

Fiona took the ring from my grasp and smiled.

She slipped it on. It was far too big for her ring finger, so she slid it on her middle one.

She twisted it in the light.

I wiped my face with my hands again. "I'm so sorry. I've completely stuffed up my proposal. You won't want to marry me now"—I bit my lip and glanced up at her—"will you?"

Fiona rubbed her hand with her chin.

"You're so sweet. Although, you should ask my dad first, if you're going to do this properly. I love the ring, though. The diamonds in a flower shape. I don't like those big solitaires. Too flashy. I'd be happy to wear this for the rest of my life."

I rubbed my eyes and raised my eyebrows. "The rest of your life? Does that mean 'yes'?"

"I suppose it must do."

I reached across the handbrake and hugged and kissed her as much as possible in the front seat of a Honda Prelude. Some of my gravel-dust and tears transferred to her face.

"At least this'll be something to tell the grandkids," she said, as she selected first gear, pulled out and pointed the car towards the mountain pass and our West Coast home on the farm.

I leant back in my seat and pressed my palms to my eyes. I'd been strip-searched, almost missed my flight and, worst of all, dropped the ring and messed up my proposal.

This day had been a complete and utter disaster.

Or had it?

I removed my hands and stared across at Fiona's hand on the steering wheel. The ring sparkled on her finger.

My ring.

Fiona wore my ring.

Veronica had been wrong.

Fiona had never wanted a big, big diamond.

I wiped my eyes again.

The tablecloth fields of the Canterbury plains stretched out towards the soaring, jagged Southern Alps.

I pushed my head against the seat back and smiled.

She'd said 'yes'.

It was time to plan.

It was time to plan the rest of our lives.

THE END

Simon and Fiona's South Pacific Shenanigans adventures comprise four books so far.
They're all available on Amazon as E-books, paperbacks and hardbacks by visiting:

https://mybook.to/southpacific

EPILOGUE:
WHERE ARE THEY NOW?

Thank you very much for reading the fourth in my *South Pacific Shenanigans* series.

I've kept up with many of the characters in the book, and I thought you might be interested to know what's happened in their lives since 1998.

Tommo moved back to Perth to live closer to his elderly parents, and he lives off the profits of his property renovation business. He has a beachside home, spends his days surfing and his nights partying. He still hasn't settled down.

I lost touch with Kylie and Leanne and would love to hear from either of them if they ever read this.

Sarah and I are still best friends, and we see each other whenever I visit England from my home in Melbourne. We're also godparents to each other's children.

I never saw Richard again. I also never discovered exactly who he worked for. And although I didn't know his exact address, I worked it out from Google maps while writing this book. I have no way of knowing whether he still lives there. But his house is completely blurred out on Google. Not just faces and house numbers, the entire property. We'll probably never know why.

And Fiona and me? Twenty-five years later, she still wears my ring, and we've had plenty more adventures. You can read about more of them in the other books in the series by visiting:

https://mybook.to/southpacific

PLEASE REVIEW
THE ANTICLOCKWISE PROPOSAL

If you enjoyed The Anticlockwise Proposal, please consider leaving a review, to let other readers know.

Even if you didn't buy the book from Amazon, you can submit a review by visiting Amazon and searching under kindle books for *The Anticlockwise Proposal.*

Thanks so much, it means a lot to me.
Simon

LATITUDE AND LONGITUDE

If you've been wondering about the strange numbers and letters in the chapter titles, wonder no more!

The world is divided into lines of latitude horizontally away from the equator in both directions, and lines of longitude vertically away from the Greenwich Meridian (which runs from the North Pole to the South Pole through London) in both directions.

This means that every location in the world, both land and sea, has an X-Y coordinate which is expressed as:

LATITUDE: degrees, minutes, seconds North / South
LONGITUDE: degrees, minutes, seconds East / West

For instance, Buckingham Palace is located at:
LATITUDE: 51° 30' 5" N, LONGITUDE: 0° 8' 32" W

The White House is located at:
LATITUDE: 38° 53' 51" N, LONGITUDE: 77° 2' 12" W

If you visit Google maps, copy and paste any of my chapter headings, and delete the words LATITUDE: and LONGITUDE:, you'll be able to see exactly where I was during that chapter.

By example, for chapter 1., enter 43° 29' 15" S, 172° 32' 15" E and it'll take you to Christchurch Airport.

Enjoy!

BOOK 1 IN THE SERIES:
THE COCONUT WIRELESS

When Simon and Fiona embark on a quest to track down the Queen of Tonga, they have no idea they'll end up marooned on a desert island.

No idea they'll encounter an undiscovered tribe, rescue a drowning actress, learn jungle survival from a commando, and attend cultural ceremonies few Westerners have seen.

As they find out who hooks up, who breaks up, who cracks up, and who throws up, will they fulfil Simon's ambition to see the queen, or will they be distracted by insomniac chickens, grunting wild piglets, and the easy-going Tongan lifestyle?

Read the first few chapters FREE by visiting the link, or scanning the QR code:

Smarturl.it/lookinsidecoconut

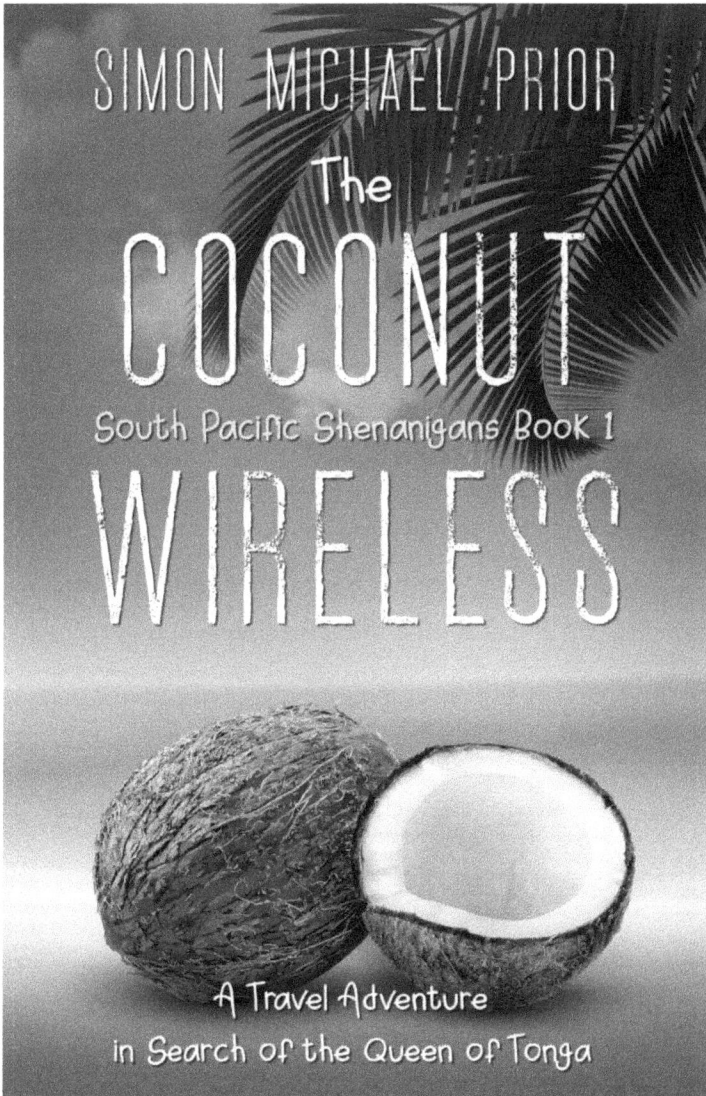

SIMON MICHAEL PRIOR

The
COCONUT

South Pacific Shenanigans Book 1

WIRELESS

A Travel Adventure
in Search of the Queen of Tonga

BOOK 2 IN THE SERIES:
THE SCENICLAND RADIO

When English city boy Simon follows his girlfriend across the world to her family farm in remotest New Zealand, he has no idea he'll be force-fed a meal of beetle larva, get pushed off the road by half a house, and be inspected by indignant penguins and flattened by a giant leaf-blower.

As he poisons the milk, dive-bombs the bulls, and loses the herd of cows in a river, will he ever learn to be a farmer, or will he have to stop impersonating a country boy, and return to London?

Read the first few chapters FREE by visiting the link, or scanning the QR code:

Smarturl.it/lookinsidescenicland

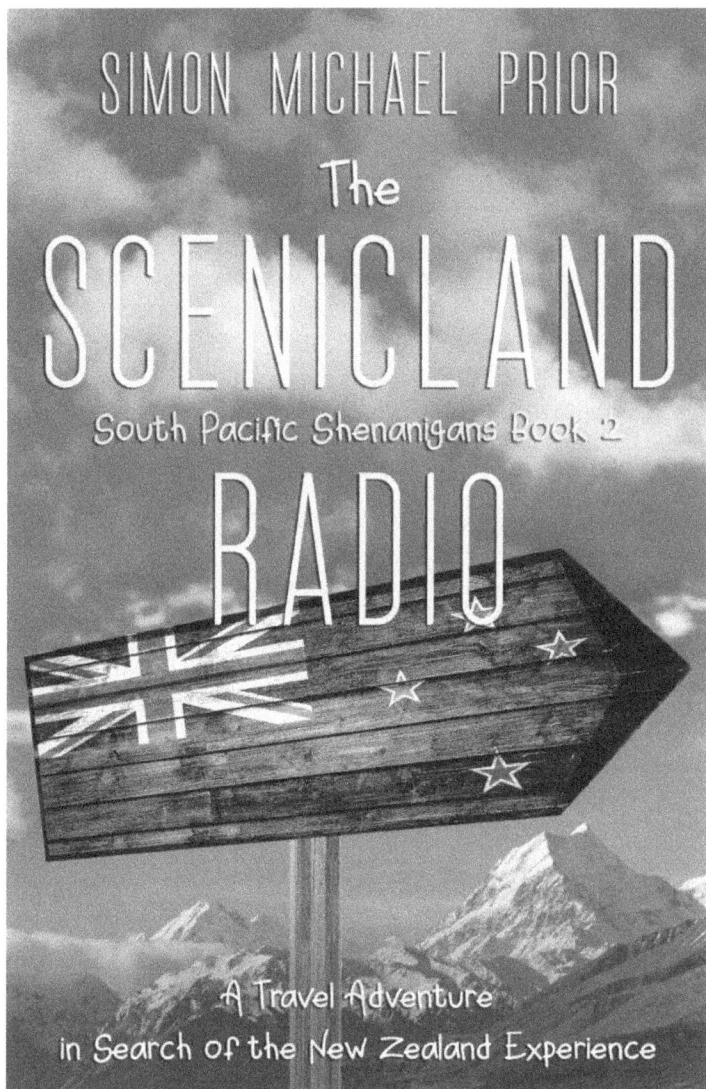

SIMON MICHAEL PRIOR

The

SCENICLAND

South Pacific Shenanigans Book 2

RADIO

A Travel Adventure
in Search of the New Zealand Experience

BOOK 3 IN THE SERIES: THE POMEGRANATE BUSKER

When London boy Simon dreams of becoming a New Zealand rock star, he has no idea he'll duet with a suspected murderer, model for posters with a dairy cow, accidentally present the weather on the radio and be upstaged by an apple crumble.

As he struggles to impersonate Elvis, forgets the most important birthday song and scares away a hen party, will he ever realise his rock star ambitions, or will he have to pack away his guitar and abandon his dreams forever?

Find out, in *The Pomegranate Busker*, the third book in the South Pacific Shenanigans series.

Read the first few chapters for free by visiting this link:

Smarturl.it/lookinpomegranate

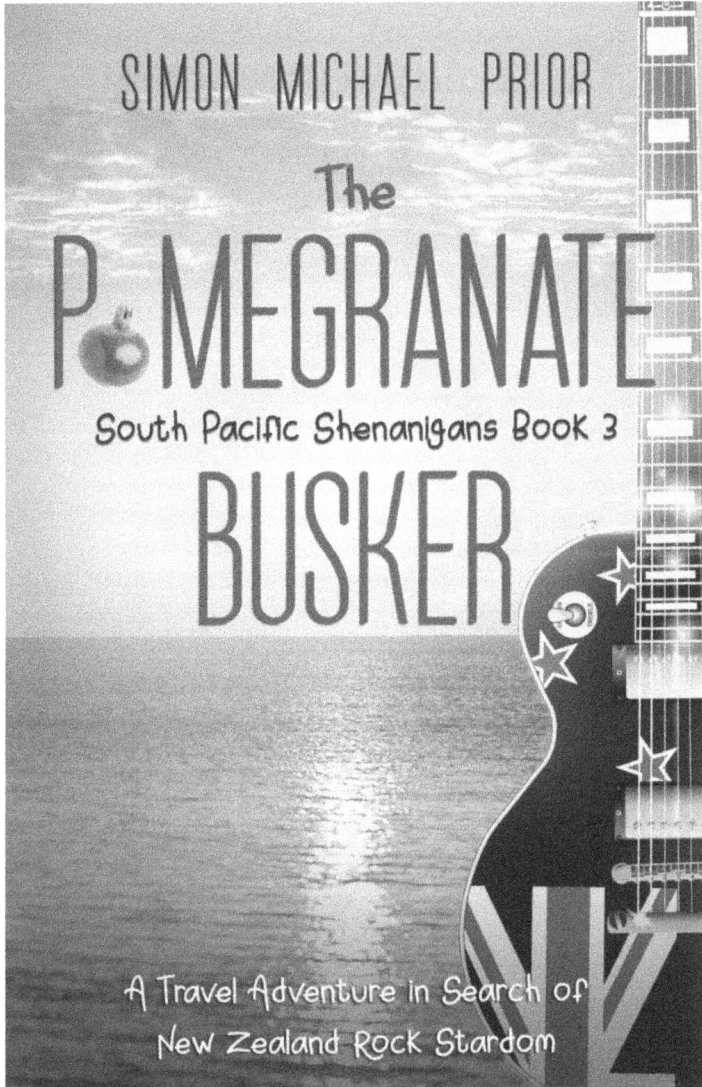

SIMON MICHAEL PRIOR

The

P:MEGRANATE

South Pacific Shenanigans Book 3

BUSKER

A Travel Adventure in Search of
New Zealand Rock Stardom

ALSO BY SIMON:
AN ENGLISHMAN IN NEW YORK

Have you ever wanted a first-hand glimpse into post-war 1940s New York?

When 21-year-old John Miskin Prior travelled by ship to New York in 1948, he had no idea he was going to meet and dine with the Roosevelts and the Rockefellers. No idea he would be among the first ever to see 'South Pacific' and 'Death of a Salesman'. No idea he would witness Truman's election victory, so unexpected, the newspapers were reprinted.

This eyewitness account of an English student living in New York for the incredible year of 1948 – 49 has been collated from his letters discovered after his death, and forms a unique account of the period.

Read the first few chapters FREE by visiting the link, or scanning the QR code:

Smarturl.it/lookinsideenglishman

ABOUT THE AUTHOR

Simon Michael Prior insists on inflicting all aspects of life on himself so that his readers can enjoy learning about his latest trip / experience / disaster / emotional breakdown (insert phrase of your choice).

During his extended adolescence, now over forty years long, he has lived on two boats and sunk one of them; sold houses, street signs, Indian food and paper bags for a living; visited almost fifty countries and lived in three; qualified as a scuba divemaster; nearly killed himself learning to wakeboard; trained as a search and rescue skipper with the Coast Guard, and built his own house without the benefit of an instruction manual.

Simon is as amazed as anyone that the house is still standing, and he now lives in it by the sea with his wife and twin daughters, where he spends his time regurgitating his experiences on paper before he has so many more that he forgets them.

Website: **simonmichaelprior.com**

Email: **simon@simonmichaelprior.com**

Facebook: **@simonmichaelprior**

Instagram: **@simonmichaelprior**

Twitter: **@simonmichaelpri**

If you would like to receive a regular newsletter about Simon and his writing, and be the first to find out about new releases, please sign up to his mailing list here:

simonmichaelprior.com

DISCLAIMER

This is a work in the genre creative non-fiction. I have tried to recreate events, locales and conversations from my memories of them. To maintain their anonymity, in some instances I have changed the names of individuals and places. Some characters in this book are composites, comprised of more than one person I met. I may have changed some identifying characteristics and details such as physical properties, occupations and places of residence. Any mistakes are all my own work. SMP.

ACKNOWLEDGEMENTS

A big thank you to Victoria Twead and all the members of the Facebook group 'We Love Memoirs', for befriending me, encouraging me, educating me, reassuring me, and driving me forward.

This book wouldn't have been possible without the help of the following people: The wonderful beta readers: Alison Ripley-Cubitt, Alyson Sheldrake, Gary Gaunt, Julie Haigh, Liesbet Collaert, Lisa Rose Wright, Pauline Armstrong and Val Poore; your feedback improved the final result so much.

Thank you to Victoria Twead, Matthew J Holmes, Meg LaTorre, David Gaughran and Dave Chesson for informative courses, tips and useful tools.

Thank you to Jeff Bezos, for giving independent authors a platform on which to publish our writing.

And thank you so much to Fiona, I couldn't have done it without you.

WE LOVE MEMOIRS

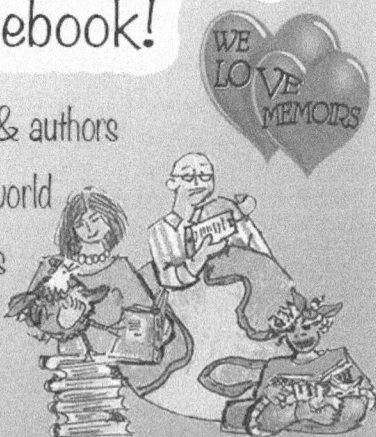

Milton Keynes UK
Ingram Content Group UK Ltd.
UKHW011314300624
444945UK00017B/79

9 780645 118759